Strategic
Family
Therapy

❖ ❖ ❖ ❖ ❖

Cloé Madanes

▦ ▦ ▦ ▦ ▦

Strategic
Family
Therapy

▦ ▦ ▦ ▦ ▦

Jossey-Bass Publishers
San Francisco • Washington • London • 1981

STRATEGIC FAMILY THERAPY
by Cloé Madanes

Copyright © 1981 by: Jossey-Bass Inc., Publishers
433 California Street
San Francisco, California 94104
&
Jossey-Bass Limited
28 Banner Street
London EC1Y 8QE

Library of Congress Cataloging in Publication Data

Madanes, Cloé
    Strategic family therapy.

    Bibliography: p. 229
    Includes index.
    1. Family psychotherapy. I. Title
RC488.5.M32   1981   616.89'156   80-26286
ISBN 0-87589-487-9

Manufactured in the United States of America

JACKET DESIGN BY WILLI BAUM

FIRST EDITION
First printing: January 1981
Second printing: May 1981
Third printing: October 1981

Code 8101

The Jossey-Bass
Social and Behavioral Science Series

In loving memory of my father, Victor Madanes

Foreword

田 田 田 田 田

Today therapists are expected to solve the problems of all the diverse people who come to their doors. Whether working in a private practice or a community agency, the clinician is expected to do therapy with children, adolescents, and adults and also expected to deal with family problems, marital distress, and extreme forms of symptomatic behavior. The psychotic, the abuser of people or of drugs and alcohol, and the delinquent have become part of the day's work for the average therapist. University training does not adequately prepare the clinician for this banquet of psychopathology. At the university, one can obtain the proper credentials and the view of therapy fashionable in a particular department. But the theoretical approach and the range of therapy techniques to deal with such a variety of problems are just not taught. This book offers the practicing therapist an extensive range of therapeutic interventions, a theoretical view of the family organization that makes sense of a client's problems, and practical examples as a guide to what to do.

Clinicians and theoreticians have always had difficulty describing the social context of people with problems. Years ago I participated in a research project with Gregory Bateson where we attempted to describe people, particularly people with symptoms, in terms of their relationships with others. Bateson proposed that communication between human beings can be described in terms of levels, and he suggested that these levels can conflict in paradoxical ways. An ancient Greek could say, "I am lying," and be telling the truth if he was lying (according to Epimenides), or a person could smile and smile and murder while he smiled (as Hamlet observed). The investigation of how messages "frame" other messages in conflicting ways in play, therapy, and ritual occupied the Bateson project for ten years. The term *double bind* was coined to describe dual messages that conflict paradoxically. In 1962, when the project ended, we had successfully made the shift from describing madness and other symptoms as individual phenomena to describing them as communicative behavior between people. However, the organizational context in which communication takes place remained largely undescribed. A mother would say to her child in some form, "I want you to spontaneously do as I say." The child would respond in a peculiar way to this peculiar set of messages. Why the mother communicated in this conflicting way could be explained only by references to her nature or to her need to respond to a child who was communicating strangely. Whether a problem child or a symptom of a marital couple was described, what was lacking was a way to conceptualize the larger social context to which family members were adapting.

Through the decades of the 1960s and 1970s, clinicians became increasingly aware that a new explanation of human motivation could be found in the social organization of the individual. Focus then shifted from the individual or a generalized "system" to the small organization of the work group and the nuclear family and extended kin. For the first time, family structures—such as the cross-generation coalition when a spouse joins a child against the other spouse, or a grandmother sides

with a child against parents, or a parental child is caught between parents and children—began to be delineated. With awareness of the importance of maintaining generational boundaries,
there was an increasing emphasis on the fact that all organizations have hierarchies. More and more, it was noted that the
hierarchies of people with symptoms are incorrect in some way,
as when parents obviously do not maintain a generation line or
when a problem child determines what happens in a family. The
developing issue was how to describe such problem hierarchies
and, for the clinician, how to think about changing a hierarchy.
It was becoming evident that symptomatic behavior is in some
way adaptive; a person must behave in abnormal ways when responding to abnormal social structures. The task was to describe
the social context of a family with problem members so that
their behavior is explainable and ways to change that behavior
more evident.

This book takes that next step. Cloé Madanes suggests
that the social organizations of problem people have a dual hierarchy which requires conflicting levels of communication, or
symptomatic behavior. Her therapy techniques are ways to
change such organizational structures so that abnormal behavior
is no longer appropriate and adaptive. Just as Bateson proposed
that there is a human dilemma when dual levels of message are
incongruent, Madanes takes the next step and proposes that in
an organization dual hierarchies can be incongruent. In fact, she
suggests that dual levels of message will be incongruent if the
organization has incongruent hierarchies.

With this organizational view, it is possible to see the conflicting levels of message in context—the conflicting hierarchies
in the organizations where people communicate. A mother who
asks her child to obey her spontaneously can be in an organization where (1) she is in charge of the child by the fact of
being a parent but (2) the child is also in charge of her because
of the power of symptomatic behavior or because of the power
given by coalitions with family members of high status. Therefore, the mother must give directives because of the nature of
her position, but she can only express helplessly the wish that
the child might do as she says. An observer would say that she is

expressing a double bind, or a set of conflicting levels of communication, because her behavior expresses the idea, "Spontaneously do what I say."

There are many ramifications to the idea that conflicting levels of communication reflect conflicting hierarchies within an organization. A major issue for the clinician is the opportunity that arises for new forms of therapeutic intervention. As the structural problem is clarified, the intervention can be planned more precisely. Madanes offers a variety of new and unusual ways to intervene to change the distressing situation of problem people. One of the more interesting interventions she offers is the use of "pretend" techniques. In a variety of ways, the family members are asked to pretend to be responding to one another.

A pretend technique falls within the category of paradoxical interventions, insofar as it can be the encouragement of the behavior that the client enters therapy to change, but it is in itself a special category that should appeal to many clinicians. Most paradoxical techniques tend to be confrontations and depend on the client's rebelling against the definition of the relationship implied in the directive. Many therapists are uncomfortable with such interventions, because they do not like the "all-or-none" confrontation quality when they must ask a client, for example, to have the symptom he came in to recover from. The pretend techniques are not confrontational in that sense and do not depend on a rebellious response. One can ask a person to pretend to have his symptom, or ask a family to pretend to respond in their distressing ways, without the directive being one that disturbs the helpful relationship between therapist and client.

One of the merits of "pretending" is that it fits within a tradition of "play" in therapy. When people are irrationally grim, the introduction of playfulness can introduce new behavior and bring about new alternatives. The reader should not underestimate the powerful influence of play and pretending. Such interventions can appear deceptively light if one does not understand that reclassifying human behavior is a powerful means of change. Probably the most important factor in human life is how behavior is classified, or framed, by people as they communicate with one another. Whether something is "pretending" or "real" is not a light and playful issue even though it can appear to be. Therapy itself has always had as a central question whether the relationship between client and therapist is "really" intimate, or "really" authoritative, or only a metaphorical response to previous authority figures. Similarly, the heart of madness has been the question whether the patient thinks that he is "really" someone else or people are "really" after him. The issue of play and pretending is not only at the center of all art and fiction, but it is also at the center of the controversies over ritual and ceremony in the world's religions. Whether in the Mass the wine and wafer are "really" the body and blood of Christ or only "symbolically" or "pretending" that they are has been the subject of heretical controversies that were burning issues. Similarly, when a wife is responding to the depressed behavior of her husband and in response to a therapy intervention is uncertain whether or not he is "pretending" to be depressed, this is not a playful issue but a serious change in the real world.

Whether dealing with the larger social situation or the marital problem, this book clarifies issues of paradox, metaphor, and hierarchy that have fascinated therapists for a number of years. The therapy techniques offered range from dispowering someone by one extreme—the use of playful paradox and pretend techniques—or by the other extreme—the requirement that relatives consistently enforce rules and resolve disagreements. Readers will learn new and lively ways of doing therapy and find them illustrated with case examples and actual transcripts of sessions to provide details. However, this book is a contribution that offers more than that. The theoretical approach is presented with a clarity and logic that should encourage readers not only to try the interventions but also to grasp the strategic point of view and discover and develop therapeutic innovations of their own.

November 1980   Jay Haley
                                                                                     Director
                                                        Family Therapy Institute
                                                            of Washington, D.C.

Foreword

Jay Haley has encompassed in his foreword the whole scope of this book. I will specifically address myself to Cloé Madanes' techniques of pretending that are masterful and unique.

The mental health field, like the world of Hieronymus Bosch, is inhabited by monsters. The more alert the therapist is, the more complex and interesting the monster becomes. Cloé Madanes' work, in contrast, is not concerned with monsters but is contained in a frame of hope. The members of a family may hurt each other in the process of living in a confined interpersonal space, but their basic motivation is to help each other. Indeed, they probably cannot do otherwise since as members of a larger organism, the family, they respond to the signals of pain in any part of this body.

Each family brings its idiosyncratic problem, wrapped in its only possible answer. But Madanes develops a custom-made alternative that is full of the creativity of children's play before the rules of the game have prescribed the correct answer. An acute observer of children, Madanes' strategies for change partake of one of the most characteristic ways in which children learn: she uses fantasy and pretending to create alternative realities.

To challenge the restrictive ways in which crystallized family systems prescribe a view of reality to family members, Madanes with a smile suggests, "Let's pretend that the world is different." She creates a therapy of "as if," where dragons are mere butterflies observed with a magnifying glass. In this therapy, a spouse who is depressed needs to pretend depression so that the symptom's communicative power to the other spouse loses meaning. A child pretends to help mother with her fears of robbers so that he can get over his nightmares that were developed to help mother with her fear of robbers. Or perhaps it is the mother who pretends in order to help the child. . . . In the imaginary field of rearranging realities, family members, in effect, break loose from the constraints of an "only" way of being.

The artistry of this strategic therapy is the utilization of very clearly organized rules for a therapy of creativity. It is the use of a narrow field of family transaction, the organization of family members around the symptom, for a therapy of expansion.

There are two possible pitfalls a reader should bear in mind. One is the danger that the clarity of this presentation and the logical order of the strategies may be transformed into mechanical meddling with families. The other is the danger that the focus on the symptomatic member's helpfulness may lead to a view of the family from the perspective of one of the participants in the transaction. Madanes is clearly aware of this when she points out that "the child might have the illusion that he can stop, that he is acting deliberately, but in fact he may be part of a system with a purpose of its own." The individual parts of the family, a multibodied organism, function with the illusion of a separate reality. Therefore, the utilization of the language of helpfulness is in harmony with the felt reality of the parts and is useful in therapy because it challenges the notion of a separate act. In that sense, the notion of the individual's control of the system to which he belongs becomes paradoxically a systemic interpretation.

One of the clearest aspects of Madanes' work is her creative ability to transform the usual routines of lives into new paths where people can find unusual ways of being. Her therapy with families creates a context in which family members and therapists regain the capacity to be curious and exploratory. She moves strategic therapy away from a group of strategies to a new conceptual whole.

November 1980   Salvador Minuchin, M.D.
                                           Professor of Child
                                           Psychiatry and Pediatrics,
                                           University of Pennsylvania

Preface

▦ ▦ ▦ ▦ ▦

Strategic family therapy developed from a concern with power in the relationship between therapist and client and in the relationship among the members of a family. Strategies of psychotherapy were developed to utilize this power in order to produce change. This book takes a further step, broadening the definition of power and offering new paradoxical strategies that emphasize metaphor and make-believe.

Power is usually thought of as involving dominance, oppression, and unsavory motivations on the part of those exercising it. The exploitative aspect of power is not, however, what this book is about; rather, it deals with the positive, benevolent aspects of power. To have power over another is not only to have the opportunity to exploit but also to have the opportunity to take care of, to reform, to comfort, and to guide the other person. The book is about this kind of power: the power

that parents have over their children and children have over
their parents and the power that spouses have over each other.

Chapter One places strategic family therapy in the context of other family therapy approaches, stressing issues relevant to most therapies. These issues include the question of
whether the past or present is emphasized, whether the therapist uses interpretations or directives, whether the goal is
growth or the solution of specific problems, whether hierarchy
is a concern, and whether the unit is an individual, two people,
three people, or a wider network. The various schools of
psychotherapy are then considered—specifically, the kinds of information that would interest the therapist of each school and
the kinds of actions he or she would take to bring about change.

Chapter Two is an overview of the basic elements of strategic family therapy, emphasizing that this book is a contribution to that school.

Chapter Three discusses marital problems. It shows how
hierarchical incongruities in a marriage can occur when a spouse
develops a symptom in an attempt to balance the division of
power in the couple. A cycle is described in which the couple
deal with the dominance of one spouse over the other by alternately focusing on a marital issue, on a spouse's symptom, or on
a child's problem. The task for the therapist is to organize the
couple so that the division of power is balanced and the couple
are organized in a congruent hierarchy. In the four case examples
presented, both paradoxical and straightforward therapeutic
techniques are used.

Chapter Four is about children's problems and how they
can be resolved. The parents are in a position superior to the
child by the fact of being parents, and yet the problem child
assumes a position superior to the parents by protecting them
through symptomatic behavior that often expresses metaphorically the parents' difficulties. Three paradoxical strategies
are presented for arranging that the parents solve the presenting
problem of the child and the incongruity in the family hierarchy. The therapeutic techniques described are characterized
by the use of communication modalities—such as dramatizations, pretending, and make-believe—that are appropriate to

children. A paradoxical approach is introduced in which the parent requests that the child pretend to have the problem or that the child pretend to help the parent. This technique has parallels in Bateson's (1972) observations of the process of play in animals and was influenced by the hypnotic techniques of Milton Erickson (Haley, 1967a). Six case examples are presented to illustrate the various strategies.

In Chapter Five, the relation of metaphorical communication to hierarchy is explored, developing the idea that disturbed behavior in a child is an analogy for a parent's difficulties as well as an attempt to solve these difficulties. The child's disturbed behavior becomes the focus for a system of interaction that is metaphorical for—and replaces—the system of interaction around a parent's difficulties. This way of conceptualizing the problem has its roots in Bateson and Jackson's (1968) description of analogical communication as both a sign for a certain type of behavior and a part or sample of such behavior. The therapist's problem is to get the child to give up the disturbed behavior that is protective of his parents and to motivate the parents to give up a system of interaction that is unfortunate but has a useful function in the family. Three therapeutic strategies and four case examples are presented.

Chapter Six deals with the problems of adolescents and young adults with diagnoses such as schizophrenia, manic-depressive psychosis, alcoholism, and drug addiction. The dilemma of the family is described in terms of the incongruities evident in the organizational hierarchy of these families. This conceptualization is a step forward from communication theory into a wider framework of organizations in which communication takes place. The main premise of the therapy is to enforce a congruent hierarchy, so that the parents are jointly in charge of the youth. This approach is a further development of Haley's (1980) method of family therapy with disturbed young adults, in which a hierarchy is established with the parents in charge, and was influenced by Minuchin's work with psychosomatic families (Minuchin, Rosman, and Baker, 1978).

Fifteen case examples are presented through the book. Of these, two are illustrated with actual transcripts of therapy sessions, with commentary, in Chapters Seven and Eight. Any identifying information in the case examples has been changed to protect the privacy of the families.

Chapter Nine reviews the key elements of the approach and offers a summary with some additional comments.

This book is based on eight years of experience teaching therapy from behind a one-way mirror. In a few of the cases presented, I was the primary therapist. In the majority of cases, however, I was the supervisor in training programs where I observed each session from behind a one-way mirror, planned the approach, called the students on the phone during the sessions, or asked them to come out of the sessions for discussions, and in these ways guided them through the therapy.

Acknowledgments

The training programs in which I taught took place at the Philadelphia Child Guidance Clinic, Hillcrest Children's Center in Washington, D.C., Children's Hospital of Washington, D.C., the Institute of Psychiatry and Human Behavior of the University of Maryland Hospital, and the Family Therapy Institute of Washington, D.C. The trainees who were the therapists in the cases presented in the book were professionals in the field—psychiatrists, psychologists, social workers, and psychiatric nurses—who were learning this particular approach. They were Judy Bankhead, Richard Belson, Michael Fox, Diane Gimber, Anne Gonzalez, Tobias Lopez, Virginia Lopez, Thanna Schmmel-Mascaro, Eugene Schwartz, Joan Shapiro, and Thomas C. Todd. I am indebted to them and to all my other students for contributing to the development of the ideas expressed in this book.

I am indebted also to Salvador Minuchin, who gave me my first job in the United States, who provided an atmosphere at the Philadelphia Child Guidance Clinic where new ideas and creative approaches to therapy could flourish, and who encouraged me to write this book. I appreciate the help of Richard Belson, Henry Harbin, Nidia Madanes, and Braulio Montalvo, who kindly read the manuscript and suggested improvements. I

am particularly grateful to my husband, Jay Haley, without
whose influence, provocations, encouragement, discouragement,
and invaluable help this book never would have been written.

Four chapters in this work have been published elsewhere
in somewhat different form. Chapter One, "Dimensions of
Family Therapy," coauthored with Jay Haley, appeared in the
Journal of Nervous and Mental Disease, Vol. 165, No. 2, 1977,
and was also published under the title "Family Therapies" in
Psychiatric Foundations of Medicine, edited by George U. Balis.
Chapter Three, "Marital Problems: Balancing Power," was pub-
lished in different form under the title "Marital Therapy When a
Symptom Is Presented by a Spouse" in the *International Jour-
nal of Family Therapy,* Vol. 2, No. 3, 1980. Chapter Four,
"Children's Problems: Three Paradoxical Strategies," was pub-
lished in different form in *Family Process,* Vol. 19, March 1980.
Chapter Six, "Severe Problems of Adolescence: Putting the Par-
ents in Charge," was published in different form under the title
"The Prevention of Re-hospitalization in Adolescents and
Young Adults" in *Family Process,* Vol. 20, June 1980.

Chevy Chase, Maryland   Cloé Madanes
November 1980

Contents

Case Studies

▨ ▨ ▨ ▨ ▨

xxix

Strategic
Family
Therapy

❖ ❖ ❖ ❖ ❖

CHAPTER ONE

卌 卌 卌 卌 卌

Dimensions of
Family Therapy

Twenty years have passed since therapists took the revolution-
ary step of bringing whole families under direct observation in
therapy. During this time, the dimensions of the different
schools of family therapy have become more evident. Until recently, the issues between different family therapies were less
clear than those between a family orientation and an individual
one. Now it is evident that "individual" therapy is one way to
intervene into a family—by seeing one person in the family and
not the others. It is also becoming more clear that therapy
works best if a person is in his natural situation. Therapy appears less successful if the person is lifted out of his situation
and treated in isolation from the community of intimates with

Note: This chapter is an expanded and changed version of a paper
originally written with Jay Haley (*Journal of Nervous and Mental Disease,*
1977, *165* (2)), published here with his permission.

1

whom he lives. With these new premises have come new explanations of psychological problems and innovations in therapy.

Even though there is more agreement that the social situation rather than the person is the problem for therapy, still there is no agreement on how to approach the problem. Some therapists oriented to the family continue with a medical model of an individual patient, while others have dropped that framework entirely. Some use an approach based on learning theory, while others do not. Many family therapists offer interpretations, while others primarily offer directives. An example might illustrate the issues. A middle-aged man presents to a therapist the problem that he is severely depressed and apathetic. He is an accountant, and he has not taken care of his business or even paid his own taxes in five years. He constantly worries about his work. He wishes to get it accomplished, but his depression prevents him from doing so. Therapists of different schools would conceptualize this problem in different ways and approach therapy differently. Some would say that the man has an organic problem or an inner depression that is based on childhood experiences with authority figures, and that is why he cannot make his presentations to Internal Revenue in spite of tremendous pressure from colleagues and clients. Others would say that the crucial issue is whether there would be consequences with his wife or other intimates should he successfully perform his work. Such contrasting views represent the differences in view between a person as a problem or a situation as a problem.

The dimensions on which therapists differ will be presented here as well as the various approaches to family therapy based on such differences. These dimensions are less those of the nature of problems but reflect more the aspects of therapy relevant to a theory of change.

Past Versus Present. One of the major dimensions on which therapists differ is whether the emphasis should be on the past or on the present. There has been a transition in psychodynamic theory from the idea that a specific past trauma caused a present symptom to a more complex theory that involves internal objects and processes of projection and introjection. The behavior therapists have gone through a similar transition.

From believing that a specific traumatic event caused a present behavior problem, they have shifted to assuming that reinforcements in the present are important to the continuation of that behavior. If one accepts the idea that the current situation is causal to the problem, past causes become less necessary as an explanation relevant to therapy. The extreme position on this dimension is that the present situation causes the problem and the past is irrelevant.

Interpretation Versus Action. Whatever the cause of a problem, the therapeutic issue is what to do about it. Those therapists who most emphasize a past cause also tend to assume that exploration and interpretation of the past will effect change. For example, if a person recalls and understands his past relationship with his father, he will behave differently toward his current employer. Those therapists who emphasize a cause in the present, while also believing that self-awareness causes change, will interpret to the person how he is behaving in the present. For example, they will point out to him how he is provoking his employer and so causing difficulties. Other therapists who believe that the present situation is the cause of the problem do not assume that understanding that situation will cause change and so do not make interpretations. The experiential therapists will provide a new experience, such as having the person rehearse in a group how to deal with an employer. More directive therapists, such as certain behavior and strategic family therapists, will suggest ways in which the person is to behave with his actual employer rather than with a simulated one. Experiential therapists tend to provide new experiences within a family interview, while directive therapists tend to require new behavior in the real life of the person outside the interview.

Growth Versus Presenting Problem. Therapists also differ in their views of the goals of therapy. Some believe that therapy should solve the problem which the client offers and think that therapy has failed if this problem is not solved, no matter what other changes have taken place. Others, although they are pleased if the presenting problem is solved, do not have this as their basic goal but instead emphasize the growth and development of the person. Family therapists are divided on this issue, with some focusing on the presenting problem and some emphasizing the growth and development of the whole family. The psychodynamic and experiential therapists tend to emphasize growth, while the behavior therapists emphasize the presenting problems.

Method Versus Specific Plan for Each Problem. When a therapy solidifies into a school, it tends to create a formal method of working. The same set of procedures and techniques is applied to every case no matter what the problem. For example, the psychodynamic therapies provide interpretations, and the experiential therapies provide specific exercises for individuals or for groups. Other therapists do not use a standard method but design a specific procedure for each person and each problem. They work on the assumption that everyone does not face the same situation and that people cannot be classified into different types, with a specific method used for each type. For example, if an adolescent steals, a method-oriented therapist will apply a "method." He may always discuss the problem individually with the adolescent, or he may always see him in a group, or he may always meet with him and his family. A problem-oriented therapist faced with an adolescent who steals might see him with his whole family, or with his siblings, or sometimes alone, or he might intervene in the school. The method-oriented therapists tend to continue using the same method whether it fails or not, while the problem-oriented therapists tend to change what they do if it is not succeeding. That is, a method-oriented therapist will, for example, continue to use interpretations or to interview only an adolescent and his parents even though he has struggled unsuccessfully in this way for months. A problem-oriented therapist who is not succeeding will, for example, shift from using interpretations to setting up a positive reinforcement schedule or from seeing the nuclear family to meeting with the adolescent alone or with the extended family.

Unit of One, Two, or Three or More People. What tends to differentiate the individual from the family therapist is the concept of the unit that has the problem: whether it is one person, two people, or three people or more. By definition, psychodynamic therapy has a unit of one, since it is the therapy of the individual psyche. When one person is the focus, the therapy tends to center on that person's feelings, ideas, perceptions, and behavior. In a family therapy with a one-person focus, the therapist tends to emphasize the feelings of the family members about each other and each one's awareness of how he deals with the others.

With a unit of two or more, the emphasis shifts to the relationship between people. A psychiatric problem is understood in terms of a contract between at least two people. For example, if a man is depressed and unable to do his work, the therapist with a unit of one person will try to understand him and help him in terms of his feelings, perceptions, and behaviors. The therapist with a unit of two will assume that his not doing his work is related to his wife. His unit will be husband and wife, since he will assume that the problem is part of the marital situation.

Some therapists think in units of three or more instead of just one or two. With a unit of three, it is possible to think of coalitions and of a hierarchical structure of these coalitions. For example, a man who is depressed and unable to do his work might be thought of as involved in a coalition with his mother against his wife.

The issue here is not how many people are actually involved in a problem or how many people are actually present in the interviews, but how many people are involved in the therapist's way of thinking about the problem. A family of eight can be thought of as eight individuals or as four dyads or as a variety of triangles.

Equality Versus Hierarchy. When the emphasis is on the individual and on groups of unrelated people, the participants are considered of equal status. When one is dealing with a family or another natural group, there is inevitably an issue of hierarchy because the participants are not all equal. They have status differences based on such issues as age, control of funds, and community-vested authority and responsibility. Therapists who think in a unit of one person tend to treat a family as a group of individuals of equal status. Children and parents are allowed to criticize each other equally, and all family members have the right to make rules. Therapists who think in units of three tend to be concerned with status and power in the family. They respect generation lines by not giving equal rights or responsibilities to children, parents, and grandparents.

Analogical Versus Digital. Communication can be classified as digital or analogical. In digital communication, each message has only one referent, belongs to only one logical type, and consists of arbitrary signs (Bateson and Jackson, 1968). The word *chair,* for example, bears no resemblance to the specific object it denotes and has no meaning other than that of a sign used to refer to a certain piece of furniture. From the point of view of digital communication, a stomachache, for example, is a pain in the stomach and nothing else.

Analogical communication has more than one referent, and an analogical message resembles the object it denotes. The clenched fist is both a sign for a certain type of behavior and a part or a sample of such behavior (Bateson and Jackson, 1968). In contrast to digital communication, analogical communication can express different magnitudes. For example, crying, tearing one's clothes, pulling out one's hair, and banging one's head against the wall are actions that, within a culture, analogically express different magnitudes of despair. An analogical message can be assigned meaning only when one takes into account a context of other messages. From the point of view of analogical communication, a stomachache is not only a pain in the stomach but may also be, for instance, an expression of dislike, a way of declining to perform a task, or a request for affection. The meaning assigned to the stomachache as analogical message will depend on the situation and the context of other messages in which the analogical message takes place.

Symptomatic behavior can be conceptualized as either digital or analogical communication. For example, the headaches of a man can be described as an event with no other referent than a pain in the head. This is a digital type of description. Another way to describe human behavior is to say that any act has more than one referent. For example, when a man is talking about his headaches to a therapist, he is talking about more than one kind of pain. From this point of view, behavior is always communication on many levels. When communication is seen as having more than one referent, the report and command aspect also appears. For example, "I have a headache" may be a report on more than one internal state, but it may also be a way of declining sexual relations or of getting a husband to help with the children.

Some schools of therapy are based on the theory that, no matter what the disturbed behavior (fears, psychosomatic problems, antisocial acts), it is a metaphorical expression of the difficulties in a person's life situation. Other schools argue that it is best to think of a symptom as a behavior with no referent other than the stimulus that precedes it or the response that follows it. The behavior therapists, who think of a symptom as having only one referent, differ in this respect from therapists who consider a symptom to be a communication about a person's life situation and therefore a referent to something else.

Straightforward Versus Deliberately Paradoxical. Some therapists make straightforward interventions that they expect will be accepted or followed. Others make paradoxical interventions designed to provoke a family to change by rebelling against the therapist. Communication is paradoxical when it involves two messages that qualify each other in conflicting ways. The messages "Be spontaneous," "Don't be so obedient," "I want you to dominate me" are common paradoxes in human relationships (Haley, 1963). They are paradoxical because if the receiver of the message complies with the request, he is not complying with the request. The paradox occurs because one directive is qualified by another, at a different level of abstraction, in a conflictual way.

It has been proposed (Haley, 1963) that all therapy involves paradox and that what produces change is the paradox involved in any therapy. The psychoanalytic method, for example, is paradoxical in that the therapist attempts to influence the patient as little as possible, within the framework of a relationship whose only purpose is to influence the patient. Even though there is a paradoxical element in all therapy, the different schools can be distinguished by whether or not they deliberately use paradoxical techniques.

Among therapists who have used paradoxical directives

deliberately, rationales for what they are doing vary as well as explanations of what brings about change, but all of them have used basically one paradoxical technique: Within a context where a patient comes to therapy in order to change, the therapist asks him to produce more of the behavior that the patient wants changed, and within a context of acceptance of the involuntary nature of the patient's behavior, the therapist requests that the patient produce this behavior voluntarily.

Schools of Therapy

A therapist who places a patient on a couch and has him free associate does not seem to have much in common with a therapist who brings in a whole family and has them mourn for a dead grandfather. A therapist who requires his client to visit distant relatives does not seem to be similar to a therapist who has parents give candy to a child every time he performs a certain act. But how similar or different they are depends on the dimensions by which they are compared. Two therapists can have quite different therapeutic approaches, and yet both can have the individual as the unit, just as they can have various ways of dealing with past situations and yet still deal only with the past. A difference thought to distinguish family therapists from individual therapists is the number of people in the room, because family therapists tend to see intimate groups of people together. However, the same therapeutic assumptions may guide therapy with a family as with a single individual.

One may compare different approaches to therapy according to the dimensions previously described. The reader is referred to Table 1 for a presentation of this description.

Psychodynamic Therapy. A therapy based on psychodynamics has an individual focus whether a person is seen alone or in a family group. The therapist is concerned with each family member's memories of the past, feelings about relevant people, motivation, and so on. More specifically, the dimensions of therapy characteristic of this school are the following. There is an emphasis on the past, both for the cause of a symptom and for the means to change it. It is assumed that a person has

Table 1. Comparison of Different Approaches to Family Therapy According to Various Dimensions

	Psycho-dynamic	Experiential	Behavioral	Extended Family	Communication	
					Structural	Strategic
Dimensions:						
Past	x					
Unit: 1 person	x	x				
Interpret (past)	x	x	x			
Interpret (present)	x	x			x	
Method	x	x		x		
Growth	x	x		x	x	
Analogical	x	x		x	x	x
Straightforward	x	x	x	x	x	x
Present		x	x	x	x	x
New experience		x	x	x	x	x
Directives			x	x	x	x
Plan for therapy			x		x	x
Unit: 2 people			x	x	x	x
Unit: 3 or more people				x	x	x
Hierarchy			x	x	x	x
Presenting problem			x			
Digital			x	x		
Paradoxical			x			x

symptoms because of a past set of experiences. These experiences are repressed and beyond awareness. The therapist focuses on the past and on bringing these ideas and experiences into awareness. The method of therapy is largely interpretive, whether interviews are with one person or a whole family, and the therapist's comments are aimed at helping the person become aware of both past and present behaviors and the connections between them (Sigal, Barrs, and Doubilet, 1976). Directives are not given, and the therapist does not take responsibility for what happens outside the session. Deliberate paradoxical interventions are not made. The emphasis tends to be on a long-term process, with the goal of helping a person grow and develop rather than just getting over the presenting problem. Usually the emphasis is on method, with each family treated in a similar way no matter what the problem. Typically the whole family is seen once a week for one-hour sessions, and there are two therapists. The theory focuses on a unit of one, and families are usually described as a set of discrete individuals with repressed ideation and emotions. Hierarchy is not emphasized. The therapy is largely analogical, insofar as the therapist is interested in metaphors and statements about the meaning of experiences (Ackerman, 1966; Boszormenyi-Nagy and Spark, 1973; Dicks, 1967; Framo, 1970; MacGregor and others, 1964; Rubinstein, 1964; Sigal, Barrs, and Doubilet, 1976).

This approach to family therapy is most congenial for a therapist who has worked with individuals in traditional psychodynamic therapy. The therapist need change little of his theory, since he can continue with the idea of repression and with interpretations and educative comments. The goal is to bring about insight and understanding and to express emotions.

In the case of the depressed accountant mentioned earlier, this approach would assume that the depression is based on past experiences with authority figures. If the man is seen individually, the therapist would help him transfer his depression from the original authority figures to the relationship with the therapist and would help him understand its causes. If seen in family therapy, he would be helped to understand how he transfers his depression in relation to original authority figures—not only to the therapist but also to his wife and other relatives.

The Experiential School. The basic contribution of this school, which differentiates it from the psychodynamic approach, is its greater emphasis on the present and the introduction of new experiences in the session as a therapeutic tool. Although the focus on expressing emotions suggests that this school emphasizes a unit of one, the focus on new experiences in the present often involves other people.

A depressed accountant would be thought of not only as repressing rage against authority but as being angry at a particular person, such as his wife. Experiential therapists with an individual orientation would put this man in an artificial group to help him break out of his inhibitions by expressing his feelings about the members of the group. Those with a family orientation would see the man together with his wife to help him express his feelings to her and would teach the couple to fight constructively. Rather than interpret about past causes, family experiential therapists tend to enlighten their clients about feelings and about the ways they deal with one another. This is the school that most emphasizes the value of honesty in expressing views and feelings and the importance of clear communication to solve interactional difficulties.

Like the psychodynamicists, experiential therapists tend to use interpretations, sometimes in the form of confrontations. They emphasize growth rather than the presenting problem, and they are not concerned with hierarchy. They do not use paradoxical interventions deliberately. They are focused on method, since they put people through a standard set of procedures. They are analogical, since they are concerned with meanings of experience rather than with individual acts. The school differs from other family therapies in the willingness to do group therapy with unrelated groups of strangers as well as with natural groups. There is wide variety, ranging from the more conservative to the most extreme, in the kinds of experiences asked of clients (Duhl, Kantor, and Duhl, 1973; Gehrke and Kirschenbaum, 1967; Kempler, 1973; Satir, 1972).

The Behavioral School. The behavioral school differs from the previous ones because the theory and practice come from learning theory rather than Freudian psychology. A dimension in common is the unit of one person. With the experiential school it also shares the emphasis on the present and on new experiences; but whereas the experiential therapists emphasize new experiences as means of expressing emotions, behavior therapists do so in order to modify specific behavior. In the case of the depressed accountant, an experiential therapist might have him act out the situation of doing his work to express his emotions. A behavior therapist might have him act out the situation of doing his work to learn how to go about it correctly and thereby gain confidence. What is unique about this school in comparison with the two previous ones is the sharp focus on the presenting problem. The emphasis is on the change desired by the clients rather than on their growth and development.

Instead of using a standard method, many behavior therapists will design a procedure for each presenting problem. They do not offer interpretations but give directives for behavior, both in the interview and outside of it. Hierarchy is not a relevant issue for this school. The concern is largely with individual acts rather than with the analogical meaning of those acts. Recently, some behavior therapists have begun to deliberately use paradoxical interventions with individuals (Ascher, 1979; Ascher and Efran, 1978).

Behavior therapists are a minority among family therapists (Hawkins and others, 1971; Patterson, 1971; Patterson, Ray, and Shaw, 1969; Stuart, 1969). Rather than the three-person orientation of many family therapists, the family behavior therapists tend to focus on a unit of two persons. For example, in the case of the depressed man, the behavior therapist might have the wife give him positive reinforcements for each step toward a more active day-to-day life. This would increase his activity at home and at work and so lessen the depression. If the patient's mother seemed involved, the therapist might have the mother, instead of the wife, reinforce him. However, the behavior therapist does not think in units of three persons and so would not think of the situation as one where a man is caught between a wife who wants him to do his work and a mother who does not, nor of his depression as a consequence of that situation.

Extended-Family Systems. In the previously described schools of family therapy, the family therapy developed out of a previous individual therapy. In contrast, other family therapies have taken ideas from different individual therapies but also have contributed novel developments, so that it is not possible to describe them as coming from one particular school of individual therapy. One such group constitutes what can be referred to as the extended-family therapists.

The main characteristic of this group is an emphasis on the wider kinship structure (Bell, 1962). Therapists in this group might conceptualize the situation in units of one, two, or three; but they will involve many relatives in the therapy. There is a tendency for the form of the therapy to take one of two foci: either the therapist brings together all the significant people in the client's life in one large group, or he sends the client to visit all the significant people in his life.

The large group, or family network therapy, is often similar to experiential therapy in its focus on growth and development of family members and sometimes on a confrontation experience (Attneave, 1969; Speck and Attneave, 1973). The focus is on the present and not on the past, on a general method that is applied to all cases and not a specific plan for each problem. Symptomatic behavior is thought to be analogical. One set of relationships in a network is changed in order to produce change in another set.

In the approach requiring a client to contact significant people in his life, relationships are thought to be analogical in the sense that changing one set of relationships in a network will change another set. For example, if a man presents the problem of depression, he would be expected to change if he activated his wider kin network and dealt differently with his parents and relatives. According to this school, family issues in one generation are replicated in the next. This repetition can be avoided if the therapist coaches or directs the patient to differentiate himself by behaving in new ways with the extended family.

Like the psychoanalytic and experiential schools, this approach emphasizes growth and method. Unlike these schools, it emphasizes directives, intergenerational processes, and hierarchy. In contrast to the experiential school, where families are encouraged to express emotions in the sessions, this approach attempts to avoid emotional interchanges and to focus on rational processes. Paradoxical interventions are used deliberately.

Despite the fact that a great deal of the literature of this school (Bowen, 1971, 1975, 1978; "Towards the Differentiation of a Self . . . ," 1972) frequently uses individual terminology (undifferentiated "ego" mass, differentiation of "self" scale, "emotional" system), the focus is on a unit of three. It is a theory of the instability of a dyad in the sense that two people involved in an emotionally intense relationship will tend to involve a third person. The therapist's task when talking to a couple is to help them while not becoming emotionally involved as part of a triangle.

One type of family therapy not dealt with here, since its theories are the same as those of other schools, is the type that brings different families together into one large group (Lacqueur, Laburt, and Morong, 1964). This is called "multiple-family therapy," and the emphasis is on group process. Extended-family therapy also has groups of married couples—not whole families—brought together; but, unlike several of the multiple-family approaches, this particular school allows no group process among the couples. The therapist works with one couple while the others observe, and then with the next couple.

Communication. The communication approach was the first family therapy that did not have its origins in a form of individual therapy. This approach did not so much become a school in itself as a body of theory adopted by other schools.

Instead of developing from previous therapy, this approach stemmed from the biological and social sciences. Unlike psychodynamic theory, which had roots early in the century, communication theory did not develop until the midcentury. In 1948 Norbert Wiener published *Cybernetics,* and through the next decade all the sciences began to emphasize homeostatic systems with feedback processes that cause the system to be self-corrective. This emphasis appeared in the field of therapy in the 1950s as part of the development of family theory. Although the ideas became evident in a number of therapies, the communication approach became most well known through Gregory Bateson's research project on communication, which ran from 1952 to 1962 (Bateson, 1972; Haley, 1963, 1976a; Jackson, 1968a, 1968b; Jackson and Weakland, 1961; Weakland, 1962). The idea of the double bind was published in 1956 (Bateson and others) and influenced many therapists to begin to think from a communication point of view. The approach suggested that the interchange of messages between people defines relationships, and these relationships are stabilized by homeostatic processes in the form of actions of family members within the family. The minimum unit was seen as two people, a sender and a receiver of messages. The therapy developing out of this view emphasized changing a family system by arranging that family members behave, or communicate, differently with one another. It was not a therapy related to lifting repression or bringing about self-understanding, nor was it based on a theory of conditioning. The past was dropped as a central issue, because the way in which people are communicating at the moment was the focus of attention. Over the decade of the 1950s, the unit shifted from two people to three or more people as the family began to be conceived of as having an organization and a structure. The unit became more and more a child in relationship to two adults, or an adult in relation to another adult of a different generation, and so on. Analogical communication was emphasized more than digital (although these terms themselves were emphasized by Bateson as a way of classifying any communication).

In the early family therapy with this approach, awareness was still thought to bring about change, and so interpretations were used because other therapy techniques had not developed to fit the new ways of thinking. By the 1960s a therapist using the communication approach was finding it necessary to defend himself for using interpretations and was not educating the family. It was assumed within this approach that new experience, in the sense of new behavior that provokes changes in the family system, brings about change. Directives were used in the interview to change communication pathways, such as requiring people to talk together who had habitually not done so. Directives were also given for outside the interview, particularly as a result of the influence of Milton Erickson's directive therapy on the communication therapists (Haley, 1967a, 1973). Paradoxical interventions were used deliberately. The tendency in the early days was to be growth oriented because of a concern with encouraging a wider range of communicative behavior in the family system. Some adherents, influenced by Erickson, focused more on the presenting problem, but even then it was a way of increasing complexity in the system. However, the presenting problem was never dismissed as "only a symptom," because symptomatic behavior was considered a necessary and appropriate response to the communicative behavior that provoked it. There was little emphasis on hierarchy in the early stages; family members were encouraged to communicate as equals. In some approaches, the emphasis was on clarifying communication (Satir, 1964). Later there was a developing concern with status in the family organization. Jackson (1968a, 1968b; Jackson and Weakland, 1961), one of the major innovators in the communication approach, was emphasizing the importance of supporting parental authority when young people were defined as psychotic. Parents and young people were not interviewed as peers, as they would be in a therapy based on free association or individual self-expression.

The communication approach tended to become part of other approaches. Satir (1972) developed a more "experiential" communication approach after participating in Esalen experiential groups. The extended-family system's theories were influenced by communication ideas. However, there were basically two branches of therapy developing out of the communication approach; one was *structural,* emphasizing the hierarchical organization in the family and describing different communication structures. The other was the *strategic,* also emphasizing organizational structure but focusing more on the repeating sequences on which structures are based.

Communication: Structural. The structural family therapy school adopted many communication ideas for therapy with lower-class families, where traditional therapy was not helpful (Minuchin, 1974; Minuchin and Montalvo, 1967; Minuchin and others, 1967). In this approach, there is a focus on hierarchy, with parents expected to be in charge of children and a family not considered an organization of equals. Families are conceived of as composed of subsystems, such as husband-wife, mother-child, and siblings. The approach is analogical, and pathology is considered to occur in families that are too enmeshed (there is little or no subsystem differentiation) or too disengaged (each person constitutes an independent subsystem). The emphasis is on the present, not the past, and the unit tends to be the triad. A transactional pattern in a family may be the following: the mother encourages the daughter to disobey the father, who attacks the daughter when he is angry at the mother. The conflict between the parents is said to detour through the daughter.

A main focus of the therapy is on differentiating subsystems. For example, parents are encouraged to talk to each other without interruptions from the children, or the parents are prevented from interrupting when siblings are talking with each other. In disengaged families, the therapist increases the flow among subsystems, so that family members will be more engaged and supportive of each other.

In the case of the depressed man, this approach would assume that depression is related to others in the family, and all members would be brought together. If both the wife and the mother were involved, the therapist would focus on differentiating the couple subsystem, so that the husband would feel more secure in their relationship and would therefore be able to leave it temporarily to be involved in outside activities such as his work. Within the sessions, the main therapeutic technique is to change the ways people relate by arranging who talks to whom about what and in what way. The rationale is that changes in communication pathways lead to important structural changes in the family. These changes are continued outside the sessions through tasks assigned by the therapist. For example, a father may be asked to spend a certain amount of time every day talking to his son about a specific subject.

In this therapy, educational interpretations are made in a

special way. Ordinarily interpretations are made with the belief that people will change once they understand the ways in which they deal with each other. In this approach, the therapist uses interpretations to define a situation that may not be an accurate portrait of what is happening but that is one the therapist can change. For example, the therapist may bring a couple together by pointing out that the daughter rules and divides them. Although this "interpretation" may be only partially true, the parents will dislike being thought of in this way and will pull together to take charge of the daughter.

In this school, the emphasis is more on structural problems in the family than on the presenting problem, except with life-threatening situations (as in anorexia and diabetic coma), where the emphasis is on the presenting problem (Berger, 1974; Liebman, Minuchin, and Baker, 1974a, 1974b; Minuchin, Rosman, and Baker, 1978). The therapy tends to be growth oriented, and paradoxical interventions are not deliberately used. This school does not have a set method but varies what is done with the family structure.

Because this book is a contribution to the school of strategic therapy, a more detailed description of the main characteristics of this school is presented in the following chapter.

CHAPTER TWO

æ æ æ æ æ

Elements of Strategic Family Therapy

Strategic family therapy is a development that stems from the strategic therapy of Milton Erickson (Haley, 1967a, 1973). It includes diverse approaches, but all of them have certain characteristics in common. A primary feature is that the responsibility is on the therapist to plan a strategy for solving the client's problems (Haley, 1963, 1967a, 1976b; Herr and Weakland, 1979; Montalvo, 1973; Montalvo and Haley, 1973; Palazzoli and others, 1978; Papp, 1980; Rabkin, 1977; Watzlawick, Weakland, and Fisch, 1974). The therapist sets clear goals, which always include solving the presenting problem. The emphasis is not on a method to be applied to all cases but on designing a strategy for each specific problem. Since the therapy focuses on the social context of human dilemmas, the therapist's task is to design an intervention in the client's social situation.

19

One set of goals for strategic family therapy is to help people past a crisis to the next stage of family life. These stages have been described by Haley (1973) as (1) the courtship period, (2) early marriage, (3) childbirth and dealing with the young, (4) middle marriage, (5) weaning parents from children, and (6) retirement and old age.

Of particular concern within this approach is the period when a young person is leaving home (Haley, 1980). The severe pathology (for instance, schizophrenia, delinquency, or drug addiction) that frequently occurs at this stage is understood as a difficulty in getting past a stage in the life cycle. In fact, all the traditional diagnostic categories, understood in the context of the individual's family situation, are seen as difficulties in progressing from one stage of the life cycle to another.

"A problem is defined as a type of behavior that is part of a sequence of acts between several people" (Haley, 1976b, p. 2). Symptoms such as "depression" or "phobias" are thought of as contracts between people and therefore as adaptive to relationships. The therapist is included in such relationships, since he or she defines the problem. To label someone as "schizophrenic," "delinquent," or "manic-depressive" is to participate in the creation of the problem that the therapy must solve. Sometimes the label creates a problem, so that the solution is made more difficult. "Depression" is more difficult to resolve than "laziness"; "schizophrenia" is not easy to cure, but "difficulty in holding a job" is more amenable to change. The approach emphasizes a distinction between (1) identifying a problem presented in therapy and (2) creating a problem by applying a diagnosis or by characterizing an individual or a family in a certain way. Psychiatric and psychological diagnostic criteria are seldom used, and the first task of the therapist is to define a presenting problem in such a way that it can be solved.

The approach is sensitive to and includes a social network wider than the family, particularly involving professionals who have power over the person with the presenting problem (Laing, 1967, 1969). When a youth is hospitalized, the social unit for the therapist is not only the young person and his family but also the professionals with power over medication, hospitalization, and discharge (Haley, 1980). Similarly, when someone is on probation, the power of the probation officer and the court is such that they must be included in the therapist's plans. Therapists are expected to influence teachers and school personnel, who can determine the way a child is identified and labeled. Sometimes it is necessary to make the dissension among professionals the focus of therapy.

The strategic approach emphasizes the analogical in the way it conceptualizes a problem. It is assumed that a problem in a child or a symptom in an adult is a way that one person communicates with another. In the case of a depressed man who does not do his work, it would be assumed that this is the way the man and his wife (and/or his mother, father, children, and others) communicate about some specific issues, such as whether the wife appreciates her husband and his work, or whether the husband should do what his wife or his mother wishes, and so on. It is possible that the couple could become unstable over the presenting problem and that then a child might develop a symptom which will keep the father actively involved taking care of the child rather than depressed and incompetent. It is assumed that a symptom analogically, or metaphorically, expresses a problem and is also a solution, although usually an unsatisfactory one, for the people involved.

The focus of therapy often is on changing analogies and metaphors. Erickson, for example, changes the patient's analogies by telling stories that resemble the patient's problem (Haley, 1967a). Haley (1963) suggests that a patient can be asked to say he has a symptom—a stomachache, for example— when in fact he has not, so that the verbal statement serves the same metaphorical purpose but without the pain. He points out that some people are able to say, "You give me a pain" and not have the pain while others must develop a pain as a way of making a statement about their situation.

The goals of the therapy are primarily to prevent the repetition of sequences and to introduce more complexity and alternatives. For example, a typical sequence is one where the child develops problems when the parents threaten to separate, the parents stay together to deal with their problem child, and as the child behaves more normally the parents threaten separation again, which leads to the child's developing problems. The task of the therapist is to change this sequence so that improvement of the child is unrelated to whether the parents separate or not.

The therapy is planned in steps, or stages, to achieve the goals. Every problem is defined as involving at least two and usually three people. The therapist first decides who is involved in the presenting problem and in what way. Next, the therapist decides on an intervention which will shift the family organization so that the presenting problem is not necessary. Usually change is planned in stages, so that a change in one situation or one set of relationships will lead to another change in another relationship and then to yet another until the whole situation changes. Interventions are planned to involve family members with one another or to disengage various family members from one another. Often the therapist attempts first to create a new problem and to solve it in such a way that the change will lead to the solution of the problem originally presented by the family.

There is a concern with hierarchy in this approach. Parents are expected to be in charge of their children, and cross-generation coalitions, such as one parent's siding with a child against another parent, are blocked. There is also a cautious concern about where the therapist is in the hierarchy, so that he or she does not inadvertently form coalitions with members low in the hierarchy against those who are higher.

Haley (1976b) describes pathological systems in terms of malfunctioning hierarchies, emphasizing that one way to design a strategy is to shift from the presenting system to a different abnormal one before reorganizing the family in a more functional hierarchy. He gives the following examples to present this idea:

> A mother may be too central to her children, so that there is no hierarchy in the family and all the children function through her as if she were the hub of a wheel. In such a case it may be appropriate to create a

system where an older child relieves the mother by taking charge. Essentially, this change creates a parental child hierarchy [a family organization with an older child who functions as an adult by taking care of the younger children]. From this new abnormal state, it is possible to shift to a more reasonable hierarchy in the family, so that all children can participate with different responsibilities.

Conversely, if the family comes in with a parental child system, one possibility is to make the mother overly central as the first stage. This change frees the parental child, and from this new abnormal hierarchy it is possible to go to a more normal one.

If the sequence involves a grandmother who is crossing generation lines and siding with the child against the mother, one can follow the procedure of giving full responsibility to the grandmother. One can then go from this abnormal stage to another abnormal one in which all responsibility is given to the mother and the grandmother cannot discipline the child at all. From this abnormal state one can go to the more normal one.

If mother and child are in an overly intense relationship and the father is peripheral, the first stage can be one where the father takes total control of the child and the mother is excluded. This is an abnormal system, and from it one can move to a more normal one. It might also be possible to use an older sibling as a parental child to disengage mother and child, thereby introducing a parental child system as the first stage. Similarly, one might introduce the grandmother and create that hierarchy as a first stage [Haley, 1976b, pp. 122-123].

Interventions usually take the form of directives about something that the family members are to do, both inside and outside of the interview. These directives are designed to change the ways in which people relate to each other and to the therapist. Directives are also used to gather information by observing the way people respond to the instructions.

The approach assumes that all therapy is directive and that a therapist cannot avoid being directive, since even the issues he chooses to comment on and his tone of voice are directive. In this therapy, directives are deliberately planned, and they are the main therapeutic technique. Insight and understanding are not emphasized, and there are no interpretations.

As an example, in the case of the depressed man in Chapter One, the therapist might ask the wife to monitor the husband's work. Ostensibly, this would be to relieve his depression, but in actuality the therapist would be changing the relationship between husband and wife—for example, by helping the wife to be more appreciative of the husband when he does do his work or by making the task a joint endeavor between husband and wife, from which other people, such as the wife's friends and relatives, are excluded.

Since this therapy focuses on solving the presenting problem, it is not growth oriented or concerned with the past. The emphasis is on communication in the present. Families go through new experiences as they follow the therapist's directives, but the experience is not a goal in itself; nor is there an emphasis on working through something or being aware of how communication takes place; if the family can get over the problem without knowing how or why, that is satisfactory, since so much necessarily is outside awareness (Montalvo, 1976).

Directives may be straightforward or paradoxical, simple and involving one or two people, or complex and involving the whole family. Straightforward directives are planned with the goal of changing sequences of interaction in the family. The interventions are directed to involve previously disengaged family members, promote agreement and good feeling, increase positive interchanges, provide information, and help a family organize in more functional ways by setting rules, defining generational boundaries, and establishing individual goals and plans to achieve those goals.

The first step in giving a directive is to motivate the family to follow the directive. The way the therapist approaches motivating a family depends on the nature of the task, the nature of the family, and the kind of relationship that family members have with the therapist. The therapist is always precise in giving directives, so that they have the effect that is intended. When directives are to be followed outside of the session, usually everyone in the family participates in the action, which is often first rehearsed during the interview.

Haley (1976b, p. 80) suggests that "a way to view the approach is to give directives going directly to the goal, such as getting the child to school. For those families in which a direct approach is not effective, the therapist falls back on an alternative plan that will motivate the family toward the goal. If that alternative is not effective, fall back on yet another alternative plan." The more clear the problem and the goal of the therapy, the easier it is to design directives.

The following are some examples of directives given by Haley (1976b, pp. 60-63):

> 1. A father and son are asked to do a minor thing that the mother would not approve of. It will be difficult for the mother to arrange what they do when the thing must be something she does not want.
>
> 2. A father who is siding with his small daughter against the wife may be required to wash the sheets when the daughter wets the bed. This task will tend to disengage daughter and father or cure the bed wetting.
>
> 3. A mother who felt she was unable to control a 12-year-old boy said that she was reluctantly going to put him in military boarding school because there was nothing else she could do. The therapist suggested that the boy did not really know what a military school would be like, and in fairness the mother should teach him about one before sending him away. The mother agreed, and under the therapist's direction she began to teach the boy to stand at attention, be polite, and make his bed every morning after rising early. It became a kind of game between mother and son to have her be the sergeant and him be the private. In two weeks he was behaving well enough so that mother did not think it was necessary to send him off to military school. Mother had found a way to deal with the son, and he had found a way to do what she asked.

Sometimes the therapist gives directives in metaphorical ways without making explicit what he or she wants to happen.

As Erickson suggests, people are often more willing to follow a directive if they do not know that they have received one (Haley, 1967a, 1976b).

In this approach, paradoxical directives are deliberately planned. The directives are paradoxical because the therapist has told the family that he wants to help them change but at the same time he is asking them not to change. The approach is based on the idea that some families who come for help are resistant to the help offered; here the therapist wants the family members to resist him so that they will change. Haley (1963, 1976b) describes several strategies:

1. The therapist restrains the family members from improving, discussing with the family what will be the consequences of solving the presenting problem, and talking only about that in each interview.

2. A couple who regularly fight in unproductive ways are requested to have a fight.

3. A spouse is asked to complain about a symptom at times when the symptom is not occurring, so that the other spouse will not know whether the symptomatic spouse is really symptomatic or only following the therapist's instructions.

4. A spouse is directed to encourage the other spouse to have the symptom.

Palazzoli and colleagues (1978) systematically use a paradoxical strategy with families of schizophrenics. The behaviors that perpetuate the dysfunction are prescribed to all the members of the family. When the therapist benevolently prescribes the rules of the system, the family may be moved to change these rules.

Papp (1980) distinguishes between directives that are compliance based or direct, referring to the therapist's expectation that the family will comply with them, and those that are defiance based or paradoxical, referring to the therapist's expectation that the family will defy them. Compliance-based interventions—advice, explanations, and suggestions—include promoting open communication, coaching parents on how to control children, redistributing jobs and privileges among family members, establishing disciplinary rules, regulating privacy, and providing information that the family members lack. Defiance-based or paradoxical directives are those that depend for success on the family's defying the therapist's instructions or following them to the point of absurdity and recoiling. Papp (1980) describes three steps in giving a paradoxical directive: (1) defining the symptom as benignly motivated to preserve family stability; (2) prescribing the symptom-producing cycle of interaction; and (3) restraining the family whenever they show signs of changing.

Since in strategic family therapy a specific therapeutic plan is designed for each problem, there are no contraindications in terms of patient selection and suitability. The approach has been used with the whole age range and all socioeconomic classes with presenting problems of various kinds, such as psychosis, brain damage, marital problems, loneliness, fears, delinquency, and psychosomatic symptoms. In each case, the therapist designs a strategy; if after a few weeks this strategy is not successful in accomplishing the goals of the therapy, a new strategy is formulated. This is not an approach where the therapist continues to do more of the same when he is failing. The approach allows the therapist to borrow in turn from all other models of therapy any techniques that could be useful in solving a presenting problem. This is a pragmatic approach where therapists are expected to keep close track of therapeutic progress. Regular follow-ups are encouraged.

This book adds to the school of strategic therapy (1) a focus that is not on levels of communication but on levels of organization; (2) a concern with hierarchical incongruities, in which two incompatible power structures are simultaneously defined in the family; (3) a concern with understanding the metaphor expressed by a symptom and by the family's interaction; and (4) a concern with understanding the specificity of a symptom—that is, why a particular symptom is chosen.

In terms of therapeutic strategies and techniques, the book contributes (1) a new approach to the use of paradox that is not based on defiance or resistance by the family; (2) additional strategies for solving problems in couples and achieving a more egalitarian relationship; (3) a focus on special techniques for changing the metaphors expressed by symptomatic behavior; and (4) techniques for persuading the parents to take responsibility and to solve their children's problems.

CHAPTER THREE

⊞ ⊞ ⊞ ⊞ ⊞

Marital Problems: Balancing Power

All couples struggle with the issue of sharing power and of organizing in a hierarchy where areas of control and responsibility are divided between the spouses. This power refers to the possibility not only of dominating the other but also of comforting, reforming, taking care of, and taking responsibility for the other spouse. Couples divide power in many different ways. In one couple, for example, one spouse may make all the decisions having to do with home and children, while the other spouse will make all the decisions involving the social context outside the family. In another couple, one spouse may have power over all the decisions involving money, while the other spouse may make all the decisions involving family and friends. Sometimes the spouses resolve their struggle by deriving power from helplessness. The spouses may, for example, capitulate to an adolescent child, who will make them equal by being superior to both of them in the hierarchy. In another couple, one spouse may make most of the decisions, but the other spouse may helplessly side with the children in a way that undermines the decision-making spouse. In other couples, a symptom, instead of a child, is chosen as a source of power. This chapter deals with those couples who choose a symptom as a way of balancing power in their relationship. Such symptoms as depression, alcoholism, fears, anxiety, and psychosomatic complaints may serve this purpose. (For another discussion of the interpersonal power of symptoms, see Haley, 1963.)

One way to describe a marriage with a symptomatic spouse is in terms of a hierarchical incongruity in the marriage. Typically, the symptomatic person is in an inferior position to the other spouse, who tries to help and to change him; yet the symptomatic spouse is also in a superior position in that he refuses to be helped and to change. While requesting advice and help, the symptomatic spouse refuses to be influenced. In this way, two incongruous hierarchies are defined in the couple. In one, the person with the problem is in an inferior position because he is in need of help, and the nonsymptomatic spouse is in the superior position of helper. In the other, the symptomatic spouse will not be influenced and helped, which puts him in a superior position to the nonsymptomatic spouse, who tries unsuccessfully to influence and change him. If the symptomatic behavior is abandoned, the problem spouse loses the superior position in relation to the other spouse, who will no longer try unsuccessfully to change and to influence him. If the normal spouse is successful in influencing the symptomatic one to become nonsymptomatic, he or she loses the superior position of being the nonsymptomatic member of the couple.

Symptomatic behavior in one spouse can organize the other spouse's behavior in many different ways. How free time will be spent, how money should be used, how to relate to the extended family—these are just a few examples of areas that can be dominated by the helplessness of the symptomatic spouse. Even the way the nonsymptomatic spouse should be helpful, and the fact that he should keep trying to help even though he always fails, is often engineered by the symptomatic spouse. The couple are caught in an interaction that defines simultaneously their power and their weakness in relation to each other.

The concept of a position that is *simultaneously* inferior and superior is important here. Spouses may be in a superior or an inferior position in relation to each other alternately and in different areas. For example, one spouse may be more affectionate and the other more intellectual; one may manage the money well, and the other may be good at doing repairs around the house. These areas of expertise may lead to a division of power and to a hierarchical arrangement that is satisfactory to both spouses. Sometimes, however, the division of power is unsatisfactory to one of the spouses, and the couple do not find a way of balancing power that is satisfactory to both. It is then that symptomatic behavior may appear (the degree of dissatisfaction before a symptom develops is idiosyncratic to each couple). One of the spouses may develop a symptom as an attempt to change the hierarchical arrangement and balance the division of power in the dyad. But symptomatic behavior in one spouse is an unfortunate solution to the power struggle in that, instead of balancing power in the relationship, it produces a hierarchical incongruity in the marriage. The couple become restricted to a situation where one behavior defines simultaneously an inferior and a superior position of each spouse in relation to the other spouse. If the symptom improves, both spouses stand to lose power in relation to each other, since equality is maintained by simultaneously defining both members of the dyad as inferior and superior to each other. If the symptomatic behavior disappears, the spouses go back to the struggle over the division of power that originally led to the appearance of the symptomatic behavior. They may struggle over this issue for some time until a symptom develops which once again will be an attempt to change the hierarchical arrangement and balance the division of power. This cycle can remain unchanged for many years. The symptomatic spouse may not get progressively worse and may not improve over time. The symptomatic behavior—although helpful in that it results in a certain equality between the spouses, often eliciting a more benevolent and positive interaction and preventing a separation —does not help the spouses deal with and resolve the issues that concern them and, in fact, prevents the resolution of these issues.

The System as Metaphor

A system of interaction develops around a sympton in one spouse and becomes an analogy for a marital struggle that the couple cannot resolve. That is, the symptom itself is a metaphor (for example, a wife who vomits compulsively may be expressing disgust with her husband), and the way the couple deal with the symptom is a *system* metaphor for other types of interaction in various areas of their lives. For example, spouses A and B may struggle over whether B should obey A in the management of money or over whether B's work problems are more important than other issues. If the struggle is so severe that the marriage is threatened, or if the inequality in the division of power becomes dysfunctional or intolerable, one of the spouses can develop a symptom. If spouse B becomes depressed, for example, or develops a psychosomatic symptom, then A and B can discuss the symptom instead of the other issue that they could not resolve. For example, instead of arguing about whether B should follow A's directives in the management of money, they can argue about whether B should obey A in what should be done about the symptom. Instead of discussing B's work problems, they can discuss B's inappropriate symptomatic behavior. The system of interaction around the symptom is an analogy for other systems of interaction in the marriage. The interaction around the symptom makes it possible for A and B to know where each stands in relation to the other on certain issues without having to explicitly discuss those issues and so endanger the marriage.

The sequence of events would be the following. Spouses A and B have a marriage in which A is dominant. A's career is considered more important than B's, and A makes the decisions (on how money should be spent, on where to live, and so on). At a certain point, B develops a symptom. By having the symptom, B puts himself down in the relationship and gives power to A, who advises B on how to get rid of the symptom and who, in contrast to B, appears even more adequate and competent. However, A fails repeatedly to help B and to solve B's problem, although there is the implication that A should solve the problem and that the very existence of the symptom is somehow A's responsibility. Also, A now has a number of things to do for B, or instead of B, or A is deprived from doing a number of things because of B's condition. In this way, the symptom gives power to B over A. The system of interaction around B's symptom is analogous to the system of interaction around other issues in A's and B's lives. That is, A and B interact around B's symptom in ways that are analogical to the way they interact around other issues. A tells B what to do about the sympton and complains because B does not do it or does not do it in quite the right way. B complains that what A wants him or her to do is not right; if A were more interested, or sensitive, or understanding, or involved, A would offer better solutions. In this way, A and B discuss A's dominant position and B's unhappiness with this situation while talking about the symptom. B expresses, through the symptomatic behavior, both the intention of not being dominated as well as the helplessness of his or her situation. A's position as the spouse of a symptomatic person constitutes both his power and his helplessness. If B abandons the symptomatic behavior, A and B will go back to struggling about A's career or over whether A should determine how money should be spent. As these issues do not get resolved, B will develop a symptom, and the cycle will be repeated. Sometimes a child will develop a symptom and save B from having one, since then A and B will focus on the child's symptom in the same way as they previously focused on B's symptom. For example, the child may begin to steal or to fail in school. The spouses' interaction around the child's problem will become a metaphor for their interaction around their other difficulties. That is, there may be a cyclical variation in the focus of interaction (sometimes they will focus on A's career, sometimes on the issue of money, sometimes on B's symptoms or on a child's problem), but the cycle will remain the same.

The case examples that follow illustrate that the presenting problem in a spouse can be solved when the hierarchical incongruity in the marriage is resolved.[1]

---

[1]The therapists were Richard Belson, Eugene Schwartz, Joan Shapiro, and the author.

Case 1: A Depressed Man

A 60-year-old man had been severely depressed for several years.[2] Group and individual therapy had failed. He woke up every morning at dawn and worried about his serious work difficulties, which were the result of neglecting his business for five years due to his depression. The wife was a therapist who, as the children were growing up, had gone back to school, with the encouragement and support of her husband, and who was now successfully involved in her career. The husband's alleged "depression" had been the focus of a system of interaction that defined an incongruous hierarchy in the marriage. The sequence of events had apparently been the following. The husband had had a dominant position during the early years of the marriage. Then the wife developed outside interests and became involved in her career as a therapist. The better she did in her work, the greater difficulties he had with his. The greater his difficulties, the more she was defined as the competent career person in the couple. He became "depressed," a problem within her area of expertise as a therapist. The depression was, for the husband, both a source of power over his wife and a source of weakness in relation to her. The wife was in a superior position, competent in her work and giving him support and advice, but she was also in an inferior position, since she failed to help him. The interaction around the husband's depression had been an analogy for the couple's interaction around the husband's reaction to the wife's increasing success and withdrawal. The husband's depression was both a metaphor for their marital difficulties and a solution to these difficulties, since it kept the wife involved with him.

The husband came alone to the first interview, because the wife had an unexpected business appointment. After listening to the problem, the therapist said to the man that this was a case of misdiagnosis. He was not a case of depression; he was simply irresponsible. He had been irresponsible in neglecting his

---

[2] A verbatim transcript of excerpts of this therapy is presented with commentary in Chapter Eight.

work for five years, and his problem was to become responsible once more. The man was surprised but accepted the diagnosis of irresponsibility instead of depression and in this way accepted the fact that his behavior was voluntary and could be voluntarily changed. To redefine the problem as one of irresponsibility took away some of the power that "depression" as a symptom gave to the husband, and it also took the problem away from the wife's area of expertise and responsibility. The interaction around the husband's irresponsibility could not be used as the same analogy as their interaction around his depression. When husband and wife had interacted in the past around the husband's depression, he had been helpless, while the wife was competent, understanding, and involved in cheering him up, even though she was exasperated with him. If the therapist had accepted the diagnosis of depression, it would have been difficult for him not to relate to the man in the same way as the wife did; therefore, he would fail to help the man, just as his wife had failed. When the husband accepted his diagnosis as "irresponsible" instead of "depressed," the therapist could demand action from him (to responsibly take care of his work) rather than feelings (to be cheerful); the therapist also could arrange that the wife relate to the husband in the same way as the therapist did. The husband could no longer draw power from the helplessness of his symptom, and husband and wife would have to deal with each other in different ways.

In the first session, the therapist also told the man that during the next week he had to set his alarm clock every night for 3:30 in the morning, and get up and worry for half an hour. He was not to worry at any other time. He was also instructed to catch up on his work; if he did not do so, he was told that he would have to do extra worrying the next week.[3]

In the next interview, the man related that he had set the alarm for 3:30 only once that week and absolutely refused to do it again because it was so foolish. However, he had slept well that week, and this problem was never brought up again during

[3] Haley (1963) and Erickson (Haley, 1967a) have described the use of paradoxical ordeals in bringing about change.

therapy. He had also not done much worrying and was beginning to organize his office.

The wife came to the second interview. The therapist explained to her that her husband's problem was not depression but irresponsibility, and he asked for her cooperation in helping her husband become responsible again. The wife, who was a pleasant woman and obviously very fond of her husband, had apparently heard about the new diagnosis from him and said that probably the therapist was right. She said that she was getting more and more exasperated with him, since their financial situation was seriously jeopardized by his refusal to do his work. The therapist sympathized with the wife and asked her to make a schedule for the husband to fulfill certain business obligations. If he did not fulfill them during a specified period of time, she would do them herself even though that would imply a considerable loss of money for the couple, since the husband was an expert and she was not. She was also to call her husband on the phone at his office regularly to make sure that he was working. With these directives, the therapist was exaggerating one aspect of the incongruous hierarchy, the one in which the wife was in a superior position to the husband, who was incompetent. The couple were expected to respond by reorganizing in a more reasonable, congruous hierarchy.

Two weeks later, the husband had improved in his work. The therapist told the wife that she had neglected her husband for many years, since she had become involved in her career. She was asked to spend two evenings the next week with her husband and to spend half an hour each day with him discussing their personal life.

When inquiring about the couple's sexual life, the therapist learned that the husband was always the initiator of sexual relations. The wife was then asked to pursue her husband sexually once during the next week. The therapist explained that the husband had been so protective of his wife that he had not given her a chance to initiate sex. By defining the husband as protective of his wife in relation to sex, the therapist was putting the husband in a superior position to the wife in this area.

Two weeks later, the wife reported that the husband was

doing much better in his work; he had been cheerful and had even made an important contribution to his field. The husband minimized his success and complained that things were the same as before. The therapist said that clearly there was a misunderstanding between them and that they needed a new way of verifying communication. The husband was told that three times during the next week he should pretend to be irresponsible and inadequate and the wife was to try to find out whether he was really feeling that way. The husband complained that it was a silly thing to do but finally agreed to do it. In this way, the therapist arranged that if the husband appeared to be irresponsible and inadequate, the wife would not know whether he was really feeling that way or whether he was following the therapist's directives. Therefore, she would not respond in her usual ways.

The next week, however, the therapist found that the husband had not followed the pretend directive. He was then asked to pretend to be irresponsible and inadequate in the session, which he did with great difficulty and under a great deal of criticism from the therapist and the wife, who found that he was not very believable as an irresponsible and inadequate person. The usual interaction between husband and wife had been for the husband to complain about his problems and the wife to offer support and reassurance. Now the husband was pretending to complain and the wife was criticizing him for not pretending realistically. Implicit in the interaction was the fact that it was difficult for the husband to appear irresponsible and inadequate. Since the husband was no longer depressed, and was working hard and making good progress, the therapist suggested that the couple should have lunch together instead of coming to the next session. In this way, the therapist began to disengage from the couple before termination.

Two weeks later, both husband and wife reported improvement. The therapist suggested termination. The couple agreed, and a meeting was arranged for a follow-up a few months later. The husband's work was going well, although he still had a great deal to do, since, as he put it, he had "to resolve five years of total irresponsibility."

In a follow-up four months later, husband and wife were cheerful, the husband had caught up with four years of work that he had neglected, and the couple had supported each other through the birth of their first grandchild and the death of the husband's mother. The husband now realized, he said, that he had to face his responsibilities and do his work, and he agreed with the therapist that he should not waste any more of his time in therapy.

The therapeutic interventions in this case were the following:

1. The therapist refused to accept the couple's definition of the problem and changed it from depression to irresponsibility. Consequently, the system of interaction around the symptom also had to change.
2. A paradoxical instruction to get up at dawn to worry was used successfully to deal with the sleep disturbance.
3. The wife was put in charge of helping the husband become more responsible; in this way, one aspect of the incongruous hierarchy was exaggerated, the one in which the wife was in a superior position of power and the husband was in an inferior position of helplessness. This was a paradoxical intervention designed to provoke the husband to rebel against this arrangement, which he did by taking control of his work.
4. A paradoxical instruction was given to the husband; he was asked to pretend to have the symptomatic behavior.
5. The interaction between husband and wife was improved, so that they were spending more time together and their sex relations were more varied. As their relationship improved, they no longer needed to use the system of interaction around a symptom as an analogy and a solution to their difficulties.

In this case, an incongruous hierarchy in a marriage was defined when a previously dominant husband developed the symptom of depression. The depression was a source of power over his wife and, simultaneously, a position of weakness in relation to her. The wife was in a superior position because of the husband's depression but in an inferior position because she was failing to help him even though helping was her business. The therapist first organized the couple so that power and weakness were no longer centered on symptomatic behavior, and then the therapist changed the organization of the marriage.

Case 2: Binge Eating and Vomiting

An attractive 35-year-old nurse, mother of three, consulted because of a problem of compulsive vomiting, which previous individual and marital therapy had failed to solve. She vomited up to five times a day and had done so for thirteen years, starting several months before her marriage. She had vomited continuously during this time except when she was pregnant (for fear of harming the baby) and for an occasional week at a time over the years.

The husband held two doctorates and was a rising executive in a complex field. The wife kept house impeccably (describing herself as an obsessive cleaner), took care of the children successfully (they presented no problems), and worked a part-time evening shift as a nurse. Several times a day, particularly while she was cleaning the house or preparing dinner, she would stuff herself with food and then vomit. She said that doing the housework made her particularly anxious because she was a compulsive cleaner. When the couple went out to dinner, she would often feel that she had eaten too much and would vomit in the restaurant and then again at home when they came back. The wife would also visit her mother occasionally and vomit there. She would often vomit before going to bed at night. When questioned about their sex life, the husband said that it was not very good, since she was usually too tired from vomiting to wish to have sex and his own interest was diminished because her vomiting disgusted him. He had recently had an affair with their babysitter, but that relationship was over. The husband angrily explained that he knew when the wife was vomiting, because she shut the bathroom door (at other times she left it open). The wife indicated that her husband was trying to stop her from vomiting, reporting that he had said to her a few days before the therapy started: "Now that I'm going out of town for a few days, you can vomit all you please."

In observing the couple, the therapist noticed that the husband presented himself as the prestigious professional who provided for the family, and the wife was the housekeeper-mother. Her part-time work as a nurse was secondary compared to his as an executive. In their communication with each other and to the therapist, he was precise and stable; she was emotional, anxious, and giggly. She constantly asked for his approval and agreement; he did not ask for hers. She was the subdued, dependent wife in every way, except that she vomited.

The vomiting was an expression of the wife's helplessness but also of her power. She was a perfect housewife and mother, except that while she performed her duties she repeatedly vomited. The symptom was a metaphor for both her submissiveness and her rebellion. The system of interaction of the couple around the symptom was a metaphor for their interaction around other issues in which the wife was overtly submissive and dependent but disapproved, rebelled, and undermined the husband covertly.

A directive was planned such that the covert power of the symptom would be replaced by an overt act of defiance of the husband, but this defiance would involve playful actions that would minimize disruption in the marriage. The therapeutic strategy was based on the idea that the symptom provided an interpersonal gain to the wife; it was a way of getting back at her husband for dominating her. If this interpersonal gain could be maintained by some other means, without the symptom, then the symptom would disappear. That is, if the symptom was a way of getting back at her husband and if another way, just as effective or better, could be provided, then the wife would stop vomiting. For the substitute behavior to be most effective, it had to be simple, playful, and related to the symptom.

The couple were told that the wife's vomiting was actually just throwing away food but going through her stomach first. Why not throw the food away directly and save herself from the unpleasantness and the destructive effect on her body? The couple agreed that it would be a better thing to do if it were possible. The therapist asked the wife to throw five dollars' worth of food into the garbage every day. Each time she felt the urge to vomit, she was to go to the kitchen and throw out food instead. If she did not have the urge, she was to throw out five dollars' worth of food anyway in periods of three times a day. The husband was to collaborate in this endeavor by doing all the shopping for food that week, making sure that each day there would be enough to throw out without having the children go hungry. He was also to check the garbage every evening to make sure that the wife had thrown out five dollars' worth of food. When he was at home, he was to watch her carefully and follow her around to see whether she vomited; if she did, he was to take her to the kitchen, sit her down, and, while he held her hand affectionately, force her to stuff herself. If she vomited when he was not at home, she was to tell him what she had eaten before vomiting, and he was to make her stuff herself. In this way, the vomiting was replaced by another behavior which served the same purpose of getting back at him, since he had to shop, look into the garbage, follow her around, and, worst of all, waste thirty-five dollars a week. Previously, the vomiting had kept the couple apart; now it would bring them together. If she vomited, the husband had to gently and affectionately sit with her and make her stuff herself. Before, the woman vomited because she stuffed herself; now she had to stuff herself because she vomited.

The husband responded to the directive by blushing, laughing, and saying: "But I am a Scotsman! Money is very important to me." Later in the therapy, the couple described how they had lived in poverty all their married life because every cent they made was invested by the husband in real estate. They now had a considerable fortune but continued to live in the same way and to invest everything they made. This life style had been the husband's idea, and the wife was pleased with the results, but she had gone through a great deal of pain over the years to raise a family on very limited funds. To throw away five dollars a day was a great offense to the husband.

With this directive, the therapist was exaggerating, para-doxically, the incongruity of the marital hierarchy. Because the wife was helpless and symptomatic, she had to throw away thirty-five dollars a week in food; and the husband had to par-ticipate in this endeavor even though it went against his values. That is, the directive made the wife simultaneously more help-less and more powerful in relation to the husband.

The couple did what they were told to do, and when they came back two weeks later, the wife had not vomited. During that session, the therapist—as a way of paradoxically preventing the discord that often follows the rapid improvement in a symptom in one of the spouses—predicted that the couple would have a serious fight the next week. If the therapist predicts a fight, the couple will make a special effort to have a harmonious relationship and prove the therapist wrong. The couple did not have a fight after that session, nor did they have one after the following session, two weeks later, when the ther-apist made the same prediction.

The same directive to throw away food was given for sev-eral weeks, during which the therapist expressed concern that the wife might become obese (she was actually very thin). It was necessary to address the issue of weight control, since binge eating and self-induced vomiting, or bulimia, is associated with extreme concern about gaining weight. In fact, at the beginning of the therapy, the woman had said that for many years she had thought of herself as a case of anorexia nervosa. The therapist was hoping that the woman could be helped to control weight in more appropriate ways than vomiting. The husband said that he was also afraid his wife would become too fat. The therapist asked the woman to keep a weight chart and to engage in exer-cise and sports activities. She joined a soccer team.

In the sixth session, the woman complained that, al-though she was not vomiting and was not gaining weight, she was still anxious—particularly on Mondays, when she had a great deal of housework and felt overwhelmed and disorganized and was afraid of vomiting again. The therapist asked the hus-band to be in charge of the scheduling of Mondays' activities for the wife. When the husband was explicitly put in charge of the wife for one day a week, the marital struggle became less covert. The wife had to either obey her husband overtly or rebel against him more openly. The husband had to request explicitly that the wife perform housekeeping duties, or he had to orient her explicitly toward other kinds of activities. The wife was told that on those occasions when she felt overwhelmed and anxious, she should call her husband at the office, ask him what to do, and follow his advice, since he knew her and understood her better than anyone else. The wife did call the husband the next Monday, and he asked her what she would like most to do if she could do anything she wanted. She said that she would like to go to the library and do some research related to her work, but it was out of the question because she was so behind in her housework. He told her to drop everything and spend the day in the library, which she did, and her anxiety disappeared. Husband and wife were now closer to each other. Through this and several sessions, the therapist referred to the husband as a particularly "understanding" man, with the purpose of making him more attractive to the wife.

In the seventh session, the wife was asked to throw away one dollar's worth of food each day, instead of five dollars' worth, and to buy something frivolous and unnecessary for herself for thirty-five dollars. The woman insisted that it was impossible for her to do this and that she did not understand the idea of "frivolous." The husband was asked to give her thirty-five dollars in the session, since it had to be *his* money that she spent in this way. He appeared surprised at the wife's difficulty in accepting this directive.

The following week, the wife came to the session with two skirts, two blouses, a pair of shoes, a shawl, and a dishcloth that she had bought at a second-hand store with the thirty-five dollars. The couple were then told that, since the wife obviously did not understand the concept of frivolous and unnecessary, the session would end early. They would then have time to go together to an expensive store, where the husband would buy a frivolous and unnecessary nightgown that was worth at least thirty-five dollars. In this way, he would show her what was meant by frivolous and unnecessary. They brought to the next

session an expensive nightgown that they had bought together
that day. The wife's symptom had been related to the husband's
miserly ideology; now the husband was being extravagant. The
symptomatic behavior had first been replaced with the act of
throwing away food—the metaphor expressed in the vomiting.
Now it was replaced with spending money on superfluous things
—another metaphor but a more normal act.

The couple were going away on vacation, and the wife
was told to exercise thirty minutes a day and record her weight.
The husband was to take a scale on the trip, so that she could
weigh herself, and he was to force her to stuff herself if she
vomited. She was also to throw away one dollar's worth of food
each day and to buy thirty-five dollars' worth of something
frivolous. They followed all the directives during the trip. She
had an upset stomach and vomited once, and the husband made
her stuff herself. The husband explained in the next session that
he wanted to spend more time with his wife, and they planned
two evenings out and two evenings at home together for the following fifteen days.

During the course of the therapy, the therapist had talked
to the wife about her career, with the idea of increasing her investment in it as a source of strength outside the home. But the
woman felt that she had gone as far as she wanted to go. She
wanted instead to increase her time practicing sports, and the
therapist spent some time planning this type of activity with
her.

Toward the end of therapy, husband and wife were
spending more time together and enjoying each other. The wife
had even eaten and drunk too much and had not vomited. Therapy was terminated a few weeks later, with a plan for a follow-
up. The wife had not vomited in four months. In the last session, the husband reported that he had cut back his work to
forty hours a week to be able to spend more time at home, and
both husband and wife said that the marriage had improved.

When the therapist met with the couple five months later,
the wife said that she had been vomiting occasionally. Therapy
was reactivated, with sessions to be scheduled occasionally. The
therapist repeated a series of directives that had proven effective

before in bringing the couple together while preventing the vomiting.

Three months later, the couple reported that their marriage was better, sexually and otherwise, but the wife had vomited four times a day during the previous four days. The husband was directed for the next two weeks to take the wife to the bathroom three times a day and make her vomit. She was to collaborate in this and do her best to vomit when he told her to do so. This was a paradoxical directive, and the wife was expected to rebel against the husband and refuse to vomit.

Two weeks later, however, it was found that they had followed the directive and that the wife had actually vomited every time her husband told her to do so, but not at other times. This vomiting was more disgusting than usual because she had always vomited immediately after eating but the husband was making her vomit when the food was partially digested. The therapist asked them in the session to pretend that the husband was taking the wife to the bathroom and telling her to vomit. She was to go through all the motions of vomiting without actually doing it. The wife performed reluctantly and was very mortified. They were told to repeat this pretend every day for five minutes in the bathroom and then to have five quiet minutes together after that. Since the directive to vomit had not had a paradoxical effect, it was replaced by the paradoxical directive to pretend to vomit. If husband and wife were involved with each other around the "pretend" vomiting, then they did not need the real vomiting to maintain this involvement.

Three weeks later, the woman had not vomited and they had followed the directive to pretend. The therapist asked them in the session to budget their time and their money together. They were directed to continue to pretend to throw up in the bathroom.

Two months later, the wife had not vomited. She called the therapist and asked her whether she thought it would be all right for the wife to participate in a "growth-type experience." The therapist said she saw nothing wrong with it. This was a mistake. The therapist should have answered that it was all right as long as husband and wife were in agreement. A few days later, the husband called and said that he was very upset and wanted a session because he had found a puddle of vomit in the basement.

During the session, the husband was upset, depressed, and said he had suicidal thoughts. The wife had been doing a great deal of reading, was taking courses, and was interested in her own development. He was jealous about the wife's involvement in the growth-oriented group, since she had not told him about her plans and did not wish to discuss the experience with him. He was upset because the wife did not show enough interest in him and was withholding affection, sex, and support. It was a session in which the husband was very distraught and the wife very indifferent. It ended with the couple, who had been asked to hold hands as they talked, promising to do things together and not make decisions separately. The vomit in the basement had not been the wife's; it might have been the cat's. She had not been vomiting.

In a session three weeks later, the couple discussed their difficulties and the efforts that they were both making, particularly the husband, to change. The therapist emphasized that they had overcome many problems together and that there would probably be more problems to overcome in the future, since normal lives are full of difficulties. The husband said that he was trying to be more affectionate and less overbearing, and the wife agreed that he was more affectionate and less overbearing.

Therapy was terminated. Six months later, it was resumed for a few sessions because the woman had been vomiting for approximately five days every six weeks during the last three months. Both spouses attributed this to a distancing between husband and wife due to the husband's long working hours. They were brought together again in therapy, and the vomiting stopped.

The therapy took place in twenty-two sessions over a period of twenty-three months. For at least eighteen of these months, the woman did not vomit. When she first came to therapy, she was vomiting five times every day. At the end of therapy, she had vomited approximately thirty-six times in

twenty-three months. The therapeutic interventions were the
following:

1. The metaphor expressed by the symptomatic behavior was
   defined as "throwing away food." A paradoxical directive
   to do more of that which was expressed metaphorically by
   the symptom (throwing away food) was used successfully.
2. The husband was requested to provide an ordeal by making
   the wife stuff herself with food if the symptom occurred.
   The symptomatic behavior was therefore changed from
   vomiting as a consequence of binge eating to binge eating as
   a consequence for vomiting.
3. A directive to replace the symptomatic behavior of vomiting and throwing away food with spending money on
   superfluous things was used successfully.
4. The therapist took care to control the woman's weight, so
   that to stop vomiting would not have unfortunate consequences.
5. By putting the husband more in charge of the wife, the
   therapist exaggerated one aspect of the incongruous hierarchy and provoked the wife to rebel against the husband
   and the husband to relinquish his exaggerated control of
   her. Later, the husband was made responsible for the wife's
   becoming more independent from him.
6. A paradoxical directive for the husband to make the wife
   pretend to vomit in his presence was used successfully. (A
   paradoxical directive to actually vomit did not prevent the
   vomiting.)
7. The couple were encouraged to agree on financial matters,
   which would be decided only with the wife's participation.
8. The interaction between husband and wife was improved,
   so that they were spending more time together, and the
   hierarchy was reorganized in a more egalitarian relationship, with the wife more independent from the husband.
9. As the wife became more independent, the husband became upset and depressed, and the therapist helped them to
   reorganize so that the husband would not begin to use
   symptomatic behavior as a source of power and weakness.
10. To deal with the possibility that the woman might vomit

again in order to continue to see the therapist, any future sessions were made contingent on not vomiting.

In this case, an incongruous hierarchy was defined during thirteen years of marriage by a submissive wife's symptom of vomiting. The vomiting gave her power over the husband and, simultaneously, increased her weakness in relation to him. The husband was in a superior position because of the wife's vomiting but in an inferior position because he could not control the vomiting and was humiliated by its consequences and implications. The therapist used paradoxical directives to resolve the symptom and reorganized the couple with the wife in a less submissive position, so that symptomatic behavior was no longer the focus of power and weakness.

Case 3: Drinking

A 30-year-old man was brought by his wife to the emergency room of a hospital because he had come home intoxicated with alcohol and said to his wife that he had had a fight in a bar and that he had been in an auto accident, although she could see no damage to the car. He thought there were people chasing him, and he barricaded himself inside the house. He was a heavy drinker who had occasionally beaten his wife, blacked out, and behaved erratically. He complained of loss of memory. The couple were referred to marital therapy.

They had been married seven years, had no children, and complained of severe marital problems. At one time, they had separated and had had marriage counseling, from which they dropped out. The wife worked as a supervisor in a government office, and the husband did custodial work in the school system. The wife had a higher education than the husband (he had not finished high school); she also had a better job, made more money, was more competent and responsible, had more friends, appeared to be more intelligent, and was more verbal and attractive than he. The wife was in a superior position to the husband in every way except that the husband drank, and his drinking made him more helpless in relation to her but also more powerful, since she put up with his erratic behavior, his beatings, and his unpredictability.

The interaction of the couple around the drinking was a metaphor for their interaction around other areas in their lives, where the wife was always struggling to make the husband behave more competently and responsibly and where the more she pushed in this direction, the more down he was in the marital hierarchy and the more he used helplessness as a way of gaining power. The more incompetent, irresponsible, and drunk he became, the more he did not follow her directives and the more power he had over her. The drinking was an unfortunate solution that defined both his weakness and his power in relation to his wife.

There were two presenting problems that had to be solved in this case. One was the drinking problem, and the other was the marital difficulties that were related to the drinking. The couple were involved in a cycle where they shifted from focusing on the husband's drinking to focusing on their marital problems and back to the husband's drinking.

In the first session, the husband went into a long diatribe about how he had been forced to drink in the war and had been abused by his superiors. The therapist dismissed these stories by saying that many men had gone through unfortunate experiences in the war and had not become alcoholics. The issue was the future and whether he wanted to change. He said he certainly did, since he had been frightened by the last episode and by his experiences of blacking out and loss of memory.

The therapy began with a paradoxical directive. The husband's usual way of drinking was to meet with a friend after work and sit drinking in the car in a parking lot until he was drunk. Then he would come home intoxicated and usually would black out. After spending some time motivating the couple to follow the therapist's directives no matter what they were, the therapist assigned them the following task. The wife would buy with her own money a good supply of rum (rum and coke was what the husband usually drank). Every day that week, the husband would come straight home from work and the wife would serve him drinks in an affectionate way, until he got drunk and fell asleep.

The next week, the couple reported that the wife had done her task but the husband had refused to get drunk two out of the five weeknights. The wife was asked at this point how much she would put up with from her husband, what were her limits. She said she would put up with anything and would never leave him. The same directive was given for the next week, with the addition that the wife also had to make the husband drink over the weekend and that every day before serving him drinks she had to make love to him for forty-five minutes. The wife complained but agreed to do this.

With these instructions, the wife, instead of nagging the husband to stop drinking, was encouraging him to drink. Before, the husband had gained power over his wife by drinking. Now, in order to refuse her orders, he had to stop drinking. Asking her to make love to him was an attempt to separate their sex life from their other struggles and to bring them closer together.

The next week, it was found that the wife had done her part but the husband had not wanted to drink. He had not been responsive to her in love making. The same task was given for the following week, with the addition that on Sunday they had to go to a movie together.

By the next week, the couple had followed all directives for five days. The husband had wanted to have only one or two drinks each evening. On the sixth day, they had had a fight over the wife's jealousy because the husband wanted to study with a girl who was in a course he was taking.

After this, the drinking was no longer a problem, with the exception of two episodes of two weeks each over a period of nine months. During these two bouts, the husband was drinking at home but was not behaving erratically or suffering from loss of memory or blackout periods, which had been the problem at the beginning of therapy. He did not beat his wife, and the paranoid ideas did not recur.

The two drinking episodes were handled in the following way. In the first one, the husband was seen alone, and he talked about how he felt put down by his wife but did not want to leave her. He said he had sacrificed a great deal for her. The wife was seen alone, and she talked about all the sacrifices that she

had made for her husband. The couple were then brought together, and the therapist revealed that both thought they had
made sacrifices in the marriage. The wife was told that she
should work even harder at taking care of her husband and sacrifice herself even more for the next week. She was angry and
said she would do no such thing. This was a paradoxical directive intended to provoke the wife to be less self-sacrificing and
tolerant. Two weeks later, the couple talked about what sacrifices each had actually made in the past and found that they
were not many. They discussed what changes there would be in
their lives if they did not make sacrifices for each other, and
they talked about their friends and the possibility of having
children. The next week, they were planning to have a baby, to
visit friends, and to have a house-warming party.

The second drinking episode began when the husband developed problems with a supervisor at work. The husband, who
was black, thought that the difficulties originated with the
supervisor, who had previously fired seven black men. The therapist discussed what could be done about the work situation
and said that, since the husband was drinking again, his family
would have to be brought into the therapy. The grandmother
who had raised him and lived in another town came to a session
with the husband's father. The husband told them that, because
he had had a psychiatric evaluation when he was a child, he had
always thought he was crazy. The grandmother and father clarified that it had been a psychological evaluation for some learning problem and that there was never any reason to think he
was crazy. The father said that the son was much like him—shy,
with difficulties in making friends, reluctant to go out. Through
his own efforts, however, he had become successful in his job
and in his social life, and he thought that the son could do the
same.

The next week the couple reported that the husband had
been drinking a great deal. The therapist said that probably he
had been pushing them too hard, that they needed to go much
slower, and that they should postpone any decisions regarding
drinking less or getting ahead in work. The husband said he had
decided not to drink any more. The therapist emphasized that it

was very important to go slowly and not to make rash decisions. The therapist's intention was to provoke the couple to improve against the therapist's wishes.

Two weeks later, the couple reported that the husband had had only one beer in two weeks. The therapist pretended to be surprised and puzzled and expressed admiration at the husband's rapid improvement. After talking about how long it had been since the couple had had a really good time together, they decided to have a party and invited the therapist. In the next few weeks, the husband replaced his supervisor temporarily at work. He continued to avoid drinking.

The marital issues were more difficult to resolve than the drinking, because some of the difficulties in the marriage were external and related to the husband's employment. The marital issues could not be solved unless the husband's position at work was improved, since his inferior situation at the job defined him as inferior to the wife in a way that was unsatisfactory to him and that resulted in attempts to balance the distribution of power in the couple through helpless and symptomatic behavior. When the husband stopped drinking, there was a brief focus on the wife's jealousy, but this focus quickly shifted to the husband's extreme jealousy of the wife—another area where he was in an inferior position. Various contracts and agreements were made between husband and wife to deal with the jealousy over a period of months. Because the husband constantly accused the wife of being unfaithful to him but never presented any proof or took any action, he was asked to agree that if he ever had suspicions about his wife again, he was immediately to pack his clothes, leave the house, and end the marriage. It took several sessions to obtain the husband's commitment to this plan, but once he agreed, his suspicions of the wife disappeared. The couple, however, continued to be unhappy with each other. They were given paradoxical directives to make each other miserable, and they responded by having a good time. The husband was referred to vocational guidance. As a result, he registered in a course that would prepare him to pass a high school equivalency examination and so qualify him for a better work situation. A year later, the husband was made a supervisor at work.

During the course of the therapy, as the drinking problem and the marital difficulties improved, the couple focused more of their interaction on good times together and on plans for the future.

The therapeutic interventions in this case were the following:

1. Outside pressures and abuse were dismissed as a cause for drinking, which was defined as a voluntary instead of a helpless act.
2. A paradoxical directive for the wife to encourage the husband to drink was used successfully, with the result that the drinking was no longer the focus of the marital struggle and the husband began to drink moderately.
3. In place of the drinking, the husband's jealousy was then used by the couple as a source of power and of weakness. This jealousy was dealt with in various ways by means of straightforward and paradoxical directives over a period of several months.
4. The husband's position was improved through a referral to vocational guidance, discussions about work plans, and a clarification of his situation in relation to his grandmother and father. A year later, the husband was promoted to supervisor.
5. The couple were brought together in a more egalitarian relationship, so that symptomatic behavior was no longer used to define an incongruous hierarchy.
6. The husband's position in the marital hierarchy was further improved when the therapist restrained him from changing too fast and then gave him the credit for his improvement.

In this case, an incongruous hierarchy was defined by the alcohol abuse of a husband whose social status was lower than the wife's. The drinking gave him power over his wife and, simultaneously, increased his weakness in relation to her. The wife was in a superior position both in her social status and because of the husband's drinking, but she was in an inferior position because she constantly tried to stop him from drinking and failed and because she accepted unlimited abuse from him. The therapist used paradoxical directives to resolve the drinking. The husband's extreme jealousy was then presented as a problem. This jealousy defined an incongruous hierarchy, just as the drinking did, and was a source of power and weakness in the marriage. The therapist dealt with the jealousy by giving various paradoxical and straightforward directives over a period of months, until the jealousy was resolved and the couple reorganized in a more congruous hierarchy with more equality between them. During this time, two episodes of drinking were contained when the therapist (1) encouraged the wife to sacrifice herself even more for the husband, as a way to provoke her to sacrifice less and be more intolerant of the drinking, and (2) brought in the husband's family of origin to clarify issues related to the husband's sense of inferiority and failure in life. As a way of improving his position in the marriage, the husband was restrained from changing too fast and was then given credit for the changes.

Case 4: Hysterical Paralysis

A psychiatric resident called to ask for a consultation. He wanted both marital therapy and supervision with his cases. The therapist explained that she would be leaving the country in three weeks and there was not enough time for either supervision or therapy. The young man insisted that he wanted a consultation for him and his wife, and an appointment was made.

When the couple came to the interview, the husband was holding the book *Strategies of Psychotherapy* (Haley, 1963) under his arm. He introduced his wife, a psychology intern. They were an attractive pair—the wife with innocent blue eyes and long straight blond hair; the husband, dark and handsome. He explained that they had a serious problem that other therapies had failed to solve. The wife had a hysterical paralysis of the tongue. Her tongue would become rigid in her mouth, so that she could hardly speak. She could only mumble and make strange noises in her effort to be understood. The symptom would go away only after she took Valium and rested for an hour. It had occurred frequently for over a year and a half; but now the young woman had to work with patients and make case presentations at meetings, and she was afraid of having the paralysis then and not being able to speak, so that everyone would find out her problem. The therapist commented on what an interesting and exotic symptom this was. It could be the last Freudian hysterical paralysis in the Western world. Husband and wife smiled and agreed, not without a certain pride.

The husband explained that psychoanalytic therapy and psychoanalysis had failed. He had read Haley's book and was certain that strategic marital therapy with the use of paradox could solve the problem. He knew that the symptom was clearly related to the marriage.

The therapist asked what had happened with the previous therapy and was told that the last therapist had been the husband's supervisor at work. He had become interested in the case because of the nature of the symptom and had been seeing the wife in therapy. The wife explained that the psychiatrist had told her that the symptom was related to guilt feelings over fantasies about oral sex. She ended the therapy when he attempted to seduce her. She had almost given in to his advances when she realized that, even though he said he was in love with her, he was taking advantage of her. She rushed out of the therapy room and never came back. This episode was a great source of embarrassment and unpleasantness for the husband, who had to continue to work in a ward where the psychiatrist was a supervisor.

The therapist asked when the symptom had occurred for the first time. Both husband and wife remembered it clearly. They were not yet married and were visiting his parents. The husband's mother told them that she was leaving her husband and would take a flight to another country in an hour with her daughter. She wanted to say goodbye to them but told them not to tell his father until the plane had left, so that he could not stop her. The couple obeyed her, and it was after she left that the young woman had the hysterical paralysis of the tongue for the first time. She was very frightened, and the young man gave her a Valium to calm her. She recovered after approximately one hour.

The therapist commented on what a painful situation

that must have been for both of them, particularly for the husband, and how sensitive the wife seemed to be to his difficulties. The wife then explained that she had always had a bad relationship with her own parents and that her father had been an alcoholic.

The wife's symptom seemed to be an important aspect of the husband's career. It provided him with a reason to become involved with teachers who interested him. In the first phone call, he had even been unclear about whether he wanted supervision or therapy. He was an expert on the wife's problem and told the therapist what approach should be used. Even though he had failed to help his wife, his was not a run-of-the-mill failure, since the problem was so out of the ordinary. The exotic quality of the symptom had to be changed if therapy was to succeed.

The therapist said that to try to understand the symptom she had to compare it to symptoms that she herself had. When she, the therapist, was upset and anxious, she had stomachaches which were the result of a tightening of the stomach muscle, a cramp. The stomach would become rigid, and she would have a stomachache. Would the husband, since he was a doctor, agree that, since the tongue is also a muscle, the rigidness was a muscular cramp, similar to a stomach cramp? The husband agreed that it could be thought of that way. The therapist then said that this seemed to her not a hysterical paralysis but a case of psychosomatic cramps in part of the digestive system, the tongue, brought about by anxiety. Husband and wife reluctantly agreed.

A psychosomatic cramp is less interesting and unusual than a hysterical paralysis. The therapist made this redefinition of the symptom, while avoiding any disagreement or confrontation, by joining the wife, in that her symptom was similar to the therapist's, and by appealing to the husband as a medical expert.

The therapist then said that she needed to place the symptom in the perspective of all the horrible things that could happen to a therapist while doing therapy; for example, vomiting, having to rush to the bathroom, fainting. Having a rigid tongue was a horrible possibility, but there were certainly many other horrible things that could happen, even more horrible than the ones she had mentioned. Husband and wife agreed with that.

The symptom was now defined not only as a psychosomatic complaint instead of an exotic hysterical paralysis but also as one of a series of embarrassing organic phenomena that could happen to any therapist. The emphasis was on the woman as therapist.

The therapist then asked the wife about her career. She talked about her insecurity, the competition with her husband, and her uncertainty about whether she could ever be a good therapist when she had such serious emotional problems.

The therapist asked the couple to describe their life together and the marital difficulties that they had. They explained that the husband not only was more involved in his career than the wife was in hers but also was more social and spent the weekends at his club playing tennis and other sports while she stayed alone at home and resented it. The wife was often anxious and sometimes could not sleep at night. She would often wake up in the middle of the night with an anxiety attack. She would then wake up the husband, asking for his support, although there was nothing that he could do to calm her. She would cry and become very regressive, talking in childish ways; sometimes her tongue would become rigid. Usually she fell asleep after taking a Valium, but neither of them liked this solution because they feared that she was becoming addicted. The couple thought that they had communication problems and should work at improving communication with each other.

The therapist said that she would think about whether she could help them in any way in the short time that was left, and she made an appointment with them for a few days later.

In the second interview, the therapist told the couple that she had been giving a great deal of thought to the meaning of the symptom, since she thought that the explanation involving oral sex was not satisfactory. The couple agreed that it was not. The therapist said that she had concluded that the rigidness of the tongue was related to a difficulty in keeping secrets. She said that the wife had probably always been very open and sincere and had had difficulties keeping secrets. These difficulties had reached an extreme when the husband's mother had asked her to keep that terrible secret. Her tongue had become rigid, preventing her from speaking and from revealing a secret that she was in such conflict to keep. Related to this, the therapist thought that the communication problem between husband and wife was not a lack of communication but too much communication. Those long nights with her anxiety attacks when they talked and talked and revealed everything to each other were evidence of too much communication. The therapist was sure that the wife had never even kept a secret from her husband. The wife said that that was true. The therapist said that therefore it was important to put some distance between husband and wife and to block some of that communication. The symptom, she thought, was completely an individual problem of the wife, related to keeping secrets, and had nothing to do with the marriage. Therefore, the therapist said that she needed to work with the wife alone, without the husband, and that everything that happened in the therapy should be a secret between the therapist and the wife. She thought that in this way she could provide some relief to the wife with a very brief intervention. The therapist stood up and accompanied the stunned husband to the door and saw him out.

The system of interaction between husband and wife around the symptom had been a metaphor for their interaction around the wife's inferior and helpless position in relation to her husband as well as for the power that she derived from this position. He was the adequate, competent expert who had to help her, but he had failed to do so; furthermore, the symptom reflected negatively on him and on the marriage and took up a great deal of his time and energy. By relating the symptom to the first episode in which it occurred and defining it as a difficulty in keeping secrets, the therapist was able to change the metaphor expressed by the symptom, so that it no longer stood for the marital problem of lack of communication between the spouses but, instead, represented too much communication between husband and wife. Previously, the metaphor expressed by the system of interaction around the symptom was one of power and helplessness of the husband as he repeatedly failed in his attempts to understand and help his wife and of helplessness and power of the wife as she asked for the husband's help but ensured his failure. The system of interaction around the symptom was a metaphor for the hierarchical incongruity in the marriage, in which husband and wife were both simultaneously in an inferior and a superior position in relation to each other. This incongruity was an unfortunate way of achieving a more egalitarian relationship and counteracting the husband's superior position in career and social life. By defining the problem as one of excessive communication and by excluding the husband from the therapy and even keeping the therapy secret from him, the therapist changed the hierarchy. The wife became more powerful and less helpless, since the symptom was hers alone, since she was blocked from asking for the husband's help, and since she alone would have the benefits of participating in this "strategic paradoxical therapy." The husband was less powerful, since he was excluded from helping his wife; but he was also less helpless, since he was no longer part of the problem or responsible for its solution.

The therapist continued by telling the wife that a paradoxical intervention would be appropriate. She opened *Strategies of Psychotherapy* to the page where Frankl's paradoxical intention is explained and asked the wife to read it. After the woman had read it, she was asked to try as hard as possible to develop the rigidness of the tongue right there in the session. The woman tried and tried but could not do it. She was then told that during the next week she was to try purposefully to have the symptom three times a day for fifteen minutes each time. The therapist then talked to the young woman about her career and about what areas she needed to develop. She said she needed more supervision and to learn more about doing therapy.

The wife came to the next interview and said that she had followed the directive and had not had the symptom. She had kept the directive secret from the husband. She was then told that something needed to be done about her anxiety attacks at night, and she was given the following instructions. She was to set up near her bedroom a desk where she would keep paper and pencils, her notes from therapy sessions, and the textbooks on therapy that she found most useful. If she could not sleep, if she was anxious, if she fell asleep but woke up with anxiety, or if her tongue became rigid, she was not to wake up the husband or say anything to him. Instead, she was to get up, go to her desk, and spend an hour writing an account of a session that she had had with a patient that week. She was to record what the patient had said or, if it was a child in play therapy, what the child had done. She was also to explain her therapeutic interventions and give the rationale for them. She could use her books to explain something that she had done or to give the basis for her understanding of a case. After an hour, she would go back to bed; if she was not asleep in fifteen minutes, she was to get up again and repeat the same task. She was to do this even if she had to be up writing the whole night. She would bring the material that she had written to the next session, and the therapist would read it and discuss it with her to help her to improve as a therapist. If, instead of at night, she had an anxiety attack during the day, she was to set her alarm for three in the morning and get up and write about a case for an hour. She was to keep all this secret from her husband and not even tell him that what she was doing was related to the therapy. The young woman agreed reluctantly to all this after complaining about how she would not get enough sleep and how difficult it would be to write when she was so anxious.

The symptom of the rigidness of the tongue was blocked through a paradoxical intervention of prescribing the symptom. The second symptom, the anxiety attacks, was blocked through the prescription of an ordeal to be carried out if the symptom occurred. The ordeal was planned in such a way that either the woman improved and the anxiety attacks were less frequent or she improved in her career by writing and being supervised in her cases. Before, her anxiety had resulted in an ordeal for the husband; now her anxiety would result in an ordeal for herself.

In the next session, the young woman related that she had not had the rigidness of the tongue but that she had had one anxiety attack. She brought in a few pages that she had written about a case. She had gone back to sleep after one hour of writing. The notes that she brought contained several hateful comments about the therapist mixed with confused comments about a child in therapy. She said she had been full of anger and hate for the therapist while writing it because she had to go through with this ordeal. The therapist said that that was understandable and discussed the notes, explaining how the woman's thinking about the case could be more clear, her description better, and so forth. The same instructions were given for the following session.

The young woman did not have any symptoms the next week. This was the final interview, since the therapist was about to leave the country. The therapist said that the woman was to continue following the directive related to her anxiety attacks; if she had any, she was to take the written material to another therapist who had been contacted to provide supervision. To discourage her from having the anxiety attacks, this therapist would charge her double the usual fee for an hour of supervision.

In a follow-up two years later, the young woman said that the rigidness of the tongue had never recurred. She had had a few sessions of supervision with the other therapist and then had discontinued, since, although she was sometimes anxious, she no longer had anxiety attacks in the middle of the night. Husband and wife were still together and involved in various activities in their professions. They were struggling over the decision of whether to have a baby and still felt that, although their relationship had improved, there was room for more improvement and growth.

The therapeutic interventions in this case were the following:

1. The therapist changed the system of interaction around the symptom by changing the symptom from hysterical paralysis to psychosomatic cramps and by changing the metaphor expressed by the symptom from sexual fantasies and lack of communication between spouses to difficulty in keeping

secrets and excessive communication between husband and
wife.

2. The husband was excluded from the therapy, and the wife
   was instructed to keep the therapeutic process secret from
   him, so that the symptom could no longer be used by the
   couple as a source of power and weakness.
3. A paradoxical instruction to voluntarily produce the rigidness of the tongue was used successfully.
4. The therapist dealt with the symptom of anxiety by prescribing an ordeal to take place every time the symptom
   occurred, so that the woman would either be less helpless,
   because she would no longer have the anxiety attacks, or
   more competent in her profession if she had to perform the
   ordeal.
5. The therapist dealt with the need to terminate the therapy
   early by transferring the case to another therapist, who func-
   tioned in the capacity of supervisor to ensure that the directive to perform the ordeal would continue for some time.

In this case, an incongruous hierarchy in a marriage was
defined when a dependent and insecure wife developed a
"hysterical" symptom. The "hysterical paralysis" was a source
of power over the husband and, simultaneously, a position of
weakness in relation to him. The husband was in a superior position because of the wife's "hysteria" but in an inferior position
because he was failing to help her even though helping was his
business. The therapist organized the couple so that power and
weakness were no longer centered on symptomatic behavior and
used a paradoxical instruction and the prescription of an ordeal
to resolve the symptoms.

Summary and Conclusion

It has been proposed here that a spouse may develop a
symptom in an attempt to change the hierarchical arrangement
and balance the division of power in the couple. Symptomatic
behavior, however, defines an incongruous hierarchy in that
equality is maintained when both members of the dyad are

simultaneously defined as inferior and superior to each other. The problem for the therapist is to organize the couple so that power and weakness are not centered on symptomatic behavior. Then the symptom can be resolved.

A symptom is a metaphor for a person's situation, and the way a couple interact around the symptom is a system analogy for other systems of interaction in the marriage. A cycle can occur in which the couple deal with the dominance of one spouse over the other by alternately focusing on a marital issue (money, in-laws, career), on a spouse's symptom, or on a child's problem. That is, there may be a cyclical variation in the focus of interaction, but the cycle remains the same and the interaction is an analogy for the spouses' power and weakness in relation to each other.

The symptomatic behavior is a solution, however unfortunate, to the couple's difficulties in that it equalizes the power of the spouses, providing a focus of interaction that stabilizes the marriage.

The case examples presented followed certain steps to change this cycle of interaction and resolve the presenting problem.

1. The therapist refused to be organized into a certain position in relation to the couples by accepting their definition of the problem.
2. Instead, the therapist changed the definition of the symptom, or the metaphor expressed by the symptom, or both, and consequently changed the system of interaction around the symptom.
3. Paradoxical instructions were given to produce the symptomatic behavior or to produce the behavior that was metaphorically expressed by the symptom.
4. An ordeal related to the symptom was given directly to the symptomatic spouse, or the nonsymptomatic spouse was asked to enforce the ordeal.
5. The hierarchical incongruity in the marriage was paradoxically exaggerated through directives designed to provoke the spouses to reorganize in a more congruous hierarchy.

6. The therapist brought the spouses together and improved their relationship so that the system of interaction around a symptom was no longer used as an analogy and a solution to their difficulties.

CHAPTER FOUR

田 田 田 田 田

Children's Problems: Three Paradoxical Strategies

When a child exhibits problem behavior, he is singled out in the family as a special source of concern for the parents who are involved in a struggle to change him. A child might have any of a variety of symptoms such as night terrors, headaches, setting fires, or wetting the bed, but whatever the difficulties of the child, the disturbed behavior keeps the parents involved in attempting to help him and to change his behavior.

A parent might have trouble at work, difficulties with relatives, or his spouse might be threatening separation, but the parents will set aside their own problems, at least temporarily, to help or to control their child. They will try to overcome their own deficiencies and hold themselves together in order to aid the child. In this sense, the child's disturbed behavior is helpful to his parents. It provides a respite from the parents' own troubles and a reason to overcome their own difficulties. Whether the child's behavior provokes helpful, protective, or punitive acts from the parents, it focuses the parents' concern on him and makes the parents see themselves as parents to a child who needs them rather than as individuals overwhelmed by personal, economic, or social difficulties. In this sense, the child is a concerned benefactor or protector of others in his family.

This view is different from other strategic and structural family therapy approaches, in which, although the protective function of the symptom is understood (Haley, 1967b, 1976b; Minuchin, 1974), the child is typically thought of as involved in a coalition with one parent against the other parent, or with a grandparent or relative against a parent, or as involved in a conflict between the parents by providing the bond that holds the conflicting parents together. In these approaches, the child is said to be used by the parents in a conflict between them. This conflict is said to detour through the child, so that, for example, the mother encourages the daughter to disobey the father, who attacks the daughter when he is angry at the mother (Minuchin, 1974). The child's involvement in a family conflict has also been seen as the replication of family issues in a previous generation (Bowen, 1978). Although the differences may not at first appear important from a theoretical viewpoint, they are important in the implications these different points of view have for the choice of therapeutic strategy. In this approach, instead of coming into the family ready to look for conflicts, coalitions, and adversaries, the therapist can look at the family in terms of helpfulness and caring. The child is seen not as a passive participant in conflicts between the parents but as an active initiator of protective sequences of interaction. Therapists often find what they look for in a family, and theoretical postures can become self-fulfilling prophecies. In this sense, it is best to look for helpfulness and caring rather than conflict and strife.

Problem behavior in children can be helpful to parents in quite specific ways. For example, a child might develop a problem that will keep his mother at home to take care of him; consequently, the mother will not have to face the issue of looking for a job. The child's problem provides a convenient excuse to the parent for avoiding unpleasant situations. If a father comes home from work upset and worried and a child misbehaves, the father can then feel angry toward the child instead of feeling worried about his work. In this sense, the child's misbehavior is helpful to his father. Also, by making the father angry at him, he saves the mother from having to help her husband by sympathizing with him or quarreling with him. In this way, the child is helping both parents.

The child's protectiveness of the parents is a function of the system of interaction in the family. This is not to say that the child deliberately plans to protect the parents by eliciting their concern, although sometimes that is the case. It is not the intention to imply that *all* symptoms in childhood are best understood from the point of view of their protective function. Sometimes a presenting problem is the result of neglect or physical suffering. Sometimes the protective element is lost in the tyranny imposed on the parents by the child. (This tyranny will be dealt with in Chapter Six.) In some instances, the child's disturbed behavior can best be understood as a bid for power through helplessness or disruption. But whether the symptomatic child is seen as a protector or a tyrant, the fact is that his disturbing behavior has a helpful yet unfortunate function in the family.

In any organization, there is hierarchy in the sense that one person has more power and responsibility to determine what happens than another person.[1] In a family organization, the parents are higher in the hierarchy than the children. When a child's disturbed behavior is protective of the parents, there is an incongruous hierarchical organization in the family. That is,

---

[1] Minuchin (1974) and Haley (1967b, 1976b) have emphasized the importance of the hierarchical organization of the family. Minuchin emphasizes the importance of defining subsystems in the family with clear generational boundaries, and Haley describes pathology in a child as involving a coalition across generational lines.

the parents, by the fact of being parents, are in a superior position in the hierarchy with respect to the child, for whom they have legal responsibility, for whom they provide, and whom they take care of. But the child, with his disturbed behavior, protects the parents by helping them avoid their own difficulties and overcome their own deficiencies. In this sense, the child is in a superior position to the parents by the fact of helping them. If the child behaves normally, he loses the power that his disturbed behavior gives him over his parents and, therefore, the possibility of helping them. To be successful in changing the child's behavior, the parents must deal with their own difficulties in such a way that the child's protectiveness is no longer necessary. The more the parents attempt to change the child's behavior, the more the function of the child's protectiveness is maintained. This protectiveness may help the parents temporarily avoid their problems, but it does not help them face and resolve the issues that concern them and can even prevent the resolution of these issues.

The therapist's problem is how to get the child to give up the disturbed behavior that is the basis of his power. This cannot be done directly by the therapist. The child's power is over his parents, and it is the parents who must take it away from him. But the dilemma is that the more the parents are focused on trying to change the child, the more the function of the symptom is maintained. Therapists have developed various ways of dealing with this dilemma. One way has been to encourage parents to ignore the symptom. Another way has been to have the parents pay attention to the child and reward him only when he does not have the symptom. Other ways to approach the problem, and the ones that will be described here, are to arrange that the child's disturbed behavior no longer serve the purpose of helping the parents and to provide a different, more appropriate, way in which the child can be helpful.

To achieve the goal of the therapy, the therapist must restore the family to a single hierarchical organization, with the parents in a superior position to the child; that is, an organization where the parents protect and help the child and where the child does not protect them. If the family hierarchy is to be restored to one in which the parents are in a superior position to the child, it is the parents who must solve the child's problem. The parents, and not the therapist alone, must be involved in changing the child's behavior.

In the therapeutic approaches described here, the therapist plans a strategy for solving the child's problem. The goal is always clearly set and is to solve the presenting problem.

1. The therapist assumes that a symptom analogically or metaphorically expresses a problem and is also a solution, although usually an unsatisfactory one, for the people involved. For example, when a child is talking about his headaches, he is talking about more than one kind of pain. That is, behavior is always a communication on many levels. The message "I have a headache" is a report on an internal state, but it might also be a way of declining to do the chores or of getting the father to help with the homework.

2. The therapist first decides who is the focus of the child's concern—who is being protected by the child and in what way. Next, he or she decides on an intervention that will change the family organization to one in which there is a single hierarchy, with the parents in a superior position. The therapist's intervention usually takes the form of a directive about something that the family is to do, both in and out of the interview. Directives may be straightforward or paradoxical and may involve one or two people or the whole family. These directives have the purpose of changing the interaction of family members with each other and with the therapist.

3. The therapist is not concerned with making family members aware of how communication takes place; if a problem can be solved without the family's knowing how or why, that is satisfactory.

4. The therapy is planned in stages, and it is assumed that the presenting problem usually cannot be solved in one step.

5. Relationships in each family are unique and may require different therapeutic plans even when the presenting problems are similar.

One way to restore the family to a single hierarchical

organization, with the parents in a superior position to the child, is for the therapist to arrange that the parents solve the child's problem. Some paradoxical techniques for doing this are presented here with case examples.

Strategies and Case Examples

Strategy 1: The Parent Requests That the Child Have the Problem. Sometimes a child's symptom expresses analogically the problem of a parent. For example, if the father's job is a "headache," the child might have headaches. The child's symptom expresses the parent's problem and is also an attempt to solve it; that is, the father forgets his own "headaches" while trying to help the child with his. The more the parents are focused on trying to change the child, the more the function of the symptom is maintained. The relationship between parent and child is based on benevolent helpfulness. That is, the child, with his symptom, helps the parent; and the parent unsuccessfully tries to help the child overcome the symptom. One way to solve the problem is to arrange that the parent encourage the child to have the symptom. In this way, both the child's and the parent's helpfulness will be blocked. The symptom will no longer have the function of helping the parents and of eliciting helpfulness from them; therefore, it will be dropped.[2]

Case 5: Bed Wetting

A 12-year-old boy was brought to therapy because he wet the bed almost every night; organic causes had been ruled out. The mother had been hospitalized at one time for depression. The father worked long hours, and the mother complained about his lack of interest in her and his attraction to other women. The therapist and supervisor hypothesized that the bed wetting was both a metaphorical expression of the father's improper behavior in bed and an attempt to help the parents by

---

[2] The therapists in the following cases were Judy Bankhead, Michael Fox, Tobias Lopez, Virginia Lopez, and Thomas Todd.

eliciting their concern and distracting them from their other problems. Because of the boy's symptom, the mother could focus on his problems rather than on her own depression, and she could nag the father to spend more time with the son and to help him rather than nagging him to spend more time with her. The father could discuss with the mother the boy's bed wetting rather than his own improper behavior in bed and the couple's marital difficulties. Mother and father could judge what each was thinking about the other by discussing the boy; in this way, the child was helping both parents.

The therapy started with several routine ways to have the father solve the son's problem. If the son wet the bed, the father—not the mother—was to wash the sheets. The son's bed wetting would be an inconvenience to the father rather than to the mother. The father also had to buy an alarm clock for the son, so that the boy could wake up in the middle of the night and go to the bathroom; and the father was to reward the son if he did not wet the bed. The father never did what was requested of him, although he excused himself and always promised that he would do it the next week.

After several weeks, the therapist told the father that, because he had not done what he promised, he would now have to carry out a more difficult task—one that would assure the cure for the son's symptom. However, the therapist would not reveal what the cure was until he had the father's commitment that he would follow the therapist's instructions. The father agreed, and the therapist told him that every evening he had to give his son a large glass of water, take him up to his room, and then demand that the son urinate on the bed on purpose and go to sleep on the wet bed.[3] He was to stay with the son in the bedroom until the son wet the bed and went to sleep in it. This was to be done every evening for one week.

The family came back after one week, and the father reported that he had gone through torture over the dilemma of whether to impose this ordeal on his son. He said he felt like

[3] This strategy is based on a procedure of Milton Erickson (see "Indirect Hypnotic Therapy of an Enuretic Couple," in Haley, 1973).

Abraham when God wanted him to sacrifice his son. He had not enforced the ordeal, although he had attempted to do so a couple of times and the boy had cried and begged him not to make him wet the bed. The father said he now understood that the therapist had not really wanted him to carry out the task. The therapist, he said, had only wanted to bring him to his senses and show him that he had to do his part or else the situation would not change. He had spent a great deal of time that week talking to his son and had even missed work one day. The boy had not wet the bed during the last four nights and as a reward, as planned earlier in the therapy, was allowed to be absent from the family session and participate in a sports event at school instead. The father said he wanted to help his son in his own way by spending more time talking to him. Since the boy had improved, the therapist agreed.

The therapist's paradoxical instructions created a situation in which the son was no longer helpful to his father through his symptomatic behavior, since it now resulted in great anxiety for the father. The father took charge of the relationship with the son and spent time talking to him and advising him. A single hierarchy was defined, with the father in a superior position and the son no longer protecting the father through his symptoms.

The son did not wet the bed again, and the couple spent a few sessions discussing their marriage. The father explained that he had been irresponsible and compulsive in his relations with other women; he called himself "a cat on a hot tin roof." The parents began to have sexual relations regularly and were pleased about it, since the father had not been sexually interested in his wife for a year and a half. The therapy ended with a better relationship between husband and wife. During the course of the therapy, the mother had quit smoking, and the son was taken off Ritalin, which he had been taking for many years for his hyperactivity. His behavior improved, and the parents no longer considered him hyperactive.

Strategy 2: The Parent Requests That the Child Pretend to Have the Problem. Rather than encourage the symptom, a therapist can encourage the child to *pretend* to have the symptom. The parent can also be encouraged to pretend to help the child when the child is pretending to have the problem. In this situation, the child no longer needs to actually have the symptom to protect the parent; pretending to have it is enough to become the focus of concern for the parent. But the parent's concern will also be a pretense, and the situation will have changed to a game, to make-believe and play. Bateson (1972, p. 180) describes this process in play in animals: "The playful nip denotes the bite, but it does not denote what would be denoted by the bite." That is, pretending to have the symptom stands for having the symptom but does not stand for that which the symptom stands for. For example, whereas a child's headaches might denote the father's difficulties at work, the child's "pretend" headaches denote his "real" headaches but do not denote the father's difficulties at work.

The directive to pretend to have the symptom is less limiting and restrictive than the directive to actually have the symptom. It provides the opportunity to respond in less structured ways. The response to the paradoxical directive to actually have the symptom is either to have it or not to have it. The response to the directive to pretend to have the symptom is more unpredictable but also more creative and spontaneous. An example of an adolescent girl and her family will clarify this approach.

Case 6: Epileptic Seizures

A 15-year-old girl was referred to therapy because she had frequent epileptic seizures and did not respond to medication. She usually had the seizures during the night, and her moaning woke up the parents and siblings, who gathered around her in great concern trying to help her. Sometimes she had the seizures during the day, and the other family members were terrified of the harm that could come to her. She was hospitalized, and a physician witnessed a seizure during the night; so there was no question that these were documented grand mal seizures with the usual postictal phenomena. She was released from the hospital and referred to therapy by her pediatrician. Considering that epileptic seizures are a physiological response that may be emotionally triggered, the referring physician hoped that with therapy the frequency of the seizures would decrease.

In the first session, the parents—particularly the father—appeared very concerned and upset about the girl. They described her symptoms and her history with a wealth of detail. The siblings were also interested and involved and volunteered information. The girl herself was mostly silent and shy. The therapist assumed that the girl's symptom had a protective function in the family, but there was no indication of what this function was—except that this mysterious illness gave a certain excitement to their lives. The therapist asked the girl, in the first session, to try to have a seizure right there in the therapy room and the family (mother, father, and several siblings) to do what they usually did at home on those occasions. The girl lay down on the floor surrounded by the family and began to make noises and shake, trying to have a seizure. The family hovered over her, particularly the concerned father, encouraging her and giving her directions. She did not succeed in having a seizure, and the therapist asked her then to pretend to have one and the family to pretend to do what they usually did in those circumstances. The girl began to shake with a little more enthusiasm, and the family hovered around her even more, especially the father, touching her and holding her.

These directives were given with the rationale to the family that if the girl could first voluntarily control having the seizures (by producing them deliberately) then she could control *not* having them voluntarily. Since she was not able to produce a seizure voluntarily, the next best thing was to pretend to have one. This would give her the practice she needed in controlling them. The family had to help her by instructing and directing her, so that the seizure would be as authentic as possible.

The parents were told to perform this dramatization at home every evening with the whole family. If the girl had a "real" seizure during the night, the parents were to wake up the other children, and the girl was then to pretend to have a seizure. They would do this no matter what time of night it was or how tired they were. This ordeal was designed to encourage the family members to change the way in which they were protecting each other.

After the first interview, the seizures disappeared. The girl, who had been previously very docile and timid, began to go out two weeks later without permission and to misbehave in various ways. The parents were asked to make specific rules and to set consequences if she disobeyed the rules. She began to be treated as the other children in her family were treated.

The therapist went away on vacation for a week and, on his return, found the family in the middle of a crisis. The girl had had a hallucination one night about a blond, green-eyed man who she said had attacked her and killed her brother and sister. She began to run around the house out of control, and the father had to hold her down. Her behavior had a similar quality to the way she behaved when she had a seizure, and the parental response was also similar. The parents took her to the emergency room, where a resident did not label her schizophrenic, although he thought she was, and referred her back to the therapist.

In the following days, the girl continued to talk about her fear of this blond, green-eyed man who she said had tried to rape her and who was after her. For a few days, the family had the whole neighborhood looking for this man, whom the girl said she repeatedly saw. Since they lived in an all-black neighborhood, the man would have been easily spotted; so the parents concluded that the girl was lying. She would suddenly act terrified about this blond man and would run away from the family, out of control. These episodes were like tantrums and occurred when she did not want to do something that the parents wanted her to do.

The therapist had the family reenact the night when she said that the siblings had been killed by this blond man and the father had had to hold her down. The therapist asked the family to replay the events of that dramatic night once a day at home, on the same schedule they had had for the seizures. If the girl woke up during the night, they were all to get up and pretend again.

The therapist reformulated the girl's conduct as misbehavior and rebelliousness and encouraged the parents to set strict rules and be in charge of the girl. If she ran off, the parents were to make her stay home all the next day. In a few days, these episodes disappeared and the misbehavior subsided as the girl became more mature and responsible.

During this time, the therapist had to give special support to the father, who had been very attached to the girl and helpful in her distress and who became upset and depressed and quarreled with his wife as the girl improved and began to go out more.

A few months after termination of therapy, the parents called to say that the girl had again had seizures during the night. A family session was held, and the dramatization was repeated. The family members were instructed in the same procedure as previously, with the girl pretending to have a seizure in the session and the family repeating the dramatization at home. At the end of the session, the parents asked the therapist for a letter stating that the girl's delicate condition was made worse because of the family's living arrangements and requesting of the housing authorities that they be transferred to a better housing project. The therapist agreed to do this (although in the letter he referred to the nervousness and fears of all the children). Up to that time, he had assumed simply that the girl's symptom had some kind of protective function in the family. Now it was clear that there was also a financial benefit from the girl's illness. The therapist told the girl, the parents, and the siblings that in the future he would be happy to help them in any way he could, whether the girl had seizures or not. In that way, the daughter did not need to have seizures to obtain help for the family. Two years later, the girl had not had any more seizures, in spite of being without medication, and had not behaved bizarrely.

Strategy 3: The Parent Requests That the Child Pretend to Help the Parent. When a child protects the parents through symptomatic behavior, he is helping them in a covert way. The symptomatic behavior is no longer necessary if the situation is made explicit and it is arranged that the child overtly protect the parents. Typically, when a child presents a problem, the parents are overtly in a superior position in the hierarchy in relation to the child; covertly, however, they are in an inferior position in relation to him, because of the power of his symptom. If the therapist encourages the parents to be overtly in an inferior position to the child, both parents and child will resist the inappropriateness of this hierarchical organization, and the family will reorganize so that the parents regain a superior position.

A similar approach is to encourage the parents to *pretend* to be in an inferior position, to pretend to need the child's help and protection, rather than to actually be in this position. The child can then be encouraged to pretend to help the parents when the parents are pretending to need his help. In order to protect the parents, the child will no longer need to behave in symptomatic ways, since the parents will explicitly ask for help and the child will overtly help them. But the parents' need for help will be a pretense, and so will the child's helpfulness. In a pretend framework, parents and child will be involved with each other in a playful way. One aspect of the incongruous hierarchy, the one in which the child is in a superior position to the parents, will be in play; it will be make-believe, and the incongruity will be resolved. Some examples will clarify this approach.

Case 7: Night Terrors[4]

A mother sought therapy because her 10-year-old son had night terrors. There were two older daughters in the family and a baby brother. The woman was Puerto Rican and spoke little English. The three older children were the product of a first marriage that had ended in divorce. The woman's second husband had died. There had obviously also been a third man, since the baby was only a few months old; but at the beginning of the therapy, the mother denied that there was a man living with the family. It was later found that she was afraid of losing her wel-

[4]Verbatim transcripts of excerpts of this therapy are presented with commentary in Chapter Seven.

fare benefits if she admitted that a man was contributing to her support.

The son appeared taciturn and preoccupied. The therapist and supervisor suspected that he was concerned about his mother, who had lost two husbands, was poor, did not speak English, and was involved with a man in a relationship that had to be kept secret even though he was the father of her child.

Since the boy had night terrors, the therapist asked each member of the family about his dreams. Only the mother and the son had nightmares. The mother often dreamed that somebody was breaking into the house, and the boy described a recurrent nightmare in which he was attacked by a witch. The therapist asked what happened when the boy had nightmares. The mother explained that she took him to her bed and told him to think about God and to pray. She made the sign of the cross on his forehead to protect him from the devil. She explained that she thought that the boy's problem was due to the influence of the devil.

It was hypothesized that the boy's night terrors were both a metaphorical expression of the mother's fears and an attempt to help her. If the boy was the one who was afraid, then the mother had to be strong and pull herself together to reassure him and protect him; therefore, she could not be afraid herself. But when she protected him, she frightened him more, by talking about God and the devil. Mother and son were caught in a situation where they were helping each other in unfortunate ways.

In the first session, the family members were asked to pretend that they were at home and that the mother was very frightened because she heard noises as of someone breaking into the house. One of the sisters played the role of the thief who was trying to enter the house, and the son was asked to protect his mother. In this way, the mother was requested to pretend to need the child's help rather than to actually need it.[5] The child

[5] This approach was inspired by Mariano Barragan, who used a similar procedure at the Philadelphia Child Guidance Clinic with a mother and a daughter who was afraid to go into a garage at night.

was encouraged to pretend to help the mother by attacking the make-believe thief. The mother's need for help was now in play, and so was the son's helpfulness.

The family had difficulty with the dramatization because the mother would attack the make-believe thief before the son could help her. The therapist had to ask them repeatedly to try again. The message that resulted from this failure to act out the scene correctly was that the mother was a capable person who would defend herself; she did not need the son's protection. This is an example of how the consequences of the directive to pretend may be unpredictable. The mother could have responded in a variety of ways, but she chose this one. If the therapist had set out to plan an intervention that would make the mother appear strong and not in need of protection, she could not have planned it better.

When the dramatization was performed correctly and the son attacked the thief, everybody sat down to discuss the performance. The therapist criticized the mother for her difficulty in expressing fear and in restraining herself so that the son would have a chance to attack the thief. The mother responded to this criticism by saying that she was a competent person who could defend herself well and that was why it was so difficult for her to play this part. This was a spontaneous message from the mother to the son that she did not need his protection.

The therapist asked the family to get together every evening at home during the following week and repeat the dramatization. During the night, if the mother heard that the son was screaming in his sleep, she was to get up, wake him, wake the sisters, and they would all perform the same dramatization. They would do this no matter what time of night it was or how tired they were. This ordeal was designed to encourage mother and son to change the unfortunate way in which they were protecting each other.

The son did not have night terrors again. The family continued to be seen in therapy for several weeks, and other issues were resolved in different ways. The therapist helped mother and son deal with the school, and the boy's behavior and grades improved. The father of the baby came to a session and was encouraged, although not very successfully, to become more involved with the boy. The mother arranged for the son to participate in activities with peers: a rock band and a soccer team. The therapist encouraged the mother in her work as a dance teacher and supported her in her difficulties with the father of the baby.

In a follow-up a year later, the boy's grades in school were so good that, as a reward, the mother had bought him a bicycle. She had become a community worker in a mental health center.

There were two stages in this therapy. In the first, the unfortunate ways in which mother and son protected each other were blocked through a paradoxical intervention. In the second stage, the mother was encouraged to be in charge of the son in relation to school and peer-group activities and to take charge of her work and the organization of her family.

Case 8: Headaches

A father and mother consulted because their 7-year-old son had frequent headaches. They described the boy's problem so vaguely that it was impossible to determine how frequent the headaches were or whether they had recently become worse or better. Behavior problems at school were also mentioned, although it was not clear what these were and apparently they had been solved by changing schools. The mother implied that the son was jealous of his 5-year-old sister because she was brighter; and the father agreed. Several times mother and father talked about the son in a way that made it difficult for the therapist to determine whether they were referring to the son or to the father.

The vagueness and confusion in the way the problem was presented, the parents' choice of words that were more appropriate to describe an adult than a child, and the difficulty in distinguishing whether the parents were talking about the son or the father led to the hypothesis that the father had problems that were painful for the couple to discuss and that the parents had established a pattern of talking about the son's difficulties as a way of metaphorically discussing the father's troubles. It was later confirmed that the father did have serious problems. He was recovering from alcoholism, there was a possibility that he would lose his job, and he had written a novel that he could not get published. The goal of the therapy was to free the child from being a metaphor that the parents could use to discuss the father's problems.

Ordinarily the son would develop a headache when he came home from school and the father came home from work feeling miserable. In the first session, the therapist asked the family to act out a scene in which the father was to pretend that he was coming home in the evening with a terrible headache. The son was to try to cheer him up by playing games with him. He was also to try to find out whether the father had a real headache by asking him about how he was feeling and what his day had been like at work. The father was to talk about make-believe problems at work and avoid discussing real problems. While father and son were involved in this way in the interview, mother and daughter were pretending to prepare dinner. (When a directive to pretend is given, everyone in the family should have a part.)

The parents were asked to perform this scene at home every evening for one week. Father would come home pretending to have a headache, son would cheer him up, father would not say whether his headache was real. In the meantime, mother and daughter would be preparing dinner.

The family followed the directive and reported the following week that the son was much improved. They continued to perform the same scene for three more weeks, and the headaches disappeared.

The hypothesis behind the intervention was that the son was protecting the father by having a symptom that elicited concern from the father and therefore helped him to pull himself together to help the son instead of feeling devastated by his own problems. Also, the boy provided a metaphor that the parents could use to discuss father's problems and, in this way, saved them from talking directly about issues that were too painful to discuss explicitly.

By asking the father to pretend every day to have a headache, and to justify it by talking about make-believe problems at work, the therapist created a situation where the son no longer knew whether the father was really upset and therefore could not help him in his usual way. A different way of protecting the father was arranged: the son had to play games and talk with him. The child no longer needed to have headaches to help the father. The father's make-believe headaches became a metaphor for his real problems and were discussed in a playful way by the family. The son was no longer used as a metaphor.

The problem of the headaches had been solved, but the mother complained that the son teased and bothered his sister. The little girl would come "screeching" to the mother, who constantly had to reprimand the son. The therapist asked the mother to pretend that she was the daughter, and the son was to tease her as he usually did his sister. The mother was to then run screeching to the little girl, who would play the role of the mother and who would say, "Don't bother me. That is your problem, not mine." This scene was rehearsed several times in the session to the great enjoyment of the family. They were also instructed that every time the son felt like teasing or bothering his sister, he was to bother his mother instead. The mother would then run screeching to the little girl, who would tell her to handle the problem on her own. Mother and children carried out these instructions at home for two weeks, and the relationship between brother and sister improved to the point that the mother did not consider it a problem any longer. The son, who was to initiate the sequence, did so several times during the first week but seldom after that.

With this sequence, the therapist had prescribed one aspect of the incongruous hierarchy, the one in which the children were in a superior position to the mother. This was a paradoxical directive designed to provoke the mother to respond by behaving in a more competent way and drawing a generation line between herself and the children. The therapist was also taking power away from the son by taking over the control of the symptom and instructing the child about how and whom he should tease. The family responded by solving the problem so that brother and sister were no longer in a superior position to mother by harassing her with their quarrels and mother was no longer complaining that she was incompetent to handle the difficulties between her children.

The family came to a termination session just before they were leaving on vacation. The father, who was often depressed, seemed particularly sad. The therapist decided to change the father's mood to relieve him of his depression and so that the family could leave in a more cheerful spirit. The father was asked to pretend that he was very depressed, that he was a failure in life and to tell his family so. However, he had to give good reasons to justify his feelings. As soon as the father started to do this, the therapist began to criticize him for not pretending to be depressed well enough and particularly for not giving good enough reasons for his depression. As the therapist continued to criticize the husband, the wife began to support him by saying how difficult it was for him to be depressed. Finally, the therapist accepted as a valid depression the father's feelings about his failure to fix the sink at his house properly. At the end of the session, the father was talking about how difficult it is to pretend to be depressed when one is really in good spirits.

Husband and wife were moved to change their usual interaction, in which husband was depressed and wife attempted to cheer him up. When the husband had to pretend to be depressed and was criticized by the therapist for not doing it well, the wife supported him because he could *not* be depressed rather than supporting him, as usual, because he *was* depressed. A new sequence of interaction was elicited between husband and wife in a playful, make-believe way.

When the family originally came to therapy, the son was a metaphor for the father's difficulties, and his symptoms were protective of the father. The quarrels between brother and sister were an analogy for the difficulties between the parents, the implicit message being that the husband was jealous of the wife's intelligence. The wife had, in fact, abandoned her career and devoted herself to supporting him in his depression. By the end of the therapy, the children were no longer protecting the parents, the symptoms had disappeared, and the parents were discussing the issues between them more openly and finding solutions.

Months after the therapy ended, the husband wrote to

the therapist that they were all doing well. The son was behaving properly, doing well in school, and involved in activities with peers. The mother had gone back to school for an advanced degree, and things were better for the father. The little girl continued to do well as usual.

Case 9: The Fire Setter

A mother consulted because her 10-year-old son was setting fires. He was a twin and the oldest of five children. The family had many other serious problems. The father had just left them and moved to another city. The mother was not receiving any financial support from him. She was Puerto Rican, did not speak English, and did not know how to go about obtaining the help she needed. The mother would not leave the boy alone for a minute for fear that he would set the house on fire.

In the first interview, the therapist gave the boy some matches and told him to light one and asked the mother to do whatever she usually did at home when she caught him lighting a match. The therapist then left the room to observe from behind the one-way mirror. The boy reluctantly lighted a match, and the mother took it and burned him with it.

By providing a focus for her anger, the boy was helping his mother. He was someone whom she could punish and blame. He made her feel angry instead of depressed and in this way helped her to pull herself together in spite of all her troubles.

The therapist told the child that she was going to teach him how to light matches properly. She then showed him how one closes the matchbox before lighting the match and how, after the match burns, one carefully puts it in the ashtray. She then asked the mother to light a fire with some papers in an ashtray and to pretend to burn herself. The son had to help her by putting out the fire with some water that the therapist had brought into the office for this purpose. The boy had to show his mother that he knew how to put out fires correctly. As all this was going on, the other children were allowed to look but not to participate in any other way. After the fire was put out, the therapist told the boy that he now knew how to light fires and put them out correctly. She emphasized to the mother that now she could trust him because he knew about fires. The therapist then asked the mother to set aside a time every evening for a week when she would get together with the boy and she would light a fire and pretend to burn herself and he would help her to put it out. The other children were only allowed to participate as spectators.

The interaction between mother and son was changed so that, instead of helping his mother by providing a focus for her anger, the son was helping her in a playful way when she pretended to burn herself. Before, the boy had been helping the mother by threatening her with fires. Now he was helping her because he was an expert on fires. Before the therapy, the child had been special in the family because he was setting fires; after the therapeutic intervention, he was special because he was an expert on fires. When the boy was unpredictably lighting fires, he was in a superior position to the mother. When he set fires under direction, he was beneath her in the hierarchy.

When the family came back a week later, the boy had not set fires. They went through the same procedure of lighting a fire and putting it out, but this time it was a bigger fire in a trash can. The therapist talked to the boy about different ways of putting out a fire. She then told the mother that, since her son had now become an expert on fires, he should be allowed a privilege that the other children did not have, such as lighting the stove at home. The mother agreed to this and said that she felt confident that the boy was not going to set fires any more. The therapist then proceeded for the next two months to help the mother with her other problems. The son did not set fires again. By helping the mother with her many other difficulties, the therapist herself was protecting the mother; therefore, the son no longer needed to do so.

Case 10: The Incredible Hulk

The staff of the department of child psychiatry of a university hospital recommended hospitalization for a 5-year-old boy who had temper tantrums and whose mother said she could not control him. After the mother went through the admission procedures, the father refused to allow hospitalization and was angry at the hospital staff for having suggested it. He was the boy's stepfather and had adopted him legally. The boy had a 2-year-old sister who was the biological child of the mother and the stepfather.

The mother came back to the hospital seeking help for the child as an outpatient, and the case was referred to family therapy. It was felt that a therapist was needed to skillfully deal with the father who was seen as undermining the staff's attempts to help the child. The father did not come to the first family session because he could not get away from his work. The mother and the two children were present.

The mother was very young, attractive, and childish. She watched helplessly every time the boy systematically hit his little sister when she tried to take one of his toys. When the therapist, however, said to the boy that hitting was not allowed in the session, the child stopped doing it. The two children were very pretty and mischievous, and the mother looked at them with a mixture of awe and wonder, as if she could not quite believe that she had produced them and did not know what to do with them. She worked part time as a waitress in the evenings to help out with the family's finances. While she worked, the children stayed part of the time with a babysitter and part of the time with the father, neither of whom complained about the boy's behavior. The teacher, however, did complain, according to the mother, about the boy's misbehavior in class.

The therapist asked the boy to dramatize a temper tantrum right there in the session to show her what it was like. The child said "OK, I'm going to be the Incredible Hulk."[6] He puffed up his chest, flexed his arms, made an ugly face, and began to scream and kick and hit the furniture. The mother was asked to do what she usually did in those circumstances. She tried to stop the boy, telling him in a weak and ineffective way to calm down. She tried to pretend that she was taking him to

---

[6] A popular television series in which a handsome doctor turns into a monster with superhuman strength every time an injustice is committed and uses his strength to right a wrong.

another room as she tried to do at home but usually failed because he screamed and kicked the door and she was afraid that the neighbors would report her for child abuse. She was asked whether the boy was dramatizing the tantrum correctly and whether this was actually the way he behaved at home when he was having a tantrum. She said the dramatization was correct, and the therapist asked the child to do it once more. This time he said, "I'm going to be Frankenstein," and proceeded to have a tantrum but now with a more rigid body and a face more appropriate to Frankenstein's monster.

The therapist talked with the boy about Frankenstein and the Incredible Hulk and asked him about his favorite television programs. She congratulated the mother on raising such a bright, imaginative child.

In the session, mother and son were then asked to pretend that the boy was having a temper tantrum and that the mother was walking with him to his room. Then they were to pretend to close the door and to hug and kiss. The boy was encouraged to act like the Incredible Hulk, with a great deal of noise and action. They did this twice. The therapist then asked the mother to pretend that *she* had a tantrum. The boy was to hug the mother, kiss her, and calm her down. Both dramatizations were performed well and with pleasure by mother and child. The therapist told them that she wanted them to perform both scenes once every morning at home before the boy went to school. That is, the boy was to pretend to have a tantrum, and the mother was to comfort him; then the mother would pretend to have a tantrum, and the boy would comfort her, as they had done in the session. The performance would end with both of them going to the kitchen to have milk and cookies. Also, every afternoon when the boy came home from school, they were to perform the two pretend tantrums again, ending once more with milk and cookies. The mother was also to keep a chart of the boy's behavior, giving him a happy face for a good day and a frowning face for a bad day.

The next week, the mother called to say that they did not need to come to the session because the boy was behaving very well and had had no more tantrums. They had performed the pretend tantrums as the therapist had indicated. The therapist said that she was pleased and that there was no need to come to therapy. During the next weeks, the therapist found out, from several telephone conversations, that the boy was still behaving well. The teacher also reported that he was behaving well in school. This improvement continued even though the mother was in a car accident and had to quit her job and stay at home for a long time. In a follow-up six months later, the child was still behaving well and did not have tantrums.

The hypotheses behind the therapeutic intervention in this case were the following. Although the mother was apparently in a superior position to the child, since she took care of him and provided for him, she was covertly in an inferior position because she could not control him. In asking the mother to pretend to have a tantrum and the child to comfort her, the therapist emphasized one aspect of the incongruous hierarchy: the one in which the mother was in an inferior position to the child. But the whole situation—the boy's pretend tantrums, the mother's pretend tantrums and her helplessness, and the child's helpfulness—was a pretense, make-believe, and play; and the incongruity was resolved. Also, mother and son would be closer together, with hugs, kisses, milk, and cookies; and the little sister (obviously an object of jealousy) would not be included.

Another hypothesis in this case was that the mother behaved helplessly and incompetently as a way of raising the position of the stepfather in the family, particularly in relation to the boy. The more she complained that the boy was uncontrollable, the more competent and effective the father appeared in relation to the boy, since he did not have any problem in controlling the child. This is a common maneuver by mothers in an attempt to introduce a stepfather into a position of respect, power, and involvement in relation to their children. The father's refusal to hospitalize and his confrontation with the hospital staff had established him even more as the head of the household. In this sense, the mother had been successful. The problem was how to resolve the child's "symptom" while keeping the father in his superior position and eliciting more competent behavior from the mother. To solve this problem, it was not necessary to see the father. Instead, the therapist provided the mother with a playful, affectionate focus for her relationship with her son; as a result, she could develop a new area of interaction (pretending, hugging, and milk and cookies) that was not competitive with the father's involvement and did not undermine his position.

Summary and Conclusion

It has been proposed here that disturbed or disturbing behavior in children is the result of an incongruity in the hierarchical organization of the family. The parents are in a superior position to the child by the fact of being parents, and yet the child is in a superior position to the parents by protecting them through symptomatic behavior that often expresses metaphorically the parents' difficulties. Three strategic approaches were presented for arranging that the parents solve the presenting problem in the child while resolving the incongruity in the family hierarchy.

The advantage that the child derives from his symptomatic behavior is to protect the parents by providing a focus of concern that helps them avoid their own difficulties and overcome their own deficiencies. This advantage is the interpersonal gain that the child derives from the symptom—similar to secondary gain in psychoanalytic theory, which in this approach is the primary gain. In the three therapeutic strategies presented here, the interpersonal gain for the child is maintained while the symptom disappears. That is, in the case examples presented, the therapist arranged for the child to maintain the interpersonal gain by organizing a different way in which he could protect the parents and/or by providing other solutions for the parents' difficulties.

The therapist follows certain steps to carry out this therapy.

1. The problem is defined clearly, and specific goals are set.
2. The therapist conceptualizes the problem (to herself or himself only) as one where the child, through his symptoms, is protecting one or both parents or a relative.
3. The therapist plans an intervention in the form of a directive

that the parent(s) will give to the child. Other family members participate in auxiliary ways. The directive includes a prescription (a) to have the problem, or (b) to pretend to have the problem, or (c) to pretend to help the parents.
4. The directive usually is first practiced in the session and then carried out at home.
5. In the next session, a report on the performance of the directive is obtained, and the therapist continues to prescribe the same directive.
6. As change occurs and the problem behavior disappears, the therapist drops the issue of the symptom and begins to deal with other problems in the same or in different ways or terminates the therapy, taking care always to give credit to the parents for the improvement of the child.

The therapeutic techniques that were described are characterized by the use of communication modalities appropriate to children, such as dramatizations, pretending, and make-believe. These "pretend" directives have been successfully used with the whole range of socioeconomic classes and with families from various ethnic backgrounds. They are helpful in bypassing resistance, because of the enjoyment that families derive from the playfulness of the directives. Flexible interventions, such as the directives to "pretend," are necessary in a directive therapy to allow for flexibility in change and spontaneity in restructuring relationships. These techniques are most effective when the relationship between parent and child is basically loving and helpful. They should be used with caution where violence and abuse are involved, since play, if forced, can become an ordeal or a punishment.

The paradoxical directives to pretend, presented in this chapter and in Chapter Three, included two strategies: (1) The symptomatic person is encouraged to pretend to have the symptom. In the case of an adult, the spouse is encouraged to criticize the performance. In the case of a child, the parent can be encouraged to pretend to help the child when the child is pretending to have the problem. (2) The parents of a symptomatic child are encouraged to pretend to need the child's help and protection, and the child is encouraged to pretend to help the parents when the parents are pretending to need his help.

In both strategies, the second stage of the therapy, after the symptom has been resolved, consists in intervening in the hierarchical organization of the family. In the case of a couple, the therapist strives for a more egalitarian relationship, so that a spouse will no longer resort to deriving power from the helplessness of a symptom. In the case of a presenting problem in a child, the parents are encouraged to be in charge of their children, providing guidance and support, and to take charge of themselves—specifically, their work and the organization of their family.

The two strategies presented—the directives to *pretend* to have the symptom and to *pretend* to help the parents (while the parents pretend to have a problem)—are similar to yet different from other paradoxical approaches. Some of the similarities and differences are explored in what follows.

1. When a person with a problem is asked to pretend to have the problem, he is not expected to be unable to pretend (as in the case of prescribing the symptom). On the contrary, he is carefully coached and helped to pretend as well as possible, since when he is pretending to have the symptom he cannot "really" have it, or else he would not be pretending. When one pretends to have a headache, one cannot be suffering from a "real" headache. The pretense precludes the occurrence of the event that the pretense represents.

2. The paradoxical directive of prescribing the symptom has been understood in terms of the resistance of patients. That is, the patient comes to therapy because he cannot help behaving in a certain way, although he would prefer not to, and family and friends have not been able to help him. He is expected to resist the therapist's attempts to influence him to change. However, if, instead of influencing him to change, the therapist requests the same behavior that he is supposed to prevent, the patient will resist by changing and no longer behaving in the symptomatic way. In the paradoxical directive to *pretend* to have the symptom, the patient is *not* expected to resist. He is expected to cooperate in pretending.

3. When a symptomatic person pretends to have the symptom, the family members are asked to criticize the performance in order to help the person to perform more realistically. In this way, the family's behavior, which is an intrinsic part of the symptomatic behavior and which usually consists of benevolently helping the person overcome the symptom, is changed. Instead of offering support and reassurance, the other family members are asked to offer criticism; instead of coaxing the patient out of the symptom, they are encouraging a better performance of the symptom. The more critical the relatives are, the greater is the implication that the symptomatic behavior does not come easily to the patient, that he is a different kind of person from what he appears to be.

4. Sometimes, instead of asking a symptomatic child to pretend to have the symptom, the therapist asks a parent to pretend to have a symptom that is similar to the child's. When a child's symptom is analogical to a parent's problem, and when that parent is asked to pretend to have a problem that is analogical to the child's symptom, the child's symptom becomes a metaphor for the parent's "pretend" problem. The child's symptom has turned into a metaphor of a metaphor and no longer expresses what it originally denoted. When a child's night terrors are metaphorical of the mother's fears, and the mother, in the context of helping her son overcome his night terrors, is asked to pretend to be afraid, the implication is that the mother is being asked to be afraid, just as the child is afraid. The child's night terrors (which were metaphorical of the mother's "real" fears) are now metaphorical of the mother's "pretend" fears, which are metaphorical of the child's night terrors. The symptom as metaphor no longer represents a "real" problem; it represents a metaphorical problem. In the same way, when a child's headaches are metaphorical of the father's "headaches," and the father, in the context of therapy designed to cure his son of headaches, is asked to pretend to have headaches, when in fact he (the father) usually has them, the symptom of the child is no longer an analogy for the father's "real" headaches but has become an analogy for the father's "pretend" headaches, which are in turn an analogy for the father's "real" headaches. The child's symptom no longer expresses a "real" problem.

5. A child's symptom not only expresses a parent's problem but is also an attempt to solve that problem by providing a focus for the parent's concern and by eliciting benevolent attention or punitive anger and orienting the parents to their situation as parents and in this way removing them from whatever disturbing situation they might have been experiencing. The directive for the parent to pretend to have a problem and for the child to pretend to help the parent replaces with make-believe the "real" situation, in which the parent does have a problem and the child does help the parent. Since the parent is pretending to need the child's help, he is indicating that he does not "really" need this help and that the child is not "really" helping him. When this message is clear, the child abandons the symptomatic behavior, and the pretense is no longer necessary.

6. The approach is similar to prescribing the rules of the system (Palazzoli and others, 1978). Here, however, what is prescribed is a playful reenactment of the rules; the rules are "pretend" rules, not the "real" ones. The family are not expected to resist by changing the rules. They are expected to pretend. As a result, the rules will no longer be "real"; they will be make-believe.

7. With the directive to pretend, a metaphor no longer represents reality. It becomes a representation of a "pretend" reality or a metaphorical reality and is therefore a different order of metaphor: a metaphor of another metaphor. Reality has disappeared. The first order of metaphor can no longer be distinguished from this second-order metaphor and therefore can no longer express a reality or be used in an attempt to change it. When a husband's "depression" is a metaphor for his situation of rejection as well as an attempt to involve his wife, and the husband is asked to pretend to be depressed so that the wife will not know whether he is pretending or is "really" depressed, the "pretense" of depression is a metaphor for a "depression" that is itself a metaphor for the man's situation. The "real" depression can no longer be distinguished from the "pretend" depression and can therefore no longer express the reality of a situation or be used as an attempt to change it.

8. When a sequence of interaction is labeled "This is pretend," it is difficult for the participants in the sequence to go

back to a framework of "This is real." This difficulty can be used by a therapist to confuse and to eliminate the reality of a symptom and to change the system of interaction on which this reality is based. When the depressed man in Chapter Three is pretending to be depressed, his wife and the therapist criticize his performance. After several attempts to appear depressed, he says in exasperation: "How can I pretend to be depressed when I'm feeling on top of the world!" The wife says, "Are you *really* feeling that way?" The system of interaction between husband and wife has changed, and the wife no longer knows whether his depression or his optimism is pretense.

CHAPTER FIVE

 ▦ ▦ ▦ ▦ ▦

Parental Problems: Changing Child-Parent Interactions

A child's disturbing behavior is helpful to his parents in that it elicits a system of interaction that is analogical to another system of interaction in the family. The sequence of events would be the following. Parent A behaves in disturbed or disturbing ways as part of System of Interaction A in the family. At a certain point in time, a child behaves in similar disturbed or disturbing ways as part of System of Interaction B (which is similar to System of Interaction A). System of Interaction B replaces System of Interaction A in the family. If System of Interaction B is abandoned, the family might return to System of Interaction A, which will eventually lead to the reestablishment of System of Interaction B. The same system of interac-

96   Strategic Family Therapy

tion may occur repeatedly, with a cyclical variation in the focus
of interaction (I. Sojit, personal communication, 1979).

In some families, a child need not actually have a
"symptom" to provide a focus for the parent's concern; a personality trait—such as extreme shyness, withdrawal, sarcasm,
cruelty, selfishness, or frivolity—may have the same function.
The personality traits observed in the so-called "charactero-
logical problems" have the same function in the family as the
symptoms described here and are amenable to the same therapeutic approach (N. Madanes, personal communication, 1979).
The therapist should approach these cases with the thought that
the trait in the child is metaphorical for the situation of someone else in the family.

The therapist's problem is to get the child to give up the
disturbed behavior that is helpful to his parents and the parents
to give up a system of interaction that has a useful but unfortunate function in the family. Several paradoxical strategies to
solve this problem were presented in Chapter Four. A different
perspective is presented here.

Strategies and Case Examples

Three approaches for changing the system of interaction
and solving the child's problems are described in what follows:
(1) changing the metaphorical action, (2) providing a metaphor
for success instead of failure, and (3) changing the metaphorical
solution.[1]

Strategy 1: Changing the Metaphorical Action. The therapist can change a child's disturbed behavior by replacing a
symptom with another action, so that the new metaphorical
action has a positive function in the family without the unfortunate consequences of the symptomatic behavior. The case
examples that follow illustrate this approach.

[1] The therapists in the cases that illustrate the approaches were
Michael Fox, Anne Gonzalez, and Virginia Lopez.

Case 11: The Self-Inflicted Wound

An 8-year-old boy was referred to therapy because he had a wound in his middle, where the stomach is, about two inches long and one inch wide, that would not heal and was constantly infected. It was the result of the child's sticking pins into himself, a habit in which he persisted to the consternation of the pediatricians.

The mother worked as a maid. There were three sons, all out of control. They were left long hours in the apartment when they came home from school, and they would spend the time destroying the furniture. The mother was a big, obese woman overwhelmed with social and economic difficulties and with serious physical problems related to her obesity. There was no adult male living with the family.

The boy not only stuck pins into his own middle; he also stuck them into his mother and into other people as they walked by him. The school had complained about his sticking pins into other children. The mother had tried punishing him in various ways but was unsuccessful in changing his behavior.

The mother and the three sons were present in the first interview. The therapist explained to the mother that the boy's problem was that he stuck pins in the wrong place. His middle was a wrong place, since it resulted in this horrible wound and since everybody knows that it is harmful to stick pins into oneself or into other people. The therapist asked for the mother's help and for her commitment to work with the child so that he would learn where and how to stick pins properly. The mother promised to cooperate. The therapist gave her a little elf-like rubber doll and said that she was to use this doll with just this one child, not with the other two boys. The therapist instructed the mother to buy a box of a hundred pins and bring it home. That evening she was to sit with her son while he stuck all the pins into the doll, one by one. He was to count them as he did it. In this way, he would practice sticking pins in the proper way, in an appropriate place; and he could also practice counting, which would undoubtedly help him with his schoolwork.

After he had finished sticking all the pins in the doll, he then was to unstick them one by one and put them back in the box.[2] Mother and son were to do this together every evening in a room by themselves with the door closed, so that the other two children would not interfere. This was just a matter between the mother and this child.

The family went home and returned the following week. The mother had bought the box of pins. She had sat with the child every evening, and the boy had stuck the pins in the doll, counting the pins as he did so, and then unstuck them again. He had not stuck pins in his middle that week, nor had he stuck pins into anybody else.

The symptom did not recur after that. The next step for the therapist was to help the mother with her health problems and her financial and work difficulties. She oriented the mother toward the medical and social agencies where she could obtain some aid. Time was also spent in organizing activities for the boy as well as for his brothers, so that they would not be left alone in the apartment for so many hours. The therapist helped the mother organize her activities, so that she could spend more time with her children and at least once a week do something special with them. It was arranged that the boys would go straight from school to a recreation center, where they could participate in sports. As these plans were made, summer approached and appropriate plans were made for all the boys for the summer. Mother and son continued to stick the pins in the doll for two or three weeks, and then the therapist abandoned the subject.

At the beginning of therapy, the child's disturbed be-

---

[2]There is a similarity between the therapeutic strategy used in this case and that used by Milton Erickson (see Haley, 1973, p. 209) in the case of a boy who picked at a sore on his forehead. Erickson replaced the unfortunate compulsion to pick at the sore with a compulsion to write accurately and provided the opportunity for the boy to pay back his strict and demanding father. In the case presented here, a child's compulsion to stick pins in his stomach is replaced by a compulsion to stick pins into a doll, and the opportunity is provided for the lonely child to be closer to his mother in a positive, affectionate way.

havior had been a metaphor for the mother's ailments. The son stuck pins in his middle and caused a wound; the mother ate too much and became sick. The system of interaction between child, mother, and doctors was a metaphor for the interaction between mother and doctors. The son would stick pins; the mother would tell him not to do that; the son would do it anyway; the mother would take him to doctors, who would tell him to stop. The mother would overeat even though she knew she should not. Then she would get sick and go to doctors, who would tell her she should not overeat.

The child's symptom was helpful to his mother in that it focused her attention on him rather than on her own physical and social difficulties. She struggled with his self-destructive behavior rather than with her own, and she was involved with doctors who tried to change him.

The first step in the therapy was to change the meaning of the metaphorical action, so that sticking pins no longer stood for inflicting a wound but only for inappropriate behavior with respect to where pins should be stuck.

The second step was to change the action of the child, so that, instead of sticking pins into himself, he would be sticking pins into a doll. Also, the sticking of pins was no longer the lonely, hostile act that it had been in the past; instead, it would take place in the presence of his mother, initiated by her and with her collaboration. Before, the mother had mostly addressed the son only to reprimand him; now, a positive emotional bond was established between mother and child around the action of sticking pins into the doll. The boy was still helping his mother by focusing her attention on him, but he could now do it through a different metaphorical action. The child's behavior—sticking a hundred pins into a doll every day—was still abnormal, but he was no longer hurting himself or others.

In the third step, the therapist helped the mother in various ways to improve her situation. As the family's condition improved and the mother was dealing with her own problems directly, the metaphorical system of interaction involving the child was no longer necessary.

Case 12: The Evil Eye

A Puerto Rican couple brought their 15-year-old daughter to the hospital because she had frequent seizures. The girl was examined, and the pediatrician recommended an electroencephalogram (EEG) to determine whether she had epileptic seizures. The parents refused to allow the EEG. A Puerto Rican therapist was asked to intervene to communicate with the family in Spanish and convince them that the EEG had to be done, since there was a concern about the possibility of epilepsy.

The therapist talked with the family and found out that the girl was constantly absent from school because of the fear that she would have a seizure there. The father was also always sick with unclear ailments and did not work. The mother went to work while the father and daughter stayed home.

The parents said that they did not want the EEG because they were certain that this was not a medical problem; it was the influence of the evil eye that was affecting the family. The therapist attempted in various ways to convince the parents that the daughter should be tested; however, they remained firm in their position. They were under the influence of the evil eye, and there was nothing that medicine could do.

The therapist consulted with her supervisor and planned a strategic intervention. She told the family that she had spent a great deal of time thinking about them that week and had concluded that in effect they were under the influence of the evil eye. Only this could explain the fact that both father and daughter were sick. She said that she had consulted her supervisor, an Argentinian more experienced than herself, who had told her that in Argentina there is an infallible cure for the evil eye. Would they be interested in hearing about it? They said that they would be interested and would do whatever was necessary to get rid of this evil influence. The therapist said that the mother had to go right away to the store and buy a few yards of red ribbon. With this red ribbon she had to make little red bows for each member of the family: father, mother, daughter, and siblings. Then she had to sew these bows to the inside of the underwear of each family member. They all had to wear these ribbons sewed to their underwear at all times, particularly when leaving the house. This would render the evil eye ineffective.

The family returned the next week. The mother had done what she was told, and the daughter had not had seizures. The father was feeling better. In talking with the family, the therapist found that father and daughter were always together, since they stayed in the house because of their ailments, while the mother, who worked, was quite removed from both of them and had relinquished to a great extent her position of wife and mother. The therapist emphasized that the parents needed to agree on decisions about the daughter and the household and began to orient them toward a joint executive function rather than having the mother abdicate her position to her 15-year-old daughter.

One week later, the daughter had still not had seizures and was back in school. The father was arranging to go back to work. The therapist suggested that it might be possible now to remove the red ribbons, since the family did not seem to be any longer under the influence of the evil eye. The family agreed to do this. They came back the next week and said that they had removed the ribbons but that the daughter had had a seizure. The therapist said that obviously it had been a mistake to remove the bows and they should continue to wear them, since it clearly was essential to keep warding off the evil eye.

The family went back to wearing the red ribbons, and the seizures did not recur. The girl went to school and the father to work. The therapist met with the family for a few more weeks, working on returning the daughter to her appropriate position in the hierarchy and on restoring the father to a superior position, which he had partly lost while he was sick at home and the mother was working.

In this case, the daughter's symptoms and the parents' refusal to comply with the doctor's request were a metaphor for the family's defiance of the American culture. That is, the presenting problem, which was not only the girl's seizures but also the parents' refusal to allow an EEG, was a metaphorical act of defiance of the culture: the evil eye was more powerful than

American medicine, than the American school which wanted their daughter to attend, and than the American factory where the father had to work. By accepting the family's interpretation of their situation, the therapist joined the family in their defiance. However, the very act of joining them against the evil eye changed the metaphor expressed by their disturbed behavior. Before therapy, the family were metaphorically defying the culture represented by the doctors, school, and work. After therapy, the family, together with the therapist, were metaphorically defying the evil eye and defeating it.

The daughter's symptom had been helpful to the parents in that it provided a metaphor through which they could defy the culture without suffering the consequences that a more direct defiance might have entailed. Her symptom was particularly protective of the father, since it relieved him to some extent from being the focus of this defiance of the culture because of his illness and refusal to go to work. The girl's condition was also helpful to the mother in that it allowed her to go to work knowing that the daughter was taking care of her husband and keeping him company.

The first step in the therapy was to accept the family's metaphor, in which they were victims of a power greater than American medicine. The second step was to change the metaphorical action of the family so that, although they were still defying the culture, they were doing so not through seizures and mysterious illnesses but by being more powerful than the evil eye and rendering it ineffective. This was accomplished when the therapist provided an "infallible" cure from a culture that was also Latin and even more far removed from the American culture than the family's Puerto Rican background. Also, by giving the mother the task of buying and sewing the red ribbons, the therapist put her in control of the action that led to the cure and, in this way, began to restore her position in the family. The child was still helping the parents by focusing their attention on her, but through a different metaphorical action. The family's behavior was still abnormal, since it is not normal to have to wear red ribbons in the underclothes to prevent ailments and seizures. However, the therapist's attempt to change this behavior proved premature in that the change brought back a seizure. Therefore, the red ribbons were reinstated, and father and daughter continued to be in good health.

In the third step of the therapy, the therapist brought mother and father together as parents to their children and as husband and wife. As the therapist helped them improve their situation in relation to work and home, they adapted better to the culture; and the metaphorical system of interaction involving the daughter was no longer necessary.

Strategy 2: Providing a Metaphor for Success Instead of Failure. When a child is helpful to his parents in unfortunate ways, the therapist can try to arrange more positive ways in which the child can be helpful. A symptomatic child expresses metaphorically a parent's failures. The therapist can arrange that the parent whose difficulties are metaphorically expressed by the child's symptoms be given credit, ahead of time, for the child's improvement. The improvement in the child should be defined, before it actually takes place, as an indication that the parent is a successful, competent person who has overcome the difficulties in his life and who can help his child do the same. The new, appropriate behaviors of the child can then become metaphors for the parent's successes, not his failures. If the parent is a successful person, the problem behavior in the child loses its function, since it can no longer be an analogy for the parent's failures.

Case 13: A Depressed Boy

A 13-year-old boy was brought to a department of psychiatry for a consultation. He had been diagnosed as a severe childhood depression at a family service agency. During the psychiatric evaluation at the hospital, it was found that his mother had been severely depressed in the past and that one of the child's cousins also had been severely depressed. This was interesting information for those members of the staff who were biologically inclined. However, an evaluation by a family therapist was recommended.

The boy had fits of crying, sat around most of the day

doing nothing, had refused to go to school for the last two months, and had threatened suicide. He had been in individual treatment with a therapist who felt strongly that the child should not be stressed. This therapist had asked for the consultation because she was concerned that the child was getting worse. As part of the boy's treatment plan, the mother had also been seeing a therapist individually in the same agency.

Because there had been talk among the hospital staff about hospitalization and long-term individual therapy for this child—and, therefore, the possibility of a career as a mental patient—it was decided before the first interview that the therapist would recommend to the parents that the child be forced to go to school as soon as possible, so that he could return to the normal life of a 13-year-old boy. It was assumed that, because the mother had been depressed in the past, the boy's "depression" was a metaphor for the mother's depression and that the child was staying at home, keeping his mother company, and helping her by eliciting concerned and protective behavior from her, so that she was focused on her son rather than on her own problems. What system of interaction had developed around the child's symptoms was not known.

It was planned that at the beginning of the session the therapist would redefine the problem as a refusal to go to school and the depression as a consequence of staying at home doing nothing. The therapist would then appeal to the mother as an expert in overcoming depression, thus defining her as a competent person who, instead of being depressed, had succeeded in overcoming the depression. On the basis of this success, the mother would be put in charge of making the boy go to school. In this way, if the boy stayed home, his behavior was metaphorical of the mother's depression; but if he went to school, his behavior was the result of the mother's success and competence.[3]

---

[3]If the focus in this case had been on cross-generation coalitions (Haley, 1976b), mother and son would have been seen as overinvolved and the father as marginal; the father might then have been put in charge of making the boy go to school. This could have increased the feelings of inadequacy and depression in the mother and resulted in marital difficulties.

The therapist started the first interview by saying that he understood that the problem they were consulting about was centered around the boy's refusal to go to school. The mother immediately corrected him, saying that they were consulting about the child's severe depression, the *consequence* of which was that he could not attend school. The father, however, stated that he had thought that the child's crying and upset were normal adolescent problems and that the boy should be made to go to school. The therapist took this opportunity to define the problem as one where the boy used to be normally sad but became depressed when he stopped going to school. The depression was presented as the consequence, not the cause, of refusing to go to school.

In the past, when the father had proposed that they should take the boy to school by force, either the mother would object or else professional helpers (his therapist or his pediatrician) would intervene and restrain the parents from taking action. The system of interaction was one where the child would cry and say that he was worried, depressed, and could not go to school; the father would say that he should go to school; and the mother would hesitate and object, saying that perhaps the child should not be stressed. This system of interaction was probably an analogy for another system of interaction that had occurred when the mother had been depressed. The father had probably emphasized that she should be active ánd take care of the children and the house, and the mother had probably replied that she could not do that, since she was depressed and could not tolerate the stress. The system of interaction around the boy's depression was the same as the system around the mother's depression. Both systems probably ended with the father's withdrawing his demands and doing something special for the mother, because she was burdened with her own depression or with her son's depression. If the son was depressed, the mother did not need to be depressed herself for the same system of interaction to take place.

The participation of professional helpers was probably the same in both systems of interaction. When the father said that the boy should be forced to go to school, he was restrained by professional helpers. When the mother was depressed, the father probably was also restrained from demanding more of her by her doctor, who had her on medication and was concerned about her depression. The system of interaction involving mother, father, son, and professionals was a metaphor for and replaced the system of interaction involving mother, father, and doctor.

The parents described the position of the pediatrician, the social worker, and the psychologist involved with the case, whose advice was not to put any pressure on the child to go back to school. The therapist explained that his view differed. He thought that sitting at home doing nothing could only intensify the feeling of sadness and that the child should do what normal children of that age did: go to school.

The plan was to use the analogy between the behavior of the mother and that of the son, so that they could be the same not only in their depression but also in their success in overcoming the depression. For this reason, the therapist asked the parents whether either of them had had any similar problems to the son's. The mother explained that after she had given birth to twins, who were a few years younger than her son, she had been severely depressed and on medication. The twins had been ill as infants and in and out of the hospital; and she had had to cope with all this when they had just moved to a new city and she was far away from her relatives, who had helped her with her older children. The therapist sympathized with her and said that she was clearly an expert at overcoming depression and, therefore, would be the best person to help her son. She knew how important it was to become active and fulfill one's obligations and that, in fact, it was the only way of coming out of a depression. The mother agreed.

The parents seemed sufficiently motivated, and the therapist proceeded to set up a plan for the boy to go back to school. The mother then said that she had a message from the child's therapist that she had to convey in private, and the therapist asked the boy to leave the room. The mother then brought up once more the objections by the other professionals to anything that might put stress on the child. The therapist emphasized again that his position differed and that the parents would have to make a choice. He said that he would be willing to speak to the child's therapist but that the therapy should be recessed until the child was going to school normally. The parents agreed to follow this plan, and the therapist brought the boy back into the room. He gave the parents the following instructions. The next day, mother and father together were to put the boy in the car and take him to school. If the boy went to class without objections, the parents would let him go. But if the boy complained or resisted, the mother was to go with him to every class and sit with him, holding his hand all the time to give him courage. It was emphasized that the mother could understand him well and reassure him because she had gone through similar difficulties. The therapist then asked each of the parents to explain to the son the plan for the next day.

Toward the end of the interview, as the parents talked, the boy, who had been sitting quietly and had spoken only when questioned, began to cry softly. The therapist said that, although it is upsetting to parents to see their son cry, nowadays boys are expected to cry as much as girls and to express their feelings; so it was natural for him to cry, and the parents should not be unduly upset by his tears. The emphasis on the difference between boys and girls reduced the dramatic impact of the boy's behavior. The child suddenly screamed at the top of his lungs that he would not go to school. The therapist pointed out that the boy was behaving in a typically rebellious adolescent fashion and that this was a good sign of developmental maturity.

That afternoon the child ran away from home and called his mother, a couple of hours later, saying that he would come back only if she promised that she would not force him to attend school. The mother promised and the son came home. The mother called the therapist and asked him what to do, since she now had promised not to take the boy to school. The therapist told her to simply say to the boy that mothers sometimes lie and that he had to go to school. The child cried and vomited that night, but the next morning he went to school without resistance and the mother did not need to stay with him.

The boy continued to go to school normally and became

very involved in skateboarding. He met with the therapist a
couple of times to discuss how he could improve his study
habits, since he wanted to do his homework as fast as possible
so he could go to the park.

The father turned out to be a very demanding man. He
wanted his son to be a Boy Scout and asked the therapist to
apply the same procedure that had been used to get the child
back in school. The son did not like the Boy Scouts and did not
want to continue his activities with them. The father also
wanted the son to go to church regularly. The therapist managed to negotiate that the Boy Scouts were not necessary, but
he could not negotiate the church issue and it was decided that
the son would attend religious services whenever the family did
so.

These issues took up four or five sessions, and the therapy was discontinued. At the beginning of the next school year,
the boy called the therapist and said he did not want to go to
school and he wanted to meet with the therapist to talk about
this. The therapist answered that he should talk to his parents
because they had helped him before and they would help him
again. In a follow-up, a year and a half after the first interview,
the boy had been attending school regularly and was involved
with friends and in sports.

At the beginning of therapy, the child's depression had
been a metaphor for the mother's depression. At the end of
therapy, the boy's success in attending school was a metaphor
for the mother's success in overcoming her depression. At the
beginning of therapy, the system of interaction—in which the
father complained that the son did not do what was expected of
him, the boy was sad, and the mother said he could not help
himself and should not be stressed—was an analogy for the
father's complaints about the mother and her arguments that
she could not help herself and should not be stressed. At the
end of therapy, the mother's success with the boy was an analogy for the mother's success in her own life, and the father was
proud of his wife's competence.

Strategy 3: Changing the Metaphorical Solution. A child's
disturbed behavior is both a metaphor and a solution to the

parent's problem. Sometimes the solution provided by the child has to do with the consequences that the child's disturbed behavior would have for the parent. If the therapist can change these consequences so that they provide an ordeal for the parent or a solution that is distasteful to the child, the disturbed behavior will no longer serve its function and will be discarded. A case example will illustrate this approach.

Case 14: Refusal to Go to School

A 14-year-old girl, Mary, refused to go to school. She was the youngest of six children. Her mother had died when she was 5 years old, and the father had raised her with the help of an older sister. This sister was now in college in a nearby city, and the father was not on speaking terms with her, since he had recently discovered that she was living with a young man. The father, a construction worker, was very fond of Mary and very involved with her.

The therapist had arranged for the father to take Mary to a meeting at the school; after the meeting, at which the therapist would be present, the father would take Mary to class and stay with her if necessary. But as soon as Mary got to school, she pulled away from the father and ran away. The meeting was held without her, and the father was very upset. It was a mystery to everyone in the school why the child did not want to attend. She had good grades and was well liked. The school psychologist mentioned, however, that Mary had told him she did not want her father to get married. The psychologist thought that perhaps this was in some way related to the problem.

The therapist brought the family (father, daughter, and an older sister) in for a consultation with her supervisor, who observed from behind a one-way mirror. Supervisor and therapist discussed the case before the interview. They decided to assume that Mary's behavior was a metaphor for being like a wife to her father. If she did not go to school, she could stay home and keep house for the father, as a wife would. The analogy seemed particularly appropriate at a time when the father had quarreled with the older daughter, who had had the position of wife and mother and had helped him raise Mary.

A strategy was planned in which the therapist would follow certain steps. She would first praise the father for having raised so many children successfully. Then the therapist would ask the father why he had never remarried, commenting that the father really deserved the companionship of a wife. The therapist would then change the subject and go back to the issue of what a successful father he had been and how all his children, except Mary, were at school or working. The therapist would discuss with the father and with Mary's sister what work possibilities Mary could have without even a junior high school education. Jobs as a waitress or a babysitter would be considered. Then the therapist would mention the unfortunate possibility that the father could be fined fifty dollars a day while Mary was not attending school, since the therapist could not testify that she was emotionally disturbed, because she was not, and since that was the usual fine for truancy in the county where the family lived. (Father and daughter had known about this for some time.) Finally, the therapist would return to the subject of the possibility of the father's marrying and would say that if Mary was not going to school the best thing would be for the father to get married. That way there would be a woman in the house to look after Mary, and Mary could keep the new wife company so she would not be lonely, since the father worked long hours. Also, the new wife could divide the housework with Mary and would not feel overwhelmed by coming into a house with several grown children. The therapist would insist that the best course of action was for the father to get married. If the girl had been behaving in a disturbed way to prevent her father from remarrying, her disturbed behavior would now lead to exactly the opposite consequence: to the father's marriage.

The plan was followed, and in the interview there was a great deal of giggling around the idea of the father's getting married. He dated often but had never brought a woman to the house. Mary said she did not care whether the father married, but, as the interview went on, she turned her back on the others and remained like that for a long time.

At one point during the interview, while talking about the sister who had moved to another city, Mary said that she would like to see her. The therapist asked the father whether Mary could visit her sister if she went to school all that week. The father said that he would drive her there himself.

The interview ended with the therapist emphasizing that the father should be thinking about marriage. The next day Mary went to school by herself and continued to attend regularly and cheerfully. She visited her sister that weekend. In a follow-up one year later, Mary had continued to attend school and was doing very well in her work, and the father was reconciled with the sister. He had not remarried.

At the beginning of the therapy, Mary's disturbed behavior was a metaphor for being the father's wife. Instead of going to school like normal children her age, she was staying home and keeping house like a wife. To a certain extent, she was also replacing the sister who had left home and with whom the father had quarreled. The therapist turned the situation around, so that Mary's disturbed behavior, her not going to school, became a reason why the father had to marry. Mary's behavior was not only no longer a metaphor for being her father's wife, but it led to the exact opposite, to the father's marriage. The therapist also made it possible for Mary to return to a previous family situation that had been better for her by suggesting that, if she went to school, she could visit her sister. In that way, it became possible for Mary to influence her father to reconcile with her sister and, therefore, to recover part of the situation she had had when she was younger and the sister had helped the father to raise her.

Understanding the Metaphor

The therapist's problem is to get the child to give up his disturbed behavior and the parents to give up a system of interaction that has a useful, though unfortunate, function in the family. In order to do this, the therapist must discover the metaphor in the disturbed behavior of the child and in the family interaction around the child's behavior.

The clues that guide the therapist are indications that

there is a similarity between parent and child—in their problem, their situation, their behaviors, their failures, or their fears. The therapist must listen to statements by the parents to each other or to the therapist that at the literal level refer to the child but that sound as if they could refer to a parent at the metaphorical level. For example, a mother consulted a child guidance clinic because her son beat up on little girls and on children who were smaller than he was, while with his peers he was unsure of himself and fearful. It turned out that the father had beaten the mother several times and that he was unsure of himself and fearful, having just lost his job and all his money. The child's aggressive behavior toward little girls and smaller children made it possible for the mother to obtain help by consulting a child guidance clinic rather than by suffering the humiliation of seeking help as an abused wife. Sometimes the clue is in the content of what a parent says, as in this case, and sometimes it is in the choice of words, the tone of voice, and the nonverbal behavior. For example, a mother said: "My son has headaches more than I think a child his age should," while she pointed vaguely in the direction of both father and son. Metaphorical communication is like a double vision in that what is visible in one track is also visible in another track. It is as if one can look in one place and get an image of what is going on in another place. Sequences of interaction repeat themselves at different levels, and one level leads to another.

The analogies between the situation of parent and child are usually quite apparent. An obese mother has a son who sticks pins in his stomach; a father with "headaches" at work has a son with headaches; a depressed mother has a "depressed" son; the child of a fearful mother is afraid to go to school. The family's interaction around the parent's situation is replaced by the interaction around the child's problem. The focus on the analogies between the situation of parent and child explains the specificity of a symptom, which is a subject not emphasized by other strategic and structural family therapy approaches (Haley, 1976b; Minuchin, 1974).

When the therapist thinks he has a clue to the metaphor involved in a child's disturbed behavior, he can obtain more information by finding out about the family's health and relations with extended family. It is also useful to ask whether one of the parents or a relative has or has had a similar problem to the child's.

Once the therapist has formulated a hypothesis about the analogy involved in the child's problem, the metaphorical action of the child can be changed, a metaphor for success instead of failure can be provided, or the solution in the child's metaphorical behavior can be changed.

Redefining the Problem

In two of the cases presented in this chapter, the problem of the child was redefined by the therapist before proceeding with a strategy for change. In the case of the boy who stuck pins in his stomach, the problem was changed so that it no longer stood for inflicting a wound—it stood for sticking pins in the wrong place. In the case of the depressed boy, the refusal to go to school was changed from consequence to cause of the child's depression. In both cases, the problem was not as drastically redefined as it was in two cases of adults presented in Chapter Three: the woman with hysterical paralysis, whose symptom was relabeled a muscular cramp; and the depressed man, who was told that he was irresponsible rather than depressed.

In cases involving a symptomatic child, the parents may be invested in a certain definition of a problem. If they are, the therapist's questioning of that definition weakens the parental position and works against the therapist's goal of reorganizing the hierarchy so that the parents are in charge of the children. This is not to say that redefining the problem should not be used at all. It can be used with caution and in special circumstances—for example, when the label to be changed comes from other professionals and not from the parents and when the redefinition involves changing the relationship between cause and consequence but without a complete redefinition of the problem. It can also be used when the parents appear inclined to accepting the redefinition without taking offense.

The pitfall of redefining the problem is that if it is not done skillfully, with proper respect and persuasiveness, the therapist can find himself in an adversary position instead of one of cooperation with the family. This is an approach where confrontation is seldom used and where the attitude of the therapist should be one of respect for the persons involved. This respect also explains why parents are not as resistant to this therapy as might be expected and why there are no severe power struggles between parents and therapist. There are also no interpretations that arouse resistance. The transcripts in Chapters Seven and Eight illustrate the tone and the style in which the therapy should be conducted.

Redefining the problem, as used in this approach, does not necessarily involve positive connotation or a positive relabeling of anyone's behavior. The point of redefining is to change the definition of a problem so that it can be solved. Irresponsibility is perhaps more negative than depression but is easier to resolve. A muscular cramp is more amenable to change than a hysterical paralysis. A child who refuses to go to school can be coped with more easily than a child who is depressed. Thus, redefining should be approached with the intention of defining a problem that can be resolved rather than with the intention of minimizing the problem or of interpreting the behavior in positive ways.

Summary and Conclusion

It has been proposed here that disturbed behavior in children is an analogy for a parent's difficulties as well as an attempt to solve these difficulties. The family's interaction around the child's symptoms becomes a metaphor for and replaces the interaction around the parent's problems. When the child is behaving in a disturbed way, the system of interaction around the parent's difficulties will be replaced by the system of interaction around the child's problem.

In such cases, the therapist's problem is to change the child's disturbed behavior and to change the participation of the parents in a system of interaction that has a useful function in the family. In order to do this, the therapist must discover the analogy in the disturbed behavior of the child. Three strategies for solving the presenting problem in the child were described.

The advantage that child and family derive from the child's disturbed behavior is that it becomes the focus for a system of interaction that is metaphorical for the system of interaction around a parent's difficulties and renders the latter unnecessary. Certain interactions can take place between family members with less risk of severe consequences for those involved. This advantage is the interpersonal gain that child and parents derive from the child's symptomatic behavior. In the three therapeutic strategies presented here, the interpersonal gain for the family was maintained while the symptomatic behavior disappeared. That is, the therapist arranged for the interpersonal gain to be maintained by organizing a different way that child or therapist could help the parents with their difficulties.

Certain steps are followed to carry out this therapy.

1. The therapist assumes that a symptom analogically or metaphorically expresses a problem of the parents and is also a solution, although an unfortunate one.
2. The therapist decides what metaphor is expressed through the child's disturbed behavior and to whom the child is being helpful.
3. The therapist determines what is the system of interaction around the child's symptoms and of what other system of interaction it is a metaphor.
4. The therapist plans an intervention that will change the metaphorical action, or provide an alternate metaphor, or change the consequences that the metaphor has for the parents. The therapist's intervention usually takes the form of an explanation of the causes of the problem, a description of the consequences of the problem, and a directive about something that the family is to do—with special emphasis on what the parent who is the subject of the child's metaphorical behavior must do.

Even though some general guidelines for therapeutic plans may be applied to a variety of families, no two families are alike, and a specific therapeutic plan must be designed for each family.

Speculations

In the suggested model, a child's symptom elicits a system of interaction in the family that is an analogy for and replaces the interaction around a parent's problems. It follows logically, although there are no data to support the hypothesis, that the opposite may also be true: that a parent's disturbed behavior may elicit a system of interaction in the family that is a metaphor for and replaces the interaction around a child's disturbed behavior. That is, a child may be a metaphor for a parent, and a parent may also be a metaphor for a child. There may be a cyclical variation in the focus of interaction; for example, from child to parent, from parent to child, from child to a marital issue, and back to the child. The cycle, however, will remain the same in that family members will help each other through behaviors that are metaphorical of one another.

Although these ideas are not based on observations of normal families, it is reasonable to hypothesize that individuals grow and develop within a family by helping one another through actions that are metaphorical of each other's behavior. That is, a cyclical variation in the focus of interaction may be characteristic not only of pathology but also of normal growth and development. For example, a youth may struggle with vocational indecisions until at a certain point her mother may become upset with indecisions about her own career. The focus of the family's concern will then shift from the young person's worries to the mother's upset. As the mother resolves her vocational dilemma and, for example, changes jobs or goes back to school, the youth will solve hers and will make decisions about her own future. Both mother and daughter will have overcome their difficulties and moved on to face more of life's opportunities and obstacles. Perhaps the main difference between normality and pathology is that normal families pass around a positive attribute, whereas disturbed families pass around a negative attribute.

From the point of view presented here, therapy can do harm if it prevents a shift in the cycle. The intervention of professional helpers may fixate the cycle at a certain point (with institutionalization or long-term therapy), preventing spontaneous change or blocking the cyclical variation in focus. Therapy may also sometimes promote a more rapid change in focus from a child to a parent or from a parent to a child or to a marital issue, giving the therapist the illusion that change is taking place. If the goal is to end this repetitive cycle, the therapist must arrange that parents and child help each other overcome their difficulties by other means than behaving in disturbing ways.

The Posture of the Therapist

The emphasis to this point has been on understanding and solving the problems presented in therapy. A summary will help clarify what the posture of the therapist should be when faced with these problems. What questions will elicit information that will lead to a hypothesis about the problem? What should the therapist ask himself or herself in order to think clearly about a family's situation? People rarely present a problem to a therapist in a way that leads to an obvious strategy for therapy. The therapist must discover what there is in the situation that will lead him or her to formulate the problem so that it can be solved.

Questions for the Therapist to Ask the Family. To begin, the therapist must formulate a hypothesis about the problem. To do this, he or she must gather certain information from the family. When does the symptom happen, how, where, and with whom? What is each family member doing while the symptom is happening? How does it go away? Who is upset by the problem, worried, sad, angry, embarrassed? Who in the family has, or has had, a similar problem? Who resembles whom in the family? What does each family member do at work or in school? Are they doing well or poorly? Do they have any special circumstances, concerns, or worries? What relatives are they involved with and in what ways? Does the person with the presenting problem resemble one of these relatives, or does he have a problem similar to theirs? Who in the family are closer together because of the problem, and who are further apart? What would change if the problem disappeared? As these questions are answered by the family (either directly or through their interaction), the questions of who is being protected by the symptomatic person; or who has an interpersonal gain from the existence of the symptom; and what is the nature of this gain, are also answered. As these issues become apparent, so does the interaction of family members around the presenting problem. It also becomes clear how this interaction is metaphorical of other interaction in the family.

Questions for the Therapist to Think About. In thinking about the presenting problem, the therapist should ask herself or himself: (1) What is the metaphor expressed by the symptom? (2) What is the request or the command implicit in the symptomatic behavior? (3) Who is the focus of concern of the symptomatic person; that is, who is being helped or protected by the person with the presenting problem and what is that person being protected from? (4) What is the interpersonal gain from the symptomatic behavior, both for the symptomatic person and for the family? (5) How can the helpfulness or the interpersonal gain be maintained without the symptomatic behavior? (6) How can family members be organized so that they are helpful to each other in a different way? (7) How can a family with children be restored to a single hierarchy, with the parents in charge? How can a couple be organized in a more egalitarian relationship? The answer to one question by the therapist leads to the formulation of another question, until a picture of the situation is formed. This image is an oversimplified version of the complexities of interaction in a family, but it does provide a perspective from which to develop a therapeutic strategy.

Questions that Lead to a Formulation of the Hierarchy. The therapist needs to ask questions that lead to a formulation of the hierarchical arrangement in the family. Appropriate questions are: Who is in charge of what in the family? Who has to ask permission of whom and about what? What are the rules in

the house? What are the consequences if the rules are disobeyed? What are the expectations of parents for their adolescent or young adult child? It is important also to ask about the
power that other professionals and social agents may have in
relation to the family. The therapist needs to plan how to influence these sources of power so that they will collaborate instead
of interfering with his endeavors.

In exploring issues of power, the therapist needs to determine who has power over whom in the following areas: (1) the
handling of money; (2) time (who decides how somebody else's
time should be spent, either directly or by impinging on the
other's time through demands or disruptions; who in a couple
determines what time will be spent together); (3) the exchange
of information (who communicates information and who keeps
secrets; who determines what information will be exchanged).

If in a marriage one spouse makes the financial decisions,
determines what time the couple will spend together, and is un-
communicative, that spouse has considerably greater power
than the other spouse, who may resort to helpless symptomatic
behavior to balance the hierarchy in the marriage. However, if
the powerful spouse loses the superior position, he or she may
seek power from symptomatic behavior. In cases of severely disturbed adolescents and young adults, the hierarchical incongruity, or reversal, becomes apparent when the therapist dis-
covers the ways in which the youth impinges on the parents'
time and money while communicating in ways that they cannot
understand and while keeping secrets from them.

As relationships are clarified, it usually becomes apparent
that the hierarchical incongruities could be approached from
different angles—for example, with a focus on time or money or
with a focus on the presenting symptom. In order to plan a
strategy, the therapist has to narrow his vision, discard valuable
information, and choose among various possible hypotheses the
one that appears most practical and economical.

The problem presented to the therapist has been understood only when it is solved. Until then, the family's response
to the therapeutic strategy is part of the information that fur-
thers the understanding of the problem.

Formulating the Problem. The formulation of the problem that the therapist makes for himself or herself does not necessarily coincide with that given *to* the family. Sometimes the problem is not reformulated to the family at all; they are simply told what to do about it. One reason for not communicating the therapist's formulation is to avoid pointless argument. When an explanation or a redefinition of the problem is provided, it is always at least partially true. The intention is not to deceive the family but to provide a definition of the problem and an explanation about it that they can act on, that will allow the therapist to lead them to change.

Planning a Strategy. As the therapist understands the problem and formulates it to himself, he develops a strategy to solve it. This strategy usually consists of directives that the therapist will give to the family, which will render the existence of the symptom unnecessary. The number of possible therapeutic strategies is at least as great as the possibilities for reformulating presenting problems.

After the therapist has formulated a strategy, he must translate it to concrete operations that will enable him to carry it out. These operations are the directives and the explanations that the therapist gives to the family.

Implementing the Strategy. Once a therapeutic strategy has been designed, it must be implemented. Objections by family members must be anticipated and answered, redefining and reformulating the situation and giving new directives. These must be based on carefully planned reformulations of the problem and on time-consuming work by the therapist to motivate family members to do what he suggests.

A directive may be an ordeal designed to discourage the symptomatic person from behaving in symptomatic ways. Directives may be straightforward or paradoxical and prescribed to the symptomatic person or prescribed for a parent or spouse to enforce. Usually several interventions are combined in a therapeutic strategy. When one operation does not succeed, another is attempted. The particular combination of interventions that are necessary to produce change is unique to each family.

Termination. If other problems exist after the presenting problem has been solved, the therapist must be willing to focus on them in the same or in different ways. After the symptoms have been resolved, the therapist must sometimes intervene further in the hierarchical organization of the family. In the case of a couple, the therapist strives for a more egalitarian relationship, so that a spouse will no longer resort to deriving power from the helplessness of a symptom. In the case of a presenting problem in a child, the parents are encouraged to be in charge of their children, providing guidance and support, and to take charge of their own lives and of the organization of their family. Often the hierarchy is reorganized as the presenting problem is solved, and a separate intervention is not necessary.

After the presenting problems are solved, the therapist must be willing to disengage quickly, with the idea of keeping in touch occasionally with the family and to be available if problems arise. The idea is that therapy will make some changes and then the family will continue to make changes on their own. It is important to give credit to the family and not to expect or try to elicit any expressions of appreciation from them. Very often, in a brief, intensive therapy, changes happen so quickly that the family can hardly attribute them to the therapist. It is important to discontinue when therapy is no longer necessary, since it is best for people to be in a situation where they solve their own problems and face life difficulties independently and not as patients.

CHAPTER SIX

Severe Problems of Adolescence: Putting the Parents in Charge

In previous chapters, problems in children and adolescents were conceptualized in a variety of ways, and various therapeutic strategies (some quite different from one another) were presented. This chapter deals with more serious and difficult problems of adolescents and young adults—problems involving aggressive or self-destructive acts, abuse of drugs or alcohol, bizarre communication, and extreme apathy or depression. The incongruity in the family hierarchy is usually long lasting and maintained by repetitive cyclical interactions. Therefore, one coherent therapeutic approach is recommended—an approach that is intended to be more rigid and less open to variation than the other approaches presented in this book. A certain rigidity of method prevents the therapist from being overwhelmed when there are issues of hospitalization, social control, and impending chronicity.

In these cases, the difficulties of the young person, the trouble he causes, and his failure in life become the main theme in the parents' lives. A parent may have problems with his own parents or trouble at work, he may be depressed or ill, or his spouse might be threatening separation, but all these problems become less important in contrast to the tragedy of the youth's life. The focus on the youth and the need to be available to him provide the parents with a primary goal. They must overcome their own deficiencies and hold themselves together in order to help him. In this sense, the young person's disruptive behavior has a positive influence on the parents, even though it tyrannizes, threatens, and incapacitates them. The youth might passively threaten that if he is stressed he will go crazy or take drugs or harm himself in some way, or he might physically attack the parents. The parents become unable to attempt to change the young person's behavior because they are afraid that they will cause him harm or that he will harm them.

Two incongruous hierarchies are simultaneously defined in the family. In one, the youth is incompetent, defective, and dependent on the parents for protection, food, shelter, and money, and the parents are in a superior position and provide for and take care of him. Yet simultaneously another hierarchy is defined in which the parents are dominated by the youth because of his helplessness or threats or dangerous behavior. If the parents are to be competent parents, they must demand from the youth the behavior that is appropriate for his age, but doing so may trigger extreme and dangerous behavior from the youth. If the youth behaves normally, he loses the power that the threats of extreme behavior gave him over his parents.

The two hierarchies are incongruous with each other or conflict paradoxically; in one, the youth is helplessly dominated and in the other he or she controls the parents. It is paradoxical to be in charge while simultaneously dominated by those over whom one has control. A hierarchical incongruity is the simultaneous coexistence of two conflicting hierarchies within the framework of one hierarchical organization, where one hierarchy frames the other and where the same people are involved in both hierarchies.

It is possible to hypothesize that this power of the youth over the parents has the function of protecting them or of holding them together.[1] With many families, a child dominates benevolently by having a symptom and being helpless. But when an adolescent, for example, sprinkles gasoline around the foundation of the house and then plays with matches, when he beats up on the parents and extorts money from them with threats, there is little question of who has power in the family, and it is difficult to see this power as benevolent. It is possible, instead, to assume that the only function of the disturbing behavior of the youth is the exploitative power derived from it. Originally, the disruptive behavior may have had a protective function; however, when the incongruous hierarchies stabilize and the system of interaction becomes chronic, the disturbed behavior persists as a function of the system and independently of what set it off. At a certain point in time, perhaps, there is no longer a hierarchical incongruity but simply a hierarchical reversal, with the youth in a superior position of power over the parents and with few or no situations where the reverse is true. (This is often the case in violence, delinquency, and addiction, but it is also sometimes the case in the psychoses.)

As the youth gains power over the parents, they try to restore their position in the hierarchy by resorting to agents of social control (the police or the mental hospital). The youth is institutionalized and consequently behaves more helplessly and with less control. This gives him more power over the parents, because they must focus more and more on him in their attempts to help him. Yet this helpfulness of the parents defines

---

[1] For a formulation that proposes that the youth's disruptive behavior has the function of preventing a separation between the parents, as well as for a detailed exposition of the stages of this therapy, see Haley, 1980.

the youth as even more helpless (or out of control) and contributes to the power that can be derived from such helplessness. In this way, a system of interaction can be established that perpetuates itself over time, particularly if there is a certain stigma attached to the situation of the youth and if society (through social agencies) contributes to maintaining it. Whether the youth's behavior originally had a protective function, whether it was meant to prevent a separation between the parents, or whether it was related only to a bid for power is quite irrelevant. The issue is that, to solve the problem, the hierarchy must be restored to one in which the youth does not dominate the parents through helplessness and abuse.

In these cases, there often is a similarity between the youth's behavior and that of one of the parents. The youth might be apathetic and do nothing, and a parent might be similarly depressed; the young person might be addicted to drugs and a parent to alcohol; the youth might hear voices, and a parent might talk to himself; the young person might be violent, and the father might physically abuse the mother. This similarity indicates that the disturbed behavior of the youth is metaphorical of the disturbing behavior of a parent.

In previous chapters, various ways of changing a child's disturbing behavior so that he would no longer be expressing metaphorically the problem of a parent were presented. In those approaches, the therapist worked on the symbolic communication of the family, changing metaphors and analogies. Here, with severely disturbed young people, a different, simple, straightforward approach is recommended. The therapist focuses on resolving the incongruity in the family hierarchy so that the parents will consistently be in a superior position to the youth. As the parents become more powerful, they are able to deal with their own problems more successfully, and the youth no longer needs to express metaphorically their difficulties. In this approach, the therapist focuses only on the literal meaning of the messages exchanged. When pathology is severe, a therapist can easily get lost in a morass of metaphorical meanings. A simple way to avoid getting caught in conflicting levels of messages by family members is to become very literal and concrete and to deal only with the most basic, mundane issues. In this approach, the therapist takes the position that a youth should go to work or to school, do his chores, avoid drugs and violence, and have one or two friends. The process of the therapy is to organize the family so that this takes place. Metaphors and analogies are largely ignored in the sense that, although the therapist might understand the analogy in the family's interaction, the therapeutic strategy will not be to attempt to change the analogy but only to deal with literal issues.

The double-bind theory (Bateson and others, 1956) describes conflicting levels of messages in families of schizophrenics.[2] The communication therapists, influenced by this theory, attempted for years to get family members to communicate clearly and congruently. There was no realization that incongruent messages are consistent with incongruous positions in a hierarchy—that for parents to talk consistently as parents, they have to be consistently in that position. The double-bind theory refers to a framework of communication. The concept of hierarchical incongruity refers to a wider framework of organizations in which communication takes place. If a parent is simultaneously defined as a person in charge of a family and as tyrannized and exploited by his own child, the family members involved in this situation will communicate in incongruent ways that reflect their incongruent positions in the hierarchy.

The approach to therapy presented here is based on the idea that the therapist must respond to only one of these defini-

---

[2] The double-bind situation was described in the following way: (1) "The individual is involved in an intense relationship; that is, a relationship in which he feels it is vitally important that he discriminate accurately what sort of message is being communicated, so that he may respond appropriately." (2) "The individual is caught in a situation in which the other person in the relationship is expressing two orders of message and one of these denies the other." (3) "The individual is unable to comment on the messages being expressed to correct his discrimination of what order of message to respond to; that is, he cannot make a metacommunicative statement" (Bateson and others, 1956, p. 257). It is proposed that a person in this situation confuses two levels of communication, the literal and metaphorical, and cannot discriminate between them. This confusion —the inability to distinguish what sort of message a message is—leads, according to the theory, to severe pathology.

tions, the one where the parents are in charge of the youth, and must discourage and block the other definition of the family hierarchy. That is, the therapist must ignore the family's presentation of their organization as one where the youth is in charge and must respond to and encourage only one hierarchy, the one where the parents are in charge of the young person.

The therapist must elicit from the parents messages that define them as competent, responsible adults and discourage communications that imply that they are weak, incompetent, or helpless. With respect to the young person, the messages that he is in charge of the parents must be discouraged, and he must be encouraged in defining his position as a member of a younger, more inexperienced generation. In this approach, only certain messages from certain family members are encouraged and allowed—in contrast to a communication approach that encourages the clear expression of all kinds of messages. The focus is not on the congruence of messages per se, but on the congruence of relationships. When the reversal in the communicational and hierarchical organization of the family is resolved, the young person will behave normally.

The hypothesized hierarchical reversals[3] in these families might not be the only relevant factors to etiology and to the reconstruction of the past. The hypothesis is relevant, however, to the most powerful factors operating in the present. It is a perspective that developed from the need to select from the multiplicity of data presented by disturbed youths and their families the events that form a pattern that is intelligible and

---

[3] For research data that support the hypothesis of hierarchical reversals in these families, see Madanes, Dukes, and Harbin (1980). Therapy outcome data also support the approach. In training programs with live supervision by the author and Jay Haley at the department of psychiatry of the University of Maryland and at the Family Therapy Institute of Washington, D.C., twenty-eight youths (age range: late teens and twenties) who had been hospitalized prior to the therapy were followed. Six were rehospitalized after therapy—a failure rate of 21 percent. The time since therapy terminated and an inquiry was conducted varied between 6 months and 2.5 years, the mean being 1.5 years. The cases included several different diagnoses, but in all cases there had been at least one hospitalization before the therapy started.

useful to the therapist for the purpose of changing the young person and his situation. More complex theories of etiology can make it more difficult to derive operations that will produce change.

It is possible to view the youth's behavior as protective of the parents in that it holds them together, preventing a separation and divorce (see Haley, 1980). It is also possible that the youth's disruption serves to prevent an agreement and an alliance between the parents. In this author's opinion, when the case involves a first break, a first criminal offense, or a few drug episodes, the therapist should carefully consider whether these behaviors have a protective function in the family: Is the youth expressing metaphorically a parent's problem? Are his acts self-sacrificing? In the more chronic cases, where there have been rehospitalizations or several encounters with law enforcement agencies, the therapist should think mainly in terms of the hierarchical reversal—the power that the youth has over the parents —and focus on understanding the problem from the point of view of how the youth's disturbing acts contribute to maintaining that power. The emphasis of this presentation is on the hierarchical incongruities in the family organization and on the communicational maneuvers that parents use to disqualify themselves from a position of authority in the family hierarchy. This emphasis developed from research on the communication of parents of schizophrenics, heroin addicts, and delinquents (Sojit Madanes, 1969, 1971; Madanes, Dukes, and Harbin, 1980; Singer, 1967). When a therapist can anticipate the communicational maneuvers of parents and youth to maintain the status quo, he can render these maneuvers ineffective.

Putting Parents in Charge

Most of the work in the therapy of these families consists in arranging a hierarchy in which the parents are in a superior position to their offspring. The parents must state explicitly what they expect the young person to be doing. Do the parents expect him to go to school or to look for a job? How is he expected to behave at home? At what time must he get up in the morning? At what time should he be home at night? The parents should reach agreement on these expectations, which must be phrased as rules for the young person. These rules should be as specific and practical as possible, and consequences should be set if these rules are not followed. Discussion of rules and consequences are the basic work of the therapy.

Each week the therapist must review with the parents whether the rules that they had set for the youth have been followed and whether the consequences were applied. As the parents begin to demand more adequate behavior from the young person, new rules and consequences must be set. The young person can be expected to put the parents to the test, and the therapist must struggle to maintain them in a superior position.

A hierarchy is defined by communication sequences. That is, if A tells B what to do, A is defining himself as being in a superior position to B in the hierarchy. If A and B discuss and agree on what C should do, A and B are defining themselves as equal and as superior in the hierarchy to C. As the therapist struggles for a definition of the hierarchy in which the parents are together in charge of the young person, he strives for communication sequences between family members that will define the situation in this way. That is, the therapist wants mother and father to talk about the young person and to agree on what he should do, and he wants the youth to listen to the parents and obey their rules. Instead, the parents typically use a series of communication maneuvers to avoid a definition of the hierarchy as one where they have power over their offspring. They do so because they are losing or have already lost their superior position in the hierarchy, because the youth is more powerful than they, because society has intervened to take power away from them, because they are afraid to do the wrong thing and harm the youth, because they are afraid that they are to blame and wish to do no more harm, or because they are afraid to lose their child. A parent can avoid a definition of the hierarchy as one where he has power over the youth by communicating (1) that he is not qualified to participate in the therapy because he cannot occupy an executive position in the hierarchy, or (2) that the other parent is not qualified, or (3) that the therapist is

not qualified to be in charge of the therapy. It is these maneuvers that the therapist must counteract so that the proper hierarchy can be defined.

Parent Disqualifies Himself

At the beginning of the therapy, parents will often disqualify themselves from a position of authority by invoking the
authority of others, by giving authority to the problem youth,
by giving authority to other relatives, by defining themselves as
inadequate, or by threatening to break up the parental unit.

Giving Authority to Experts. Parents might invoke the
authority of experts by saying, for example, that the therapist
or the chief of the ward should make the decisions concerning
the disturbed young person. The therapist must decline giving
power to the professional experts, including himself, and give it
to the parents. To transfer power to the parents, the therapist
must relabel the young person's problem so that it is in the area
of expertise of the parents rather than being a medical or
psychological problem. When the therapist describes the youth
as misbehaving, confused, childish, rebellious, in need of guidance, instead of using words like *mental illness, schizophrenia,
emotional problems,* and *psychological conflicts,* the parents, if
reluctant to take charge, will protest that this is not the way the
youth has been described by other experts, who have talked
about years of intensive therapy and the need to avoid any
stressful situation. The therapist must use all his authority and
the backing of his institution to counteract such statements,
whether or not they were truly made by other experts, or it will
be impossible to achieve the goals of the therapy.

Each inappropriate behavior of the youth must be carefully reformulated so that it is not a psychiatric symptom but a
behavior that the parents can change. It is important for the
therapist to relabel even the most bizarre behavior as dis-
courteous communication, in that others cannot understand it
or in that it upsets others. Then the parents can be asked to
require that the youth communicate more clearly and politely.
If the problem is apathetic behavior, it can be reformulated as

laziness, so the parents can be moved to demand regular activities. If the case involves drug addiction, the therapist can emphasize that it is not a physiological dependence that cannot be overcome. The parents must be convinced that the young person's problem is one that they can handle by establishing clear rules and severe consequences if these rules are not followed. If the youth is on medication, the therapist must state that he will reduce the medication and discontinue it altogether as soon as possible. As long as the young person is on medication, he is a mental patient under the care of psychiatrists instead of a misbehaving son whose behavior must be changed by the parents. A similar issue often comes up with the question of whether the youth should be on disability benefits. If the therapist accepts this idea, he is defining the youth as a mental patient incapable of making a living like a normal person.

Parents often disqualify themselves from the tasks of the therapy by communicating their ignorance about what expectations and rules to set for the young person or what consequences to set if the rules are disobeyed. Parents will typically express ignorance as a response to broad questions from the therapist (such as "What are your expectations of your son?") and in relation to very concrete and practical issues (such as "May your son use the family car on Saturday night?"). The messages that express ignorance are of the following variety: "I don't know," "That's a lot of thinking," "That's a difficult question," "I wouldn't know where to start," "It depends on so many things," "I couldn't make rules that would contemplate all the possible eventualities," "How could I know what is good for him." To counteract these messages, the therapist can state and restate the goal of the therapy, or the goal for that particular family meeting, and use his authority as a therapist to keep the focus on his goal. The therapist can also repeat a request, giving a rationale for it that the parents will have difficulty in arguing against. For example, if the parents are expressing ignorance about what rules to set for the son, the therapist can say, "I know it is difficult to set rules for him, but your son was hospitalized because he was confused. For him to be clear in his own mind, you, his parents, have to be very clear with him about the rules for his behavior in your house when he comes home from the hospital." It would be a mistake for the therapist to believe that the parents are actually ignorant. Their expressions of ignorance serve the purpose of arranging for others to take charge. The therapist must assume that the parents are committed to communicational sequences that define a hierarchy in which they are not in charge.

The therapist should start by requesting a statement of position from the parents that is general enough so that they can address the issues that they consider important. However, if the parents respond to this request with an expression of ignorance, then the therapist should narrow down the question to help the parents agree on a clear issue. For example, the therapist should start by asking the parents to agree on expectations and rules for their offspring when he comes home from the hospital. However, if the parents are not able to formulate any rules, the therapist should say something like "What I'm driving at are very simple, concrete guidelines for your son. For example, is he allowed to break furniture in your house? Is he expected to get up by a certain time in the morning?" Questions that allow for a yes-or-no answer are useful in forcing the parents to take a position and agree with each other, thus beginning to correct the hierarchy.

Often parents will make abstract statements in which they seem to be saying something when in fact they are again expressing ignorance; for example, "I want him to be a decent human being." The therapist can answer that that is a reasonable expectation, but does it mean that he is to come home every night at twelve or that he cannot hit his parents? The general idea is for the therapist always to bring the conversation back to concrete issues and concrete behavior. It is then more difficult for the parents to avoid taking charge.

The therapist should avoid the temptation of taking over the parents' task and himself setting the rules and consequences for their son. Since the therapist wants a hierarchy with the parents in a superior position, he cannot put them down in front of the offspring by taking over a parental position. Only if the therapist feels strongly that the parents' decisions about the young person are seriously wrong should he undermine their authority by suggesting an alternative, and then this should be done with the parents alone, not in the presence of the youth.

Giving Authority to the Problem Youth. Sometimes the parents will offer the authority to the disturbed youth. For example, when asked to make a decision about him, the parents might turn to the youth for advice or say that it all depends on what the young person wants for himself, that they just want him to be happy and to do what is best for him. The therapist should emphasize that the young person needs parental guidance and that only when he is behaving properly will he be in charge of himself. If the youth objects, the therapist can explain to him what there is in this approach for him. It can be emphasized that the youth will live in a predictable world, knowing exactly what his obligations and privileges are and will, therefore, not find himself in situations where he will be punished or mistreated arbitrarily or without warning.

When the parents begin to talk to each other and there is the possibility of an alliance between them, which will give them power over their offspring, the youth will behave in bizarre and disruptive ways. The threat of a parental alliance will end as the parents focus on the youth. It is important for the therapist to know that, at the beginning of the therapy, the young person probably will intervene and call attention to himself whenever the parents begin to talk to each other. The therapist must quiet the young person or ask the parents to do so.

In describing these sequences of interaction, Haley (1980) has emphasized that the youth behaves disruptively to prevent a disagreement between the parents. There are two ways to describe the function of this behavior by the youth: one is that it prevents disagreement and conflict; the other is that it interferes with the possibility of reaching agreement. In this writer's view, the youth's disruption has the function of preventing an agreement or an alliance between the parents. When the parents are talking in a context where a therapist is trying to bring them together in agreement, so that they can be jointly in charge of their offspring, and the youth erupts, what the disruption prevents from happening is the joint agreement to be in authority, not the disagreement. Even if the conversation starts with a disagreement, as long as the parents are talking, and with the help of a therapist, the possibility exists that they will be able to express their disagreements, communicate about them, and reach agreement. It is this possibility that is blocked by the youth's disruptiveness. This difference in interpretation of the function of the youth's disruption leads to different therapeutic interventions.

There is no question that when a family with a severely disturbed youth come to therapy there is a split between the parents. But this split may quite probably be the result and not the cause of the pain, bickering, accusations, and guilt that happen inevitably around this kind of problem. The disturbing behavior of the youth perpetuates this problem; and, although it often prevents a separation and divorce, since the parents must stay together to take care of their defective offspring, it also prevents the parents from coming together in joy and good feeling. It may be that the youth behaves disruptively both when the parents are too far apart (if they threaten to separate or divorce) and when they are too close together (when there is agreement between them), because in both cases the young person loses power over the parents.

Sometimes the parents will give authority to the problem youth by threatening to expel him from the family home. In this way, the parents threaten to renounce their position in the hierarchy as parents who are responsible for and in charge of their offspring. This threat must be blocked. The therapist must emphasize that this separation from the parents can happen only when the youth is behaving competently and when the parents know and approve of where and how he is going to live. Expulsion is a threat that is rarely carried out; in any case, the chances are that soon parents and youth will be involved with each other again, and the cycle will be repeated.

Often the parents are in disagreement over expulsion from the home as a consequence for the youth's misbehavior. Most frequently the father will threaten the offspring with expulsion while the mother will side with the youth to protect him from the father's threat and will withhold information about the offspring's activities from father for fear that the expulsion will take place. Sometimes the mother will threaten the father with separation and divorce if he expels the youth. Sometimes the father will insist that either the youth leaves the house or he will. In these cases, the threat of expulsion from the home is clearly at the service of preventing an agreement between the parents in which they are jointly in charge of the offspring. The youth is in a superior position in the hierarchy, since he has the power to divide them. The therapist must use all his authority and the backing of his institution to block this threat, so that leaving home is postponed until it is planned properly and until it happens not as a punishment but as a step forward for the youth and with agreement from both parents.

Sometimes the young person makes a powerful bid for power by threatening suicide. In this case, there are two possibilities for the therapist: (1) to hospitalize the youth, which means that the therapy will have to start all over again when the young person is discharged; or (2) to put the parents in charge of the youth and help them organize to prevent suicide. This is a difficult decision to make and should depend on the seriousness of the suicide threat, on whether there have been previous attempts, on an evaluation of the parents' investment in keeping their offspring alive, and on their ability to work together to prevent the suicide. If the therapist decides against hospitalization, he should carefully help the parents organize to prevent the suicide. They should institute a twenty-four-hour watch, and the parents should take turns watching him so that the youth is never alone. This usually tests the limits of the parents' patience and helps them take a more firm position in demanding normal behavior from the youth.

When a young person makes suicide attempts and extreme threats, the therapist can make a threat to the parents' marriage contingent on these disruptive behaviors, so that the parents will suffer if the young person continues to misbehave. In this way, the therapist exaggerates paradoxically one of the two incongruous hierarchies—the one in which the youth has power over the parents. The family will react by reorganizing more congruently with the parents in charge.[4]

Case 15: A Self-Destructive Girl

A 15-year-old girl had had several suicide attempts and behaved bizarrely, sticking needles in her arms, cutting her wrists with razor blades, and hurting herself in various ways. She heard voices that called her obscene names and told her to harm herself. The therapy was with the girl, her mother, and her stepfather. The stepfather was ten years younger than the mother, very handsome, and as close in age to the daughter as he was to the mother. The girl was very beautiful and very interested in her mother's marriage. She once said in private to the therapist, "My father reads novels about teenage sex, and my mother worries." It was clear that by acting crazy the girl was threatening the stability of her mother's marriage, since the stepfather had to put up with a daughter who not only was too old to be his but also was constantly acting crazy and attempting suicide. Mother and stepfather were afraid of the girl's dangerous behavior, and the girl was in charge of the situation. After several sessions, during which the parents were put in charge of the daughter, the girl's behavior improved, but she was skipping school and had gotten drunk. The family was told that, although there was improvement, the daughter was not completely well, and, therefore, the mother and the stepfather would have to bring up and discuss the issues in their marriage, since the therapist felt that marital difficulties might somehow be related to the girl's problems. The mother said that she did not want to bring up these issues because she felt it would endanger her relationship with her husband. The stepfather, who was a quiet man, mumbled that he agreed with his wife. The daughter stated emphatically that her problems had nothing to do with her parents' marriage. The therapist insisted, saying that, even though it might be unpleasant, the marital difficulties

---

[4]The therapist in the following case was Diane Gimber, supervised by the author.

had to be openly discussed and that this was a sacrifice that the mother should make for the sake of her daughter. The mother cried and said that she had already gone through a divorce and knew that this marriage too would be broken if she brought up these issues. The daughter cried and said that the mother's marriage was irrelevant to her problems and that, in any case, she did not have any problems and would not cause any more trouble. The stepfather remained silent. The therapist pointed out that the girl had promised this before and therefore could not be believed and insisted that the parents talk about their marriage. This went on for an hour and a half, with each one sticking to his position. The therapist's intervention exaggerated the power that the daughter's disruptive behavior had to endanger the parents' marriage. The family left the session without a resolution.

From that day on, the girl behaved properly. During the next week, she contacted her biological father, who lived a few miles away, and told him that she needed to see him and that she wanted to visit with him regularly. She had not seen him for years. The father was pleased, visited her, and promised to see her regularly. The daughter continued to behave normally and reestablished her relationship with her biological father. By involving herself with him and by behaving normally, the girl withdrew from the position of disruptive power that she had had in relation to the mother's marriage.

Giving Authority to Other Relatives. The more disturbed the young person is at the beginning of the therapy, the greater the possibility that, as soon as the hierarchical organization of the nuclear family begins to become congruent, a relative will be brought in who will have influence over the youth, allying with him, and there will be the danger that two incongruous hierarchies will again be defined in the family. The therapist must shift the relatives from allying with the disturbed youth to supporting the parents in their efforts to guide him.

Defining Himself as Inadequate. In struggling to provide guidance to the youth, a parent might become more aware of his own deficiencies and failures and, consequently, become upset or depressed. Sometimes the upset is related to a struggle with his own parents as he tries to keep them from allying with the youth across generation lines.

As the youth improves, relationships between family members change in ways that can sometimes be very painful to those involved. It may then be a parent who threatens suicide or mental breakdown, and it may be necessary to have some sessions alone with one or both parents to support them through this difficult time.

Threatening to Break Up the Parental Unit. As relationships change, the difficulties of the parents can become exacerbated. Demanding more of their child, the parents may also begin to demand more of each other, which may result in a threat of separation. It is then sometimes useful to exaggerate the power of the youth in bringing the parents together to take care of him because of his extreme and incompetent behavior. If this power is presented benevolently, emphasizing the young person's concern and self-sacrifice, the family will not be antagonized, since no one will be accused of bad intentions. They will respond, however, by reorganizing in more appropriate ways. This intervention is similar to those described by Palazzoli and colleagues (1978). The facts are that the youth's extreme behavior does bring the parents together to take care of him and that the kind of power that the young person holds over the parents requires extreme involvement at the cost of other attachments. The youth's behavior, however, although preventing the parents from separating, causes so much disruption and pain in the family that it also prevents the parents from coming together in happiness.

Parent Disqualifies Other Parent

Sometimes one parent will define the other parent as incompetent or defective. If one parent is incapacitated and disqualified from taking charge of the offspring, the two parents cannot reach agreement and ally to be jointly in charge of the youth. There are a series of tactics that the therapist can use to counteract this maneuver by one of the parents. He can say that the past behavior of one of the parents—whether he or she was too harsh or too weak or too withdrawn or depressed—is not the issue; this is a new situation where they will be working with the therapist, who will help them get together, agree, and jointly take charge of their offspring. Whatever happened in the past is irrelevant. The therapist can reformulate the disqualification of one parent by the other parent so that weakness becomes sensitivity, harshness and brutality become desperate attempts to provide clear guidance to a disoriented youth, depression and emotional instability become dedicated concern. Once the incompetence has been reformulated, it can be discarded.

Sometimes both parents may state that agreement with each other is impossible because they have different views about how to deal with the young person. In such instances, the therapist should emphasize that this will be a new experience of reaching agreement, since the therapist will be acting as mediator and will help them find a common ground for agreement. At times the parents may quarrel in the session. The therapist can prevent the quarrel from getting out of hand by asking each parent to address him rather than each other, so that the therapist will be acting as interpreter for each parent in relation to the other parent. Usually this tactic helps the parents be more polite to each other and prevents an escalation that could end with one parent leaving the session.

Disqualifications of one parent by the other parent can sometimes be avoided or corrected if the therapist reformulates the behavior of the disqualifier. This reformulating may be inaccurate and closer to what the therapist wishes the parent did than to what he or she actually does. If a parent who is critical is defined by the therapist as supportive, he or she will behave more supportively.

An example will illustrate this approach.[5] The parents of a 17-year-old user of phencyclidine hydrochloride (PCP), a synthetic hallucinogen, reluctantly brought her to family therapy. In the first interview, the mother objected to the use of videotapes and to the consultant behind the mirror. She also

[5] The therapist was Thanna Schmmel-Mascaro.

objected to the approach that their daughter needed guidance
and clear limits on her behavior. She wanted to explore why the
daughter was so depressed that she needed to resort to drugs.
She questioned the therapist thoroughly on her qualifications
and on the results of her method, even though the referral was
the recommended follow-up by the clinic where the girl had
been hospitalized. By the end of the first session, the father had
agreed with the approach and proposed to the mother a series
of rules for the girl and consequences if the rules were disobeyed. The mother was hesitant, afraid of being too harsh,
fearful that the girl's feelings were not taken into account. However, the parents did reach some agreements by the second
interview, although the father was constantly disqualified by
the wife for not understanding the girl, not communicating with
her, proposing a police state, and the like. Toward the end of
the second interview, the father proposed that the girl should
provide an accounting every week of the money she spent, since
in the past that money had been used for drugs. The therapist
thought this was a good idea, and before the mother could object, the therapist said: "And your wife is very supportive; she is
going to go along with you."

Mother: Oh, yes, I am very supportive of him.
Therapist: She has been so far.
Mother: Yes, we almost always agree and support each
                other. That, at least, is not one of our problems.

The mother was moved, there were tears in her eyes, the father
looked at her fondly, the parents agreed that the money would
be monitored, and the session ended in an atmosphere of good
feeling between the parents.

    When one parent is disqualified from being in a superior
position in the hierarchy by the other parent, the therapist can
also ignore this disqualification and proceed with the therapy as
if nothing had been said. This is a strong message about the inappropriateness of such statements.

    Sometimes a parent will suggest that there are secret, un-
savory facts about the other parent, so that the other parent is
disqualified from being in a superior position in the hierarchy.

For example, a parent may suggest or imply that the other parent has sexual relationships outside of the marriage. A father may say in passing that the mother has the same temperament as her disturbed, violent young daughter. A mother may suggest that the father is involved in shady business dealings and, therefore, cannot provide moral guidance to his son. The therapist must deal with these messages in much the same way as when a parent qualifies the other parent as incompetent or defective; that is, by emphasizing that the therapy is a new situation and the past is irrelevant, by reformulating the disqualification so that a defect becomes a positive quality, or by simply ignoring the disqualifying message.

Often the suggestion that there are secret, unsavory facts about a parent is made with the purpose of arousing the therapist's curiosity, so that he will become interested in these facts and will focus on the parent's difficulties rather than on the issue that the parents must jointly take charge of their offspring. The therapist should be prepared to avoid being distracted from his goal by other issues. It is a good idea for the therapist to say that he will be interested in the parent's difficulties and willing to discuss them, if this is the parent's wish, only after the disturbed youth is leading a normal life. The first priority now is the young person, who needs the parents to take charge and guide him. This message implies that, no matter what secret or unsavory facts there are about a parent, he or she must take charge of the youth and provide the necessary guidance. Also, in this way, the therapist is only postponing, without rejecting, the parent's bid for attention. This postponement is necessary because otherwise the therapist will quickly find himself involved in helping the parent with his difficulties and ultimately neither solving the youth's problems nor the parent's difficulties.

Parents Disqualify Therapist

The parents can ignore the therapist's requests that they be in charge of their offspring by disqualifying the therapist from being in charge of the therapy. If the parents put the therapist down, it is difficult for him to help the parents be in a superior position in their family. They need not follow the directives of a therapist they do not respect.

The parents might disqualify the therapist by suggesting that he is incompetent and does not know what he is doing. They can object to the therapist's age, sex, or professional degree. They might quote the opinion of other professionals whose position differs, or they might state that the therapist will fail as other therapists have failed in the past. In order to counteract these maneuvers effectively, the therapist must realize that often the parents would rather discuss the therapist's competence than face the difficulty of taking charge of their family. The parents, however, have the right to information on the therapist's qualifications. Therefore, the therapist should briefly describe his qualifications without telling the parents that they may have brought up these issues in order to avoid dealing with other matters.

When the issue of conflicting opinions from other professionals is brought up, the therapist must state that he is aware that there are different positions in the field and does not agree with some of them. To the prediction that the therapist will fail as other therapists have failed in the past, the answer can be that this approach to therapy is different and the family should give him a chance to do his job. The therapist can suggest that the parents try this approach for a limited period of time; for example, for three months. They will then understand the modality of therapy, and after the three months they can decide whether to continue. Also, after three months the young person might be on his feet, and the therapy might no longer be necessary.

Sometimes the parents refuse to comply with the therapist's requests as a way of disqualifying the therapist from being in charge of the therapy. The therapist may ask a father to talk to his wife, and the father may turn and talk to his daughter instead. Family members may argue loudly with each other and ignore the therapist's attempts to get them to speak one at a time and to listen to each other. Parents may refuse to address issues that the therapist insists are important and choose instead to talk about matters that are irrelevant to the therapy.

A family member may refuse to participate in the conversation and leave the room abruptly. Simple directives given by the therapist to be carried out at home may not be followed, and the family may come back week after week to report that father, for example, did not sit down with his son every morning to look through the employment ads in the newspaper or that mother did not report to father every evening on the activities of the offspring during the day.

The therapist needs to use certain tactics to ensure that his directives are followed. He must state and restate the goal of the therapy, which is to prevent hospitalization or prison and to organize a normal life for the youth. He can explain the cycle of hospitalization, discharge, and rehospitalization that can occur if the issues are not resolved. Sometimes what the therapist asks is denied on the basis that the requested behavior took place many times before. The therapist should reply that this is a new situation, since he, the therapist, is now involved with the family. The therapist should repeat his requests time and time again until he succeeds. A great many of the therapist's tactics within this approach involves repetitiousness and tenacity.

When the youth's behavior is extremely bizarre, the parents may threaten hospitalization. Apart from other negative effects, hospitalization usually means that other staff become involved with the case and the therapist loses control. To hospitalize would also be an error because it invalidates all the therapist's efforts to put the parents in charge of the problem. If the parents threaten to put the youth back in the mental hospital, the therapist must state that this is no longer an option because parents and therapist have agreed that the goal of the therapy is to keep the young person out of the hospital. Medicating the youth for a short period of time to reduce acute symptomatology and parental anxiety is sometimes necessary to prevent rehospitalization. The therapist can help the parents by suggesting alternative consequences if the young person misbehaves, such as no money, no food, or confinement in his room. If there is violence or the threat of violence, the therapist might suggest that the parents call the police. If there have been previous hospitalizations, the police will probably take the youth to the hospital; however, this is better than if the parents directly resort to hospitalization themselves. The ideal situation is one where the therapist has power to say that if the patient is brought to the hospital he will not be admitted; but even when the therapist can arrange for this at one hospital, the parents can always take the youth to another one. Therefore, it is very important for the therapist to obtain a commitment from the parents that they will not hospitalize the youth. Another consequence that the therapist may suggest to the parents is to restrain the youth in his room, locking him up there if necessary. This can be presented benevolently as providing the youth with an experience of what his life will be like in jail. Another possibility is to lock the young person out of the house for one night. This consequence may be used when the youth does not come home at the time stipulated by the parents.

Sometimes the young person demands to be taken to the mental hospital. The therapist should anticipate this possibility with the parents and suggest that they refuse to do this. If the youth wants to go to the hospital he must get himself there. If hospitalization occurs, the therapy must start all over again, following the same steps that were carried out previously.

In summary, during the course of the therapy, the therapist must simultaneously work to change the organization so that instead of incongruous hierarchies there is one clear organization, with the parents in charge. He must change the parents' incompetent and conflicting behavior so that they can jointly be in charge of the youth, rejecting his bid for power.

The Single Parent

In cases where there is a single parent, it is best to obtain the cooperation of a relative in the treatment, such as a grandmother, an aunt, or the mother's boyfriend. This relative should be the most significant parental surrogate in the young person's life. The therapy will then proceed in the same way, except that instead of two parents there will be one parent and one parental surrogate. If there is no relative to involve in the therapy, the stages and the treatment plan are still the same. The only difference is that, instead of having two parents talking to each other and making decisions jointly, the therapist will have to use himself more in the discussion with the single parent. That is, the therapist needs to become more involved with the single parent in encouraging her or him to make the decisions that are necessary during the course of the therapy.

Organicity

The question of whether certain types of pathology that typically occur in young people, such as schizophrenia and manic-depression, have an organic basis is quite irrelevant to this therapy. Even if these pathologies had an organic or a genetic basis, the medications that are known today, although useful in the acute phase to reduce symptomatology, have clearly failed in the psychosocial rehabilitation of patients and must be used sparingly and with caution because of dangerous side effects. The goal for the therapist still must be to organize a life for the young person that is as normal as possible, keeping him out of the mental hospital. In fact, the same approach has been used with mentally retarded youths, young people with irreversible neurological damage from PCP use, and epileptics.

Summary of the Therapeutic Strategy

In cases of severely disturbed youth, the therapist is typically presented with a situation where there is an incongruity in the family hierarchy. Based on his disturbing and helpless behavior, the young person is in a position of superior power with regard to the parents.

Hierarchy in a family is defined by repetitive sequences of who tells whom what to do. Sequences in which the parents tell the children what to do and the children do it usually occur more frequently in families than the opposite kinds of sequences. In families of severely disturbed young people, the therapist faces a situation in which the youth is still economically and emotionally dependent on the parents; however, the most frequently recurring sequences are ones in which the parents tell the youth what to do but he does not do it, or the parents do not tell the youth what to do but complain about what he does, or the youth tells the parents what to do and the parents do it.

The therapist must intervene to change these sequences to ones in which the parents tell the youth what to do and the youth obeys. Through the repeated occurrence of these sequences, a hierarchy will be defined in which the parents will be in a superior position to the young person. The content of the communication sequences between parents and youth must be one in which the parents set expectations and rules for the youth and establish consequences if these are not followed. Since at the beginning of treatment the parents are at a power disadvantage, the therapist must influence them to establish rules and consequences that are stringent enough to build up their power vis-à-vis the youth. When the young person loses his power over the parents, he will behave normally and eventually become independent.

The strategy used in this therapeutic approach is based on the manipulation of power, with the therapist redistributing power among family members. The process for carrying out this strategy consists of eliciting from family members the communicational sequences that define an appropriate hierarchy and counteracting the communication maneuvers that disqualify that hierarchy.

CHAPTER SEVEN

✠ ✠ ✠ ✠ ✠

Night Terrors:
A Case Study

This chapter consists of transcripts of excerpts from a whole therapy, edited and with commentary. A summary of this case was presented in Chapter Four. The therapist was Virginia Lopez, who was in training at the Philadelphia Child Guidance Clinic. The writer was the supervisor behind a one-way mirror, planning the approach, calling the therapist on the phone during the sessions, or asking her to come out of the sessions for discussions, and so guiding her through the therapy. The purpose of presenting this transcript, as well as the transcript in Chapter Eight, is to acquaint the reader with the actual process of conducting this therapy.

A mother sought therapy because her 10-year-old son had night terrors. There were two older daughters (12 and 14 years old) and a 7-month-old brother. The whole family, except the baby, had been born in Puerto Rico. They had been living in the United States for eight years. The mother, a 29-year-old dancing teacher, had been married twice; she had divorced her first husband and separated from the second one shortly before his death the previous year.

The mother and her four children were present in the first interview. The children were slender, with long, dark, straight hair and a very Spanish air. Raoul, the 10-year-old son, had a melancholic expression and his face was frequently covered by his dark, long hair. The mother was somewhat overweight and looked older than her age. At the beginning of the interview, she was anxiously chewing gum. The family sat in a semicircle with the mother at one end; Raoul at the other; and the daughters, Maria and Clara, in the middle. Maria, the 14-year-old daughter, held the baby boy in her arms. The therapy was conducted in Spanish because, although the children spoke English well, the mother spoke only Spanish.

Supervisor and therapist met before the first interview, and the supervisor suggested the following plan to the therapist:

1. Begin by asking the mother for information about Raoul's problem.
2. Find out about the sleeping arrangements in the house.
3. Inquire of each family member whether she has or has had a problem similar to Raoul's, as a way of looking for a clue to the metaphor expressed by the symptom.
4. Ask the boy to dramatize the symptom in the session, in order to bring it into the interview and thus have it happen under the control of the therapist.
5. Find out what happens before and after the symptom occurs, in order to gather information on who is involved with the child around the symptom.
6. Find out how the mother has attempted to solve the problem and what her theory is about the cause of the problem (without disagreeing or arguing with the mother).

First Interview

Lopez: You gave me some information on the telephone. Could you make it a little more specific, the information that you gave me? What is the problem?

Mother: Well, the problem is that sometimes he can't sleep until late at night and he says that he hears voices that call him, that he hears people shouting.

Lopez: And for how long has this happened?

Mother: Like a month and a half, something like that.

Lopez: And before this started, he didn't . . .

Mother: Never, he never complained or talked to me about this, he never said anything.

Maria: Mummy, this began when we moved to the new house, that you put him in a room by himself.

Mother: Yes, because before we had an apartment that wasn't too comfortable, you know, and I had the three of them in one room. Then when we moved to the house, I gave him a room because he is a boy and he has to be alone in his room, right? It was then.

Lopez: And Clara, you sleep alone?

Mother: No, the two of them sleep together.

Lopez: In the same room. And you?

Mother: I sleep with *him* [*pointing in the direction of the baby*].

The supervisor called the therapist on the phone and asked her to find out about the fears and dreams of the other family members. This inquiry had two purposes. First, it was a way of leading into a redefinition of the problem as a more normal event (fears and dreams related to childish fantasies) rather than as hearing voices, with its connotation of madness. Second, the reply from the mother and sister might give a clue to who was involved in the presenting problem of the child. If the mother had similar fears, it was reasonable to hypothesize that the child's symptom was metaphorical of the mother's problems and that it had a protective function toward the mother.

Lopez: And you are not afraid?

Mother: Not me. [*Short laugh.*]

Lopez: And you sleep well all night?

Mother: M-hmm.

Lopez: You don't dream or anything?

Mother: Well, I dream, but I don't pay attention to any of that. [*Short laugh.*]

Lopez: What kind of dreams do you have?

Mother: Well, sometimes I dream that somebody is breaking into the house, that kind of thing.

Lopez: M-hmm.

Mother: I have that tendency, you know, I have a certain tendency, because sometimes I am alone, well then—I hear anything and I think that someone is going to break in. Those are things that happen, it's natural, you know.

Lopez: Do you discuss your dreams with the children?

Mother: Sometimes. And sometimes they discuss theirs with me.

This information about the mother's fears was enough to formulate the hypothesis that the boy's problem was metaphorical of the mother's fears and that it was also helpful to her. However, before a strategy could be designed, it was necessary to know more about the function of the symptom and the involvement of the siblings.

Lopez: M-hmm. Do you dream, Clara? What do you dream sometimes?

Clara: Sometimes I dream that I find money . . .

Lopez: That you find some money?

[*They laugh.*]

Clara: I always find the money.

[*Laughter.*]

Lopez: And where do you find the money?

Clara: In the street.

Lopez: True?

Mother: M-hmm.

Lopez: How nice! [*To Maria*] What did you tell me your name was?

Maria: Maria.

Lopez: Maria. I don't know why I forget because I have a daughter who is also called Maria.

Mother: M-hmm.
Lopez: And you, don't you dream, Maria?
Maria: Yes.
Lopez: Yes? And what kind of dreams do you dream?
Maria: I don't remember what I dream. Mmm, I don't re-
            member.

The sisters did not have nightmares as the mother did, and they did not seem to be involved in Raoul's symptomatic behavior. But they were friendly and helpful. It would be possible to engage them to participate in a therapeutic plan.

The therapist then asked Raoul about his symptoms. The boy described a recurrent nightmare in which he was attacked by a witch, and the terror that followed those dreams.

Lopez: And what are the things you dream?
Raoul: Bad people.
Lopez: Bad people like what?
[*Silence.*]
Lopez: What do you dream? Tell me a dream that you had.
Raoul: One day I dreamed about witches and . . .
Lopez: M-hmm.
[*Silence.*]
Lopez: What did they do to you?
Raoul: Hm?
Lopez: What did they do to you?
Raoul: They wanted to break into the house.
Lopez: They wanted to break into the house?
Raoul: In the house where we lived before, on Fourteenth
            Street.
Lopez: And what are you afraid of?
[*Silence.*]
Lopez: When you go to bed at night, are you afraid?
Raoul: Sometimes.
Lopez: And what are you afraid of?
Raoul: Sometimes I hear shouting.
Lopez: You hear shouts?
Raoul: Sometimes.

Lopez: And what do you hear? A man, a woman, or a baby?
Raoul: A woman.
Lopez: Hm?
Raoul: A woman.
Lopez: A woman shouting?
[*Silence.*]
Lopez: Many times you hear it?
[*Raoul nods affirmatively.*]
Lopez: How many times do you dream at night?
Raoul: I always dream. Sometimes, like three times I didn't dream.
Lopez: Like three times you didn't dream? Since you moved to this house?
Raoul: No, I always dream. In the other house also.
Lopez: Ah, you dreamed! And what are the dreams you had there?
Raoul: The one I told you.
Lopez: The one of the witch? You always dream about the witch?
Raoul: No.
Lopez: And what else do you dream about?
Raoul: Sometimes I haven't dreamed, in this house . . . it's been like three nights that I didn't dream.

The family came with the presenting complaint that Raoul heard voices in the night that frightened him. At this point in the interview, the therapist has already, almost inadvertently to the family, reformulated the problem as one of nightmares. The issue was no longer hearing voices but nightmares, a normal experience of everyone. The supervisor called the therapist on the phone and suggested that mother and son should dramatize the dream of the witch. The mother would be the witch and would attack the son while he slept. The symptom was then no longer something that the family only talked about in therapy but that happened at home, out of the therapist's control. Bringing a symptom into the therapy room is the first step toward changing it.

Raoul: A witch . . . a witch . . .

Mother: It was coming with a knife on top of him.

Lopez: OK. Do you think that we could dramatize a dream that you dreamed?

[*Silence.*]

Lopez: Hm?

[*Silence.*]

Lopez: A woman shouting, to kill you? A witch? OK, let's suppose that mummy is the witch that comes to kill you. You are dreaming. OK?

Raoul: I can't do it like this.

Lopez: Why?

Raoul: Because the . . . the witch was taller.

Lopez: Well, suppose it is she, OK?

Raoul: She was bigger than her; it was a complete woman.

Lopez: What do you think your mother is?

Raoul: You know, a real tall woman.

[*Mother laughs.*]

Lopez: A real tall woman?

Maria: He says that he realized, that he saw, that when he saw that she was going to stab him with the knife—that he couldn't move and that he stayed . . .

Mother: M-hmm, he stayed inert, eh . . .

Lopez: [*Superimposed with Raoul*] OK.

Raoul: [*Speaking with great excitement*] No, it was . . . I woke up, and I was like this . . . [*folds his arms rigidly*]. Afterwards when I was still like this, I couldn't . . . I couldn't . . . I couldn't sleep . . . a . . . a . . . and afterwards I woke up but I couldn't move.

Mother: M-hmm.

Lopez: OK, that is one we will dramatize, OK? You . . . Mummy will be the witch, and you will imagine that she is real big, OK? So you will . . . you will tell us the dream and then we will dramatize it.

Raoul: But . . . but I woke up when she talked to me later . . .

Lopez: OK, then, when she stands over you, then you wake up.

[*Laughter.*]

Mother: Put her [*pointing to one of the daughters*] put her,
             let's see . . .

Lopez: No, I want it to be you, OK?

[*Laughter.*]

Mother: She knows that I'm a performer.

[*Laughter.*]

Lopez: OK, then you will be the witch, he is sleeping. You
             take this as if it were a knife [*gives her a pencil*].
             OK? And he is sleeping.

[*Raoul is sitting with his eyes closed and his arms crossed over
his chest. The mother rises slowly from her chair, holding the
pencil in her hand as if it were a knife, walks toward her son
and stops in front of him, holding the pencil with her two hands
over his head. Raoul looks at her, frightened.*]

The therapist then found out what happened at home
when Raoul had nightmares. The mother explained that she
took him to her bed and told him to think about God and pray;
she made the sign of the cross on his forehead to protect him
from the devil. She thought that Raoul's problem was due to
the influence of the devil.

Lopez: That was how you woke up?

Raoul: Yes.

Lopez: And you were very frightened?

[*Raoul nods his head affirmatively.*]

Lopez: And what happened afterwards?

Raoul: I told mummy. She made the sign of the cross on my
             head and then I fell back, asleep.

Lopez: A-ha, and you slept more peacefully?

Raoul: I was like this . . . I was like this . . . still . . . mmm
             . . . you know . . . afterwards . . . I couldn't move.

Lopez: You couldn't move?

Raoul: I couldn't move my hands.

Lopez: You couldn't move your hands?

Raoul: No, neither one.

Lopez: You were like this [*makes gesture with her hands*]?

Raoul: Like in shock.

Lopez: M-hmm, how were you, let's see, put your hands like they were.

Raoul: I was like this [*demonstrates making his body look rigid*].

Lopez: M-hmm, and then what happened?

Raoul: I also couldn't speak.

Lopez: You couldn't speak. And after that, what happened?

Raoul: Afterwards, when I lay down again, it happened again.

Lopez: It happened twice in the same night?

Raoul: No, like three times.

Lopez: Like three times in the same night. The three times it was the witch that was going to kill you?

Raoul: No, m-hmm . . . three times it was that . . . you know . . . that I couldn't . . . move.

Lopez: Three times it happened that you couldn't move. And what did your mother do?

Mother: I put him to bed with me. Right? Wasn't it like that, that I put you in bed with me?

Lopez: After you dream and your mother comes, she talks with you and leaves and it goes away?

Raoul: Yes, she takes it away.

Lopez: After she talks to you?

Raoul: Yes, some dreams.

Lopez: Then you lie down to sleep.

Raoul: M-hmm.

Lopez: What do you talk about to him, Mrs. Sanchez?

Mother: I tell him to pray.

Lopez: To pray.

Mother: I talk to him about the self and grief, and to think about God, ask God . . . because above God there is no one, ask God, above God there isn't . . . there isn't evil . . .

Lopez: M-hmm.

Mother: They are the devil's doings.

Lopez: You think that these are the devil's doings?

Mother: Of course.

The therapist did not argue with the mother concerning her ideas about the devil, nor did she attempt to change her point of view. It was now possible to conclude the formulation of the hypothesis about the problem. Raoul's night terrors were both a metaphorical expression of the mother's fears and an attempt to help her. If he was the one who was afraid, then the mother had to be strong and pull herself together to reassure him and protect him; therefore, she could not be afraid herself. But when the mother tried to protect and help Raoul, she frightened him more. Mother and son were caught in a situation where they helped each other in unfortunate ways.

The first therapeutic intervention was designed to block the special way in which Raoul was protecting his mother and the mother was protecting him. The supervisor called the therapist out of the therapy room and instructed her to ask the family to pretend they were at home and the mother was very frightened because she heard noises as of someone breaking into the house. One of the sisters would play the role of a thief who was trying to enter the house, and the son would protect his mother by attacking the thief. In this way, the mother was requested to pretend to need Raoul's help rather than to actually need it. The son was encouraged to pretend to help the mother. The mother's need for help was now in play, and so was the son's helpfulness. What follows is the first attempt to dramatize this scene.

Lopez: Now we are going to dramatize [to Maria] that you
          are a thief that is going to come in here.
Maria: A what?
Lopez: A thief. [She explains it in English.] Someone that
          will rob the house.
Maria: Oh!
[Mother has finished feeding the baby, and Clara is walking him
around the room.]
Lopez: [To mother] You are going to be very frightened,
          very nervous. OK? [The children laugh.] OK. [To
          Maria] You are going to come in as if you are going
          to rob the house, OK? And then . . .
Mother: I don't have the feeling that they are going to rob.

Lopez: No, but that's what I want to see. Do you understand? That you are going to get scared, very scared.
Then Raoul, you are going to try to help your
mother. OK?

Maria: Let's see you. If somebody comes into the house,
what are you going to do? You go like this [*making
gesture of hiding*]?

Mother: He runs away. [*They laugh.*]

Lopez: OK. We will see what happens. OK?

[*All the children talk at the same time. Maria gets up from her
chair and goes to stand near the door of the room.*]

Lopez: Raoul, you are going to help your mother, OK? She
is very frightened; they are coming to rob her.

Maria: Mother, stand up because . . .

Lopez: She doesn't necessarily have to be standing.

Maria: I was only saying . . .

Lopez: Go over there and come in as if you are going to
steal.

[*Maria leaves the room.*]

Raoul: And what am I going to do?

Lopez: Well, see what you will do.

[*Raoul looks for something in his pockets, Maria comes into the
room on tiptoe, nobody moves. Mother says something in a
whisper to Raoul. After a few seconds, Maria and Mother look
at each other and smile. Maria fixes her hair, and Raoul stands
up and looks for something in the pockets of his coat that is
lying on a chair. Maria laughs.*]

Several rehearsals of the scene failed. The mother attacked the thief before her son could help her. The message that
resulted from this failure to act out the scene correctly was that
the mother was a capable person who would defend herself; she
did not need the son's protection.

Finally, the therapist said that she would observe from
the other room. This time they dramatized the scene correctly.

Lopez: I am going to leave you alone, and you are going to
act it out again. I'll look at you from behind here.

But I want you to give it life, you know . . . if you
want to scream, scream, as if it were true. Raoul,
what are you going to do?

Raoul: I don't know.

Lopez: I'll be looking at you, to see what you will do.

[*The therapist leaves, and the mother tells Maria to go out.
Maria leaves and comes in again. Mother takes a chair and lifts it
over Maria's head with a threatening gesture. Raoul has remained seated.*]

Raoul: But she has to take something, Mummy.

Mother: [*Standing in the middle of the room, holding the
             chair with one hand, and shouting at Raoul*] Listen,
             you have to do something. What would you do if
             something happened to me?

Raoul: [*In English*] All right, all right, begin, begin.

Mother: I already did everything I can.

[*The mother puts the chair in its place while Maria leaves the
room again. Mother remains standing and Raoul walks toward
the door. When Maria comes in, mother runs to pick up the
chair, but Raoul is faster and he pushes Maria out of the room,
hitting her on the arm.*]

While the therapist was observing behind the mirror, the
supervisor proposed a plan: (1) The therapist would discuss the
dramatization with the family and would criticize the mother in
her difficulty in expressing fear and in restraining herself so that
the son would have a chance to attack the thief. (2) The therapist would praise the mother for her efforts to help Raoul and
ask for the mother's commitment to follow the therapist's instructions. (3) The therapist would instruct the mother in the
following ways: (a) Raoul was to sleep in his own room always.
(b) Every evening the family would pretend for a few minutes
that the mother was frightened because somebody was breaking
into the house, and that Raoul would protect her. (c) During
the next week, if Raoul woke up screaming, the mother would
wake up the whole family, and they would pretend the same
scene that they were to practice every evening.

The therapist returned to the room, discussed the dramatization with the family, and criticized the mother for her diffi-

culty in expressing fear and in restraining herself. What follows shows how the mother responded to the therapist's criticism. She talked about how she was a competent person who could defend herself well and that was why it was so difficult for her to play this part—she did not need Raoul's protection.

Mother:	But it is that I am not . . . not . . . naturally I am not like that. When I . . . if I see something, I look for how to defend myself and how to defend them. Naturally I am not frightened in that way.
Lopez:	How are you frightened?
Mother:	I try to attack the one that comes.
Lopez:	M-hmm.
Mother:	Do you understand? I hear something, I stand up and look for something, I am always like that.
Lopez:	And after you look for something?
Mother:	I go to see, to attack. Do you understand?
Lopez:	But . . .
Mother:	That is, I don't . . . my thought is that I won't give him a chance not even to talk to me or anything. Do you understand?
Children:	Whew!
Mother:	My idea is to attack, because since I was little I was used to fighting.
Lopez:	Ah! You fought?
Mother:	Yes.
[Lopez laughs.]	
Mother:	You know, I had this thing to attack, see?
Lopez:	M-hmm.
Mother:	Because I am a person that has been raised almost alone and I have defended myself, see, and I have even defended other people, friends, and I have this thing.
Lopez:	M-hmm.
Mother:	Do you understand? I do here naturally what I think I must do if . . .
Lopez:	M-hmm.
Mother:	Other people . . . other people even lose consciousness and scream and everything, but not me.

After talking for a few minutes about the dramatization, the therapist congratulated the mother for everything that she had done to help Raoul and told her that if she wished to help her son get rid of his symptoms, she must follow the therapist's instructions.

Lopez: You were telling me that you were teaching Raoul to be responsible, right?

Mother: M-hmm. What I want is for him to have his own initiative, you understand? That as soon as he gets up in the morning, he should leave his room picked up. I always tell him that the clothes that he takes off he must hang up; what he wears to school he shouldn't wear around the house or to play.

Lopez: Well, you have a wonderful idea, and if you want to help your son to be a man . . .

Mother: You know, because I want him to be a completely independent person . . . I know that there are children at his age that even wash their socks and things. He doesn't yet, because at home I put everything in the machine . . . and I wash his things. I do everything.

Lopez: Well, but there are other ways of making the children responsible.

Mother: M-hmm.

Lopez: If you want to help him to be like a man.

Mother: Yes.

Lopez: Then we will have to do three things for a week.

First, Raoul must sleep in his room, and for no reason whatsoever would he sleep in his mother's room again. Second, every evening the family must get together and they must pretend, as they did during the interview, that someone is coming into the house, that the mother is afraid, and that Raoul protects her. Third, during the following week, until the next interview, if during the night mother hears from her room that Raoul is screaming in his sleep, she must get up, wake him, wake the sisters, and they all must act out the same scene that they are to practice every evening. They must do this no matter what time of the night it is or how tired they are. This ordeal was designed to encourage mother and son to change the unfortunate way in which they were protecting each other. Maria was asked to keep notes of when and how the family performed these tasks. A second session was scheduled for five days later.

Second Interview

Lopez: And how are you, how have you been?

Mother: Fine.

Maria: More or less. Let's see . . . Saturday we did it . . . we did the drama, we went to sleep, this one didn't wake up.

Lopez: He didn't wake up?

Maria: Sunday we did it, but there was the Spanish program. Monday we didn't do it.

Lopez: Why?

Maria: Because we went . . . Monday I . . . I wanted to go to sleep later, and this one went to sleep earlier. Wednesday we did it, I mean Tuesday.

Lopez: And Raoul, have you had some dreams?

Mother: He dreamed, yes, but he didn't get up. He dreamed, in the morning he told me but he didn't get up like other times when he used to get up like this.

Lopez: M-hmm. Tell me, Raoul, then you didn't have any dream?

Raoul: I dreamed, but I don't remember.

Lopez: Hm?

Raoul: I don't remember.

Lopez: You don't remember? Very good! And you slept alone?

[*Raoul nods affirmatively.*]

Lopez: M-hmm. And you didn't have to sleep with mummy not even one night? Wonderful!

Mother: Last night he got up saying to me . . . what was it that you were saying to me last night? Ah! That . . .

Lopez:	that he had forgotten part of the Father, Thou Art in Heaven.
Lopez:	Oh!

Raoul had not had symptoms. The next step for the therapist was to encourage and advise the mother in her work as a dancing teacher. If the mother were more successful and competent, the son would need less to protect her.

Lopez:	I think it's wonderful that you can teach . . .
Mother:	Yes, I give lessons in ballet, flamenco, baton. Do you know what the baton is?
Lopez:	Yes, m-hmm.
Mother:	And oriental dances, and tango, latin dances, see, tango and things like that.
Lopez:	Aha.
Mother:	I have specialized in children, teenagers, and adults.
Lopez:	Wonderful!
Mother:	That is my field.
Lopez:	M-hmm.
Mother:	Because I was always in this from the age of nine.
Lopez:	And have you found . . . haven't you talked with a person that could help you?
Mother:	Well . . . already they gave me the place, see. They said, "You can do there what you want," and you know . . . we need a place, see, to be able to be there giving your lessons, you can do what you want, until you make it, like people say.
Lopez:	Yes.
Mother:	And if ever I have a very big group, well I give them a part.
Lopez:	I see, do you have a big group? How many do you have?
Mother:	Well, at the moment . . . it is the second lesson that I have, the third today, tonight I have it. Tonight in the baton class I have eight.
Lopez:	M-hmm.
Mother:	Then in the flamenco I have four, and ballet I have three.

Lopez: They are all Puerto Rican?
Mother: Aha, they are all Puerto Rican. Because I am inter-
            ested in making a big group of baton twirlers, Puerto
            Rican.

The therapist ended the interview by asking the mother to do something special in her profession during the next two weeks and to have a surprise related to her work for the next interview. She repeated then the same instructions of the first interview.

Third Interview

The family did not come to the next interview, and the mother said on the phone that the child no longer had problems and she thought it was not necessary to come. They were asked to come anyway. In the meantime, the psychologist of Raoul's school called the clinic to refer the case. She was concerned about Raoul's nightmares and because he was not doing well in school. There had been a delay from the time the psychologist found out about Raoul's problem until she called the clinic; therefore, she did not know that the family were already in treatment. The psychologist was then asked to come to a session together with the family, with the idea of facilitating communication between the psychologist and the mother, since one spoke only English and the other only Spanish. In this third interview, three weeks later, it was clearly observed that Raoul was sharing his fears and his fantasies with the school psychologist, who was very interested in him and concerned about him. By becoming involved with an outside expert who intervened—encouraging him in his symptomatic behavior through her benevolent interest and concern and thereby taking power away from the mother—Raoul was again defining an incongruous hierarchy in the family.

Psychologist: Raoul told me that he has a hard time because
                  he thinks about other things when he is in
                  school.
Lopez: M-hmm.

Psychologist:	And I know that that dream was bothering him and I think it still is.
Lopez:	M-hmm.
Psychologist:	Raoul . . .
Lopez:	[*To mother*] She says that Raoul told her that he thought about other things . . . when he was in school.
Mother:	Like about what?
Lopez:	Raoul, do you want to tell your mother?
Raoul:	Hm?
Lopez:	Do you want to tell your mother?
Mother:	What do you think about?
Raoul:	About the dreams I had.
Psychologist:	He dreamed about a man . . .
Mother:	One dreams so many things! To pay so much attention to dreams!

[*The psychologist says something to the sister.*]

Clara:	Oh, she said that the dreams he had, well, of a man beside a post, with . . . a cape . . . a cape . . .
Lopez:	A black cape.
Clara:	A black cape.

[*The psychologist continues explaining her concern about Raoul for a few minutes. The therapist reassures her that she and the mother will take care of the boy, and the psychologist leaves.*]

Lopez:	Well, how are things . . . with the family? Did Raoul wake up screaming sometime?
Mother:	No.
Lopez:	Raoul, did you wake up screaming some time?

[*Raoul shakes his head negatively.*]

Lopez:	And why do you think he doesn't wake up screaming?
Mother:	Because I don't hear him.
Lopez:	You haven't heard him? Why do you think Raoul doesn't wake up screaming, Clara?
Clara:	I don't know, because he doesn't have any more bad dreams, because all he tells me is that he

	dreams about superhero, or cartoons, things like that.
Lopez:	M-hmm.
Clara:	He always dreams about that.
Raoul:	Eh . . . sometimes I hear people, like always.
Lopez:	You hear people like always, and what happens when you hear people?
Raoul:	[*Coughing*] I see also. [*Coughs a great deal.*]
Lopez:	What do you see?
[*Raoul coughs.*]	
Mother:	Tell her, tell her what you see.
Raoul:	People.
Lopez:	How do you see them?
Raoul:	The same people that I saw in the dream.
Lopez:	But you tell me that you haven't had that dream any more, right?
Raoul:	Yes, but the dream that Mrs. Violet [*the psychologist*] . . . the one . . . you know.
Lopez:	M-hmm. When did you have that dream, Raoul?
Raoul:	I didn't have a dream, but I saw it when . . . you know.
Lopez:	It wasn't a dream?
Raoul:	No.
Lopez:	Ah, and what was it then?
Raoul:	Like when Mrs. Violet, you know, she was saying that I close my eyes, well I saw it. I told her.
Lopez:	When Mrs. Violet . . . you were talking with Mrs. Violet?
Raoul:	Yes.
Lopez:	You saw that? What was it that you saw?
Raoul:	Yes. She told me to close my eyes and afterwards I saw it.
Lopez:	When you closed your eyes . . . you saw it? And what was it that you saw, Raoul?
Raoul:	A man, you know, all black, with a black face.
Lopez:	With a black face?
Raoul:	M-hmm. I could see everything well but he was on top of a post [*very agitated*] for . . . high,

	and afterwards he hid and hmm . . . afterwards I saw . . . I didn't see him, and afterwards I opened my eyes and I closed them again, and afterwards I saw many people beside the post taking a photograph with a man or somebody.
Lopez:	M-hmm. And you saw that while you were awake, talking with Mrs. Violet?
Raoul:	No, I was thinking.
Lopez:	You were thinking, oh, it was that you were imagining that. But you didn't see it.
Raoul:	Hm?
Lopez:	You didn't see it?
Raoul:	Hm . . . I . . . you know, when she . . . she told me to close my eyes . . .
Lopez:	And to think?
Raoul:	And afterwards she told me . . . yes . . . what was I thinking.
Lopez:	M-hmm. Then you thought about a black man with a black cape.
Raoul:	No, I didn't think of a man, she told me that, you know . . . "Let your mind go."
Lopez:	M-hmm.
Raoul:	And afterwards that's what I saw.
Lopez:	M-hmm.

The supervisor advised the therapist to block this relationship by asking the psychologist, in private, to talk with the child only about matters related to his schoolwork and to avoid discussing anything related to his dreams and fears; that was the task of the therapist. At the end of this interview, the family were asked to dramatize again the scene in which Raoul protected his mother from a thief, and they were told that if Raoul had nightmares again, on the next day they should dramatize this scene. The mother, who seemed not to have forgotten the instructions given to her weeks earlier in the second interview, invited the therapist to a show in which she was going to dance.

Fourth Interview

The man who was currently living with the family came to the fourth interview, one week later. This was managed after a great deal of insistence from the therapist. The mother had mentioned him for the first time at the show. Up to then, she had denied that any man was living with the family. Apparently she was afraid of losing her welfare benefits if she admitted that a man was contributing to her support. This man had separated from his wife, with whom he had four children, and he was the father of Raoul's younger brother; he had two jobs and was rarely at home. When the mother had finally talked about him, she complained of the way he treated her children. The therapist tried, in this interview, to strengthen the relationship between Raoul and his stepfather, in an attempt to stabilize a congruous hierarchy by having both mother and father involved in parenting Raoul. Although the stepfather promised to collaborate, he did so reluctantly. He had little time, and this attempt was not successful.

Fifth Interview

The supervisor then instructed the therapist to focus directly on the boy and to have an individual interview with him to help him to control his fantasies better and so to free him to seek relationships in which to share other things besides his fears. The therapist was to ask the boy to purposefully see his usual frightening image of a man and then to patiently and repetitiously suggest that he could change this image by changing the clothes, the posture, and so on, and finally change him into an attractive character like Superman or Bugs Bunny. Then the therapist was to explain to the boy that his mind was like a television set, and he could change what he thought and imagined just as one changes TV channels. What follows is an excerpt from this individual session with the boy.

Lopez: Raoul, you told me that you haven't had any more nightmares or dreams. [*Raoul nods affirmatively.*]

Now I want you to do something for me. I want you
to close your eyes [*Raoul closes his eyes*], and I want
you to imagine . . . that man. That one that you say
you dream about him, to see him . . . are you seeing
him? [*Raoul moves his head negatively.*] Tell me how
you see him. What color is his face?

Raoul: Peach.

Lopez: Peach. OK.

[*Long pause. Raoul holds his head with his hands. His eyes are
closed.*]

Lopez: You saw his face. His peach face. I want . . . I want
you to see a body [*pause*] with a black cape. [*Raoul
puts his head down, obviously trying to concentrate.*]
With a black cape . . . with a black cape. Do you see
him like that and a big hat? How do you see him? Are
you seeing him, Raoul? He doesn't laugh? [*Raoul
moves his head negatively.*] Maybe you can make
him laugh, Raoul. He doesn't want to laugh? Does he
have a hat, Raoul? See if you can put a hat on him,
Raoul . . . how does he look with a hat? [*Pause.*] Let's
make him wear a coat instead of a cape; let's make
him wear a coat to see how he looks better. Does he
look a little bit better with a coat? Hm? Does he look
better? Are you seeing him now with a coat? Does he
have a hat, Raoul? Let's put a hat on him to see how
he looks. How does he look? Does he have a scarf,
Raoul? Is he well dressed? [*Raoul nods his head affirmatively.*] To go out? OK, let's take off his hat,
OK? Did you take off his hat, Raoul? Did you take
off his scarf? Did you take off his coat? And we are
going to make him wear a Superman outfit, hm? Did
you dress him with the Superman outfit? Superman's
cape? [*Raoul nods affirmatively.*] Now he is going to
fly. [*Raoul nods affirmatively.*] Now you are going to
imagine him flying, OK? Imagine that you have a television. Do you see the TV set? And do you see the
buttons? Do you see the buttons of the TV? And you
have Superman flying, right? [*Raoul nods affirma-*

tively.] See if touching some of those buttons of the TV, what you can do. We have Superman on one channel, OK? You have him flying. Do you see the buttons? Change a button. We are going to change to another channel. Who is there, Mickey Mouse? [*Raoul shakes his head negatively.*] No? Who is there? [*Long pause.*] Who do you see now? Superman? Nobody? [*Raoul moves his head negatively.*] When you changed the TV, Superman disappeared, hm? That means that you can change what you are thinking, hm? [*Raoul nods affirmatively.*] OK. Now we are going to imagine something else, OK? [*Raoul nods affirmatively.*] But raise your head because I can't see you like this. Now we are going to imagine Bugs Bunny. [*Long pause.*] Are you seeing him? Well, think that you are seeing him, OK? You can think that you are seeing him, Raoul? [*Raoul nods affirmatively.*] Yes, right? Now he comes running, no? He is standing on a post? Yes? [*Raoul nods affirmatively.*] And he goes jumping on the floor. Is he jumping, Raoul? Hm? He is going to start to run. He is beginning to run. He has climbed on the post. Hm? [*Raoul nods affirmatively.*] Now imagine that he is getting off the post. And that he is running. [*Raoul nods affirmatively.*]

[*After a few minutes, the therapist tells Raoul to open his eyes.*]

Lopez: I want you in school, for example, when you have those thoughts that you say you see men, to remember that I told you that you have a TV, and that the mind is like a TV and to change it. You can do that. You know what I mean? [*Raoul nods affirmatively.*] What did I say?

Raoul: That if in school . . .

Lopez: M-hmm.

Raoul: I think of a man, to remember that the mind is like a television. And to change it.

Lopez: And that you can do it. You can do it because you did

it here, so in school when you think that you are having a thought like that—well, you say, let me change
to see what there is on another channel, OK?

Sixth Interview

Lopez: And tell me, have you dreamed?

Mother: This morning he dreamed. He told me that he
dreamed that he had climbed on a post. [*Laughs.*]

Lopez: Did you dream, Raoul?

[*Raoul shakes his head negatively.*]

Lopez: No?

Mother: He dreamed that he was climbing on a post.
[*Laughs.*]

Lopez: Have you had nightmares, Raoul? You didn't get up
screaming?

[*Raoul shakes his head negatively.*]

Lopez: No? And you didn't imagine any more that ugly
man? [*Raoul shakes his head negatively.*] And have
you been able to imagine nice things? [*Raoul shakes
his head negatively.*] No? But you can change it, no?
When you think about seeing an ugly person, you can
change it to a pretty one, true? [*Raoul agrees.*] [*To
mother*] And how do you feel now that Raoul
doesn't get up screaming?

Mother: I feel better, because I was worried, I was, because he
would get up every time with the fixed idea in his
head. I see that he is happier.

Lopez: [*To Clara*] And how do you see him?

Clara: Hm?

Lopez: How do you see Raoul now that he doesn't have
dreams or anything?

Clara: Well, better.

Lopez: You see him better?

Clara: M-hmm.

Lopez: And why do you think he doesn't have the dreams?

Clara: I don't know. I know he doesn't have them.

Lopez: [*To Maria*] Why do you think that Raoul doesn't
have dreams any more?

Maria:	Because he doesn't get up like before at night to tell mother.
Mother:	Before he used to get up . . .
Maria:	He walked all around the house.
Mother:	It's been a long time since he doesn't get up.

Raoul was participating in new activities with groups of children. The mother had listened in silence when, during the fourth interview, the therapist explained to the stepfather that Raoul needed friends. Now she explained with great pride how she managed to get Raoul involved in a rock band and a soccer team. Raoul was now more involved with children while the mother continued to be very interested in her own work.

Lopez:	Yes. I can tell that you are very interested in helping your family, and with Raoul you have helped very much.
Mother:	Yes, I try as much as possible, see? Now I met a friend, a man there who is his friend and who plays with him the trombone.
Lopez:	Ah, yes!
Mother:	So he told him that sometime he is going to take him to the orchestra.
Lopez:	Yes?
Mother:	For a start, then on Saturday . . .
Lopez:	Do you like it, Raoul?
Raoul:	Yes.
Mother:	On Saturday, when we went we had a show, because the boys' orchestra was there, and he didn't leave the stage there with them. [*Laughs.*] I had to take him away because the music was so loud, see.
Lopez:	Do you like that, Raoul? And how do you feel now that you have a friend?
[*Raoul smiles.*]	
Mother:	Then another American man from around there also takes him . . .
Lopez:	This man is Spanish?
Mother:	One is Spanish and the other man is American. He lives a block from our house, so he picks up all the

boys in the block and he takes them . . . to baseball.
There they give him a shirt, bats, and all that. And he
goes. I give him money, half a dollar I have to give
him and something to eat there. I always give him,
every Sunday, and he goes. Those things. He didn't
have that.

Lopez: How do you feel now, Raoul, that you can go to play
ball and to play . . .

Raoul: Good. [*Smiles.*]

Mother: M-hmm. Very happy.

[*Raoul nods his head affirmatively.*]

Mother: And I too feel happier, see, because I know he feels
well.

The treatment was reaching its end. Since the goal was to
stabilize the change and facilitate separation, it was important
to give the mother all the credit for what had been achieved.
The therapist also thanked Raoul and his sisters for their collaboration.

Lopez: You brought him in time so that his fears could be
treated, the fantasies and the dreams.

Mother: M-hmm.

Lopez: And with your help, because your help was tremendous . . .

Mother: You think?

Lopez: For the boy . . .

Mother: You think?

Lopez: Certainly, I didn't do anything, you did everything.

Mother: Thank you.

Lopez: With your help and with the girls', well, Raoul could,
you know, get ahead with his dreams.

Mother: M-hmm.

Lopez: Now he doesn't get up screaming, nightmares or anything, and this he owes to you. Because, after all, you
did everything.

Mother: M-hmm. Everything that could be done. M-hmm.

[*Later in the interview.*]

Mother: And that's why I tell him he can be in baseball, he
            can be in music, he can do everything . . . study and
            everything, he can do a little of each thing.
Lopez: And Raoul, you?
Raoul: [*In English*] I want to be a scientist and a musician.
Lopez: You want to be a scientist and musician?
Raoul: [*In English*] A musician. And I want to be a singer,
            and I want to be an actor.
Lopez: And you want to be a singer and an actor?
Raoul: And I want to be in baseball . . . and I want to be . . .
Lopez: Oh, my God!
Mother: True.
Lopez: Well, you still have a lot of time to think about these
            things.
Mother: Sure.
[*Later in the interview.*]
Mother: I'll give you a dollar when you come home if you do
            it [*a flamenco dance*] well. Come on!
Raoul: Really?
Mother: By God! Well look, I have a few coins there, and we
            change them and I give you a dollar.
Raoul: [*In English*] You promise?
Mother: Sure!
Raoul: [*In English*] All right.
Lopez: Let's see, let's see.
[*Raoul dances flamenco.*]
Mother: There. See how he knows.
Lopez: Ah! Yes! [*Applauds.*] Very good! It's very nice. See
            all you can do.
Clara: He is always practicing it.
Lopez: Yes. Look, you have a family of performers!
[*Mother laughs.*]

Seventh Interview

This was the last interview. The mother, Clara, Maria, and
Raoul were present. Raoul had not had any symptoms. The
therapist talked first with the whole family and then stayed
alone with the mother.

Lopez: How long did you tell me that you have been living with your husband?

Mother: Like . . . I told you a year and a half, a year and eight months, see.

Lopez: Because I was thinking that you are a very responsible person and a very respectful person, and . . . you have achieved so much with your children, you know. There is such a great change. Maybe . . . you could also try, if you see that this man is the person that is right for you . . .

Mother: In part he is right for me, in part he is right for me.

Lopez: Since you have a son . . .

Mother: He . . . In other things he is very irresponsible also.

Lopez: Maybe you would like to try . . . maybe you would like to try to see if one can suggest any ideas, you know . . .

Mother: M-hmm.

Lopez: That one can try, to see if your situation can be straightened out . . .

Mother: I, eh . . . as for me, I have the best disposition to fight, see, my idea is to fight. Do you understand? I never . . . when I . . . I . . . and I think about breaking up, see? But I say while I can fight, I fight.

[*Later in the interview.*]

Lopez: Raoul looks very . . . quite changed, no?

Mother: Yes, the change is quite amazing.

Lopez: Yes, you have noticed the change a great deal?

Mother: Yes, for me it is an amazing change.

Lopez: M-hmm. What is the change that you have noticed?

Mother: He looks calmer, more sure of himself. He goes to bed calmly and he gets up peacefully, not like before that he had like that. He looks happier. Before he was always I don't know . . . and he went to bed with that fear, and he kept turning around from here to there before going to bed because he didn't want to be in his room alone and all those things.

Lopez: M-hmm.

Mother: He didn't sleep peacefully and all those things.

Lopez: And now he does.
Mother: M-hmm.
Lopez: And how do you feel?
Mother: Hm?
Lopez: How do you feel?
Mother: I feel quite grateful, see . . .
Lopez: M-hmm.
Mother: That you have taken that . . . have taken real interest, that you have worked with your heart, because here, if one looks around, I have noticed that here the Puerto Ricans are not interested in other Puerto Ricans, you understand? When they get certain jobs, well, they fall back and it's the same one thing as the other, see. [*She swallows with emotion.*] And all those things, I . . . I can appreciate them, see.

A follow-up, one year later, revealed that Raoul had not had symptoms again. He was still in the band and playing baseball. He had had several A's in his report card, and his mother bought him a bicycle, which was something that, during the course of the treatment, she had promised to do if he had good grades. The baby's father was still living with them. The mother seemed happier, and she was now working as a community aide in a local hospital.

The key elements of this therapy were the following:

1. Understanding the Problem
   The mother presented as a problem that the boy heard voices in the night. The son presented as a problem that he had nightmares, particularly a recurrent one about a witch who attacked him, and that he heard voices at night of women shouting. The mother was the only other family member who said she had bad dreams and was sometimes afraid. The boy's symptoms were seen as metaphorical of the mother's fears. When the boy was afraid, the mother reassured him and protected him while defining the problem as due to the devil's influence, which made the child even more helpless. The hypothesis was that the son was helpful to his

mother through his symptomatic behavior by eliciting competent, nurturing behavior from her. When helping her son, the mother was not afraid herself. She pulled herself together to reassure her child. However, the helpfulness of the son was expressed through behavior that was disturbing to the mother. The helpfulness of the mother was expressed in ways that were disturbing to the child. It was necessary to arrange that the mother help the child successfully and that the son help the mother feel like a competent parent in a different way.

2. The Interventions
   a. *Defining the Problem.* The therapist became interested in the issue of nightmares, ignoring the issue of hearing voices. She discussed with the family their dreams and had mother and son reenact one of the boy's nightmares. In this way, the problem was defined as one of nightmares—a problem much more within the range of normal behaviors than hearing voices.
   b. *Bringing the Problem into the Interview.* The reenactment of the nightmare brought the problem into the session, giving the therapist more control than if it had been only something that the family talked about.
   c. *Requesting That the Mother Pretend to Be Afraid and That the Son Pretend to Help Her.* The mother was asked to pretend to need the boy's help and protection, and the boy was told to help her. The child no longer needed to behave in symptomatic ways to protect the mother, since the mother was explicitly asking for help and the son was overtly helping her. But the mother's need for help was a pretense, and so was the child's helpfulness. In a pretend framework, mother and son were involved in a playful way. When the son was symptomatic, the mother was overtly in a superior position in relation to him; but, covertly, she was in an inferior position because *he* was helping her. Two incongruous hierarchies were simultaneously defined. With the pretend directive, one aspect of the incongruous hierarchy, the one in which the child

was in a superior position to the mother, was in play. It was make-believe, and the incongruity was resolved.

d. *Giving the Pretend Directive for the Home.* The family were instructed to repeat the dramatization at home every evening and to do it once more if the boy woke up screaming, even if they had to do it in the middle of the night. In this way, the boy's night terrors resulted in an ordeal for the whole family. In this way also, the mother was instructed to respond to the child's fears in a different way. The usual response was further blocked by the directive that the child could sleep only in his own bed.

3. The Obstacles

a. *The School Psychologist.* The school psychologist encouraged the boy's symptomatic behavior through her benevolent interest and concern. She was an outside expert who intervened, taking power away from the mother. Her intervention was blocked, and a clear hierarchy was established, with the therapist in charge of the case and the psychologist taking care of school issues. The boy, however, had responded to the psychologist's concern by talking about frightening people he was seeing when he closed his eyes. He was seen alone and was taught to voluntarily imagine he saw different things and to voluntarily change what he was seeing.

b. *The Mother's Boyfriend.* The man who was functioning as a stepfather in the home was asked to collaborate by becoming more involved with the child around activities that were appropriate for a boy his age. The attempt to engage the man was not successful.

4. The Reorganization
The relationship between mother and son was reorganized in a congruous hierarchy. Both became involved in activities that were appropriate to their age and situation. The mother was in a superior position to her child, not only because she helped him become involved in interesting things but also because she helped him overcome his problem.

CHAPTER EIGHT

✠ ✠ ✠ ✠ ✠

A Depressed Man:
A Case Study

This chapter consists of excerpts from a whole therapy, edited and with commentary. A summary of this case was presented in Chapter Three. The therapist was Richard Belson, training with "live" supervision by the author. The client was a 60-year-old accountant who was referred for marital therapy after previous therapy had failed. He had been diagnosed as a case of depression. His wife, a therapist, did not come to the first session of marital therapy.

In the first session, the man complained about his depression, saying that he was ineffectual, had neglected his business for many years, had let all his clients' work go, and had not paid his own taxes in five years. These complaints were made in an obnoxious, irritable manner. He also talked about his wife, who had recently become a therapist; his mother, whose taxes he failed to pay; and his two daughters, who were very concerned about him. One was expecting a baby, and the other would soon become a therapist herself and had long telephone conversations with her father, trying to help him to overcome his depression. It would have been possible and reasonable to formulate the problem and plan a strategy not only around the relationship between husband and wife but also including the mother and the two daughters, since all of them appeared to be supportive in similar ways and since obviously the man was very fond of all four women. The therapist and his supervisor decided, however, that it would be more practical and effective to intervene only in the marriage. Once the marital situation changed, they believed that there would also be positive changes in the other relationships.

In the first interview, the therapist redefined the problem. He told the man that he was depressed because he had been irresponsibly neglecting his work and defined him as a case of irresponsibility, not of depression. The problem was for him to become responsible once more. In the second interview, the wife was put in charge of seeing that the husband got his work done.

Third Interview

Belson:	What's happened since you were here?
Wife:	David finally, during the first week of the contract, did a number of client matters that he had contracted to do.
Belson:	Did you call him and check on him?
Wife:	I called him every day and checked up on him, and he was doing very fine.
Husband:	I'm not very happy with that.
Belson:	[*To wife*] Well, you did what you had agreed to do. He took care of his business?
Wife:	He certainly did.
Belson:	Very good.
Wife:	And then he got part of his mother's business organized during the first week and ran into a lot of problems; it took him much longer than he antici-

pated, so he couldn't get on the other business, which he did this past week, so he got this all out of the way. The work in relation to his mother's business is completely finished.

The wife had followed the therapist's directive and had called her husband at work every day, checking to see whether he was doing his work. The husband had been taking care of his business and had begun to catch up with the work he had neglected. By putting the wife in charge of the husband's work, the therapist was exaggerating her superior position. The expectation was that the husband would respond by taking charge of his work himself. In the past, the wife had commiserated with her husband and supported him in his depression. Now she was pushing him to do his work.

It was assumed that the husband's depression coincided with a change in the marital relationship. The wife had gone back to school after the children were grown and had become a therapist. The husband had had a dominant position during the early years of the marriage, but as the wife became more and more interested in her new career he developed more and more difficulties. The greater his difficulties, the more competent the wife appeared and the more focused she was on his helplessness and his problems. He became "depressed," a problem within her area of expertise as a therapist. The husband's depression was both a source of weakness and of power to him: weakness in that the wife had to support him and advise him, power in that she failed to help him no matter how she tried. The marital hierarchy was incongruous in that husband and wife were both simultaneously powerful and weak in relation to each other. By exaggerating paradoxically the superior position of the wife, the therapist provoked the couple to reorganize in the direction of more equality.

Wife: [*To husband*] There were several days there where you started your same old shit about, you know, I'll do it, I'll get around to it, I can't get around to

	it—the same exact phraseology that you've used in the past.
Belson:	You mean irresponsibility?
Wife:	Right, and so I said, "Look, let's not get back on to that old thing. I wanted to know a list of every single responsibility that you have to clients by the fifteenth of the month, and I'm going to call you every day and all this." He promised to bring a list home. He did not bring it home.
Husband:	I did bring it home, I left it in my pocket.
Wife:	At this point I said, "You better make sure that you have the list with you this morning for the session, so we don't have to waste the whole hour coming up with what your irresponsibilities are."
Belson:	[*To wife*] We have to talk about when you're going to get to work on your own financial affairs.

The therapist threatened that the wife should file the tax returns herself. This had already been mentioned in the previous interview, to the great displeasure of the husband.

Wife:	Well, I could start on it right away, but he wouldn't allow me to do anything about it. He says it's going to cost too much money.
Belson:	I know, but what we're doing is we're making a breakthrough and we're knocking aside the impasse.
Wife:	I would say so.
Belson:	I thought that what you did was really good, would you agree? [*No answer.*] You don't have to agree.

[*Wife and Husband laugh.*]

The playful, confusional style of the therapist counteracted the obsessive, depressed style of the husband.

Belson:	The fact is that it's being done and that's what's important. Did you thank her, did you thank her for her help, incidentally?

Husband: No, I . . .
Wife: [*Laughing*] For being a bitch?
Husband: I resent it.
Wife: First, he resented it. I felt like a mommy. I felt like a mommy, having to say: "Did you do your homework?"
Belson: I don't think of it that way. I think of it as a couple helping each other.

It is important for the therapist to emphasize the benevolent aspect of the wife's intrusion in the husband's work, since the goal is not for the husband to resentfully quarrel with his wife. The goal is for him to do his work.

[*Later in the interview.*]
Belson: Look, let's just look at the facts. The fact is [*turning to wife*] that you did take care of him during that week, and the other fact is [*to husband*] that if you would become more responsible, that she wouldn't have to do this. So this is only a temporary thing till you get back on track. Obviously, what you need is for her to do this. So I just want you to understand that this is only temporary.
Husband: I'm well aware of it, but I don't really think that it's getting to the heart of the issue.
Belson: Right, the heart of the issue is: when you start taking care of it, it'll be done.
Husband: Well, I know, but Rome wasn't built in a day, and I can't take three or four or five years of neglect and correct them in one week.
Belson: It's amazing how it can be done.
Husband: Well, I can't do it.
Wife: We have corrected a tremendous amount of it in one week.
Husband: Well, all right, but I can't do it all.
Belson: By the way, it may be from what you're saying that you hate to take credit for what you did.
Wife: That's for sure. He did a tremendous amount.

Husband: Well, I don't feel like taking credit for what I did, because in the first place I didn't do it a long time ago, and I'm only doing what I should have done.

Belson: In that case you shouldn't take credit. In that case don't take credit and just do it.

The therapist skillfully turned the object of the man's oppositionistic arguments away from whether he would do the work to whether he was willing to take credit for doing it.

Husband: Well, that's what I'm trying to do.

Belson: Because maybe you're the kind of person who doesn't want to take credit for what he did, and in that case you shouldn't.

Husband: I want to just do it.

Belson: Right.

Husband: Right. I'm delighted that I got rid of it.

Belson: [*To wife*] Don't give him the credit.

Husband: I didn't do it the way I wanted to do it.

Belson: Yeah.

Husband: But I did it. I got it out of my mind and I'll settle for that.

Belson: Good enough. So what has to be done now?

[*Later in the interview.*]

Belson: [*To wife*] I'm wondering whether you should file the tax returns yourself even if it's costly, just as a lesson for the future.

Husband: They'll put me in jail too.

Belson: Otherwise, we'll be on the same road again. I think that you should keep after him and call him at regular intervals. What are the intervals that you found to be working?

Wife: Once a day, and I call every evening.

Belson: [*To wife*] How many days, at what point will you do the tax returns yourself? I think that you should take the loss, because that would freshen things up for the future.

Wife: I think that as long as David keeps on progressing,

> every day doing a little bit, or at least putting out a certain amount of time a couple of days a week toward this end, then we will be able to see that we can get the thing done.

The couple were beginning to reorganize, with the husband behaving more competently. The therapist continued to put the wife in charge of scheduling the husband's activities, while the husband protested that he was doing his work and would continue to do it. It was time to begin to encourage the couple to reorganize in a congruous hierarchy, with more equality between the spouses. Since the therapist had previously put down the husband by calling him irresponsible, he now shifted to the wife and accused her of being neglectful. He made this sound like a serious offense by apologizing for insulting her. The husband then talked about his loneliness and the change in their relationship since the wife became involved in her career.

[*Later in the interview.*]

Belson: The whole idea is that he should become responsible and this will move him in that direction. And once that happens, that will become self-perpetuating because in his heart he likes it better that way. I'd like to move on to something else. I'd like to say something, and it's not a pleasant thing to put in the way that I'm going to put it. So, will you be able to take it when I say it? Yes? [*Looks at husband.*]

Husband: Yeah.

Belson: I think that she's been neglectful to you. And I . . . [*to wife*] I don't mean to be insulting.

Wife: That's OK.

Husband: You mean neglecting me?

Belson: Yes.

Husband: Neglectful to me, what's that mean?

Belson: The same thing.

Husband: Neglecting me . . .

Belson: Yes, and I think what happens is because you're both highly accomplished people that often it happens in such a relationship that the people don't give each other the amount of time that they need in a more social way. So [*to wife*] I think that you should spend at least two evenings with him socially.

[*Later in the interview.*]

Belson: In some way, I sense that she's not involved enough in your life.

Husband: Well, she isn't involved in the things that she used to be. But that was only because I told her about what was going on with me more than I do now. But now she has her own business.

Belson: I want some sort of detail. Could you just fill that in a little bit?

Husband: Well, I used to have the habit for many, many years, of coming home and spilling my guts out in terms of what was going on at my office. Whatever it was, what was not happening or was happening, and she listened. I wondered whether she comprehended or not; I felt she did. I thought she was rather sympathetic, and it just helped to spill it out. But it was—I realize it could have been very boring to her because a lot of the stuff she didn't understand. I would get very excited about something technical and try to explain it to her. Then she became a psychotherapist in the last four or five years and developed a lot of her own interests, and her work seemed to be infinitely more interesting in a humanistic kind of way, you know, than my work, which is highly dry and technical, and consequently I don't talk about my work to the same extent. I'm also a little ashamed of complaining about things that are happening constantly. I refer back to some letters. For example, I was reading some letters to my sister that I wrote about two years ago. And they're the same thoughts that I'm feeling now—I'm harried, I can't get the stuff out, apologizing for being late—and I just haven't changed and it's getting worse, not better. And so I don't discuss cases or matters with her except when it is something very fascinating and interesting, out of line, out of the way. And I'm very interested in what she's doing. But she doesn't discuss too much about it with me. She feels it's a breech of confidentiality, I think, to discuss therapy cases, which is OK.

[*Later in the interview.*]

Husband: In other words, I don't see that any of this is negative. Obviously, she's not as closely intertwined in my life as I would . . .

Belson: As you would what? She's not as closely intertwined in my life as I would what?

Husband: I was going to say as I would like her to be, but I'm not sure if I would like her to be.

Belson: Well, I think we should try it.

Husband: Because on an intellectual basis, I enjoy the fact that she's got her own sphere of interest—her jobs, her work, her practice.

Belson: Absolutely.

Husband: Her friends. It's great. I haven't been—been able to fill that void.

Belson: Fill what void?

Husband: The void of not having her highly involved in my own affairs.

Belson: Absolutely.

Husband: The farm, for example, that we bought several years ago. A schoolhouse with a farm acreage that we have been involved in furnishing and getting up there almost every weekend, at the cost of our social life here in New York. She's got less involved in that.

Belson: M-hmm.

Husband: She just doesn't seem to have any interest in doing much about it.

Belson: M-hmm.

Husband: Unless I push her to something.

The husband's description of the change in the marital relationship since the wife became involved in her career confirmed the assumption on which the therapy strategy was based. In the past, husband and wife had shared an interest in the husband's work, in their social life, and in their farm. Then the wife had developed new interests, new friends, and a life that was separate from her husband's. The husband became depressed, and his depression gave him an entry into the wife's new interests as a therapist. He derived power from the symptomatic behavior and kept his wife attached to him. The therapist then began to bring the couple together in a different way, directing them to spend time talking to each other.

Belson: I'd like to make this recommendation for the next week. I understand you're busy, and so on and so forth, but I want you both to set aside a time and spend half an hour each night. You don't have to do it mechanically, but [*to husband*] you should use your half an hour to talk to her, not in a complaining way, just to talk about what your work is like. [*Turning to wife*] I want you to use up your time discussing your cases with him. OK. Let's decide on what time that will be done.

Husband: Well, that's impossible.

Belson: Half an hour is not impossible. In fact, it will give you both a new burst of energy because it will fill up an energy void. It's very necessary.

Husband and wife presented various objections, but the therapist insisted. The couple's difficulty in finding a half an hour that they could spend together was indicative of how distant they were from each other.

Belson: I know that you're a little bit reluctant to make this demand on her, but I think that we should go ahead with this.

Wife: Well, I would say I could do it at ten thirty.

Belson: All right, let's begin; tonight is Tuesday? OK, what time tonight?

Wife: Either ten thirty or eleven.

Belson: Ten thirty or eleven?

[*Later in the interview.*]

Belson: He's afraid to make this demand.

Husband: I am.

Belson: 'Cause he wants to be nice about it.

Husband: No, I'm not being nice about it. I don't see the use, I don't see the utility of it.

Belson: Well, it does, anyway.

Husband: You know, I'm subjecting myself to a lot of crazy . . . I think they're nuts, these suggestions. I don't think they go to the heart of the issue.

Belson: They are crazy.

Husband: They sure are.

Wife: Well, what is the heart of the issue?

Husband: Well, the heart of the issue is my inability to organize my time.

Belson: I don't want to discuss the heart; I just want to discuss the . . .

Wife: [*Laughing*] The lungs.

Belson: The lungs? I want to discuss the *mouth,* when you're both going to speak. OK?

Wife: OK.

Belson: We'll get to the heart later.

Wife: All right.

Belson: OK. What time on Wednesday?

Wife: Eleven o'clock.

Husband: Eleven o'clock each time.

Belson: That's being organized.

Husband: That's the way the English live. On Monday I go to my club, on Wednesday I go to my club, and Tuesday I have an appointment, and Thursday and Friday we have intercourse.

[*Wife and Belson laugh.*]

Wife: OK. So.

Belson: Do you have sexual relations?

Husband:	Occasionally.
Belson:	What's occasionally mean?
Husband:	Once every couple of weeks.
Wife:	You're kidding.

[*Husband laughs.*]

Wife:	Stop being so funny.
Belson:	There seems to be some disagreement.

[*Pause.*]

Wife:	You say once every couple of weeks.
Husband:	OK, once a week.
Wife:	Twice a week.
Husband:	Twice a week?
Wife:	Yeah.
Husband:	In your mind it's twice a week?
Wife:	In my mind? What about my calendar?
Husband:	Do you write it on it?
Wife:	No, but I would say, it doesn't feel like it to you?
Husband:	Approximately. I guess it hasn't been that bad.
Belson:	What is it? It's not enough for you, or the sex is not exciting enough?
Husband:	I guess it's a little bit of both.

[*Later in the interview.*]

Husband:	I have constantly complained about the fact that I don't seem to turn her on. I have to work at it, although there has been some improvement in the past. I don't find her being aggressive, with some exception in the recent past. If I'll initiate the sexual foreplay, either before we get into bed or after we get into bed, she seems to be satisfied, and she is aggressive sometimes.
Wife:	Sometimes. [*Laughs.*]
Husband:	And you are aggressive sometimes, like last night; I thought you were indicating a little bit of aggressiveness. And I wasn't particularly interested for one reason or another.
Wife:	Yeah.
Husband:	You give up.
Wife:	So what's wrong with that?

Husband: When I feel aggressive, I never give up.
Wife: That's your style.
[*Later in the interview.*]
Husband: Yeah, I've been arousing her for thirty years. [*Wife laughs.*]
Belson: [*To wife*] This is how you've been, excuse me for saying, neglectful. Could you write down next on your orders . . . [*Belson is referring to the list that the spouses keep of things they are to do in relation to the therapy.*]
Husband: I'm tired of having to play the game of arousing her all the time.
Belson: That's true, that's really very old fashioned.
Wife: It is.
Belson: No matter what he's doing, I want one time during this week, whether or not he's working or reading his novel, I'd like you to make sure that you bring him to a strong climax even if he fights you off. Once during the coming week.
[*Husband laughs.*]
Wife: I'm going to write down: persistent.
Belson: Persistent; in other words, even if he runs around the room away from you, you must knock him down.
Wife: He wouldn't do that. He wouldn't protest that much.
Belson: Well, he might, as a way of trying to fight you off. But I think that that's been a question of neglect [*to husband*] in terms of your sexual needs, which I think that you're absolutely entitled to.
Husband: No doubt about that, but should I try to find out what she wants?
Belson: It's up to you. I think that it's really been sort of one sided, frankly, and that I would say that you don't have to do anything in regards to her; you know, you're doing enough. This should be her job.
Wife: I agree.
Belson: OK.

[*Later in the interview.*]

Belson: In regard to a number of things she has been ne-
             glectful. But you have allowed her to be neglectful.
             In other words, even in regards to sex, because you
             take so much upon yourself, you don't give her a
             chance to do the things that she's supposed to do.
             So you have to give her a chance.

Husband: It hasn't appeared to me that way. I don't think
             that . . .

Belson: Yes, you, in some way, you've encouraged her to be
             neglectful, and now it's time for her to take charge
             a little bit more of the things that are more impor-
             tant. In any case, let's just go ahead and let her take
             care of the sex this time. At least once, all right?

Husband: Be my guest. [*Laughs.*]

A more egalitarian division of power between the spouses
was encouraged by this redefinition of the husband as responsible and protective and the wife as neglectful in relation to sex,
and by the directive to the wife to initiate sex once during the
next week. Ostensibly, the wife would be in a superior position
because she would be the pursuer; yet being pursued would
make the husband feel wanted and important. The routine of
the couple's sex life would be changed, and they would come
closer together in a new way. The husband reported on the
wife's efforts in the next interview. The wife did not come to
this session because she had an unexpected business appointment.

Fourth Interview

Belson: What about her pursuing you sexually; what did she
             do on that?

Husband: Ah, she did reasonably well, very well.

Belson: What did she do?

Husband: Well, the last time, we've had sex a couple of times,
             she's been very aggressive.

Belson: Did she pursue you to the finish?

Husband: Yes, yes, I think she showed quite a lot of aggres-
            sion, that I wasn't quite used to.
Belson: M-hmm.
Husband: And it was enjoyable, as far as I was concerned.
[*Later in the interview.*]
Belson: Do you mind if I say something that will sound a
            little bit critical?
Husband: No.
Belson: I think that you're too forgiving of her.
Husband: Well, OK, I . . . I . . . What other course do I have?
            In other words, you know, what other choice? I
            have to forgive her and to be forgiving to have an
            enjoyable life.
Belson: I think last week you took a different stand. And
            you put her, it sounds too strong, a little more in
            her place, sexually, by demanding what you have
            coming to you.
[*Later in the interview.*]
Husband: Well, I'm beginning to get the value of the nature of
            this therapy or whatever you call it. You're coming
            up with some things . . .
Belson: Well, I think what's happening is that you're com-
            ing to your senses . . .

The therapist pushed the husband to overtly demand
more of his wife rather than covertly requesting her involvement, as he had been doing in the past by being depressed.

Fifth Interview

The wife reported in this session that the husband was
doing much better in his work; he had been cheerful and had
even made an important contribution to his field. The husband
minimized this and complained that things were the same as before. The therapist said that clearly there was a misunderstanding between them and they needed a new way of verifying communication. The husband was told that three times during the
next week he should pretend to be irresponsible and inade-

quate, and the wife was to try to find out whether or not he was really feeling that way. The husband complained that it was a silly thing to do but finally agreed to do it. In this way, the therapist arranged that if the husband appeared to be irresponsible and inadequate, the wife would not know whether he was really feeling that way or whether he was following the therapist's directives. Therefore, she would not respond in her usual ways.

Sixth Interview

Wife: He didn't complain at all last week, as far as I can remember.

Belson: You mean the whole week?

Wife: That's right. Not even three times out of six. [*Laughs.*]

Husband: Well, I've reached the point, frankly, that I have sort of an inner realization that nobody can do it for me. I just got to work, work, work, pay the price, until I get the goddamn thing done. I mean, all the therapy in the world isn't going to help, I just got to do it. I was up till twelve working in the office, till twelve, twelve thirty last night.

Belson: You mean the whole week, he didn't complain about not taking care of his business and being upset and all that kind of stuff?

[*Wife shakes her head negatively.*]
[*Pause.*]

Belson: I'm sort of disappointed with that. I have to speak with them. [*Belson stands up and leaves the room to consult with the supervisor behind the one-way mirror.*]

[*Husband and wife laugh.*]

Wife: [*To husband*] He's disappointed. It's not working out the way he wants.

The therapist was pretending to be disappointed because the husband had not followed his directive to pretend. In fact, he was pleased because the goals of the therapy were being accomplished. The husband had not complained or been upset, and he had worked very hard. The husband also said that now he had this "inner realization" that he had to do his work. The directive to pretend to have the symptomatic behavior is often followed with some kind of insight about what "really" has to be done. In this case, what really had to be done was the work. It would have been premature for the therapist at this time to be pleased and not to pursue the directive to pretend any further.

The therapist consulted with the supervisor behind the one-way mirror. The supervisor suggested that, since the husband had not pretended to feel irresponsible and inadequate during the week, he should practice pretending to be irresponsible and inadequate right there in the session. The therapist was then to criticize the husband for his performance and encourage the wife to criticize him, saying that he was not very believable as an irresponsible and inadequate person. The usual interaction between husband and wife had been for the husband to complain about his problems and the wife to offer support and reassurance. Now the husband would be pretending to complain, and the wife would be criticizing him for not pretending realistically. Implicit in the interaction would be the fact that the husband could not present himself as irresponsible and inadequate because he was not irresponsible and inadequate.

Belson: What has he been doing as far as taking care of his business? Has he been taking care of it?
Wife: He's done considerably. He's finished now all the coding and filing as of last night. He got in by twelve o'clock last night. He's doing this XYZ work at night, so he's getting at least that one—one more very big thing out of the way now.
Belson: In other words, he's finally becoming more responsible in terms of his being a professional? He is?
Wife: Ah, I guess you could say that. [Laughs.]
Belson: I felt that what you didn't do was really a lapse, that you were supposed to have done that for three

times. [*Belson is referring to the directive to pretend.*]

Wife: What for three times?

Belson: That you were supposed to have . . . that you didn't know.

Wife: Oh! M-hmmm.

Belson: I'd like to do something—I know that you people are a little bit playful, so I can do this with you.

Husband: That we are playful?

[*Wife laughs.*]

Belson: Yes, you are. I had misread you; I thought you were always serious, but I see that you both have a sense of humor. So I'm going to ask you to do this right here in the office; I want you to do it.

[*Husband laughs.*]

Belson: I'd like you to speak to her. I'd like you to do it in a way that you didn't do last week. You obviously weren't convincing enough because—what you were supposed to have done was to be convincing enough during those three times that she wouldn't know whether or not you *really* were taking care of your business, not taking care of your business, being upset, not being upset. You were supposed to—I'd like you now, just for a few minutes, to tell her about your office, and your work, as *though* you're upset but you're really not. But be convincing.

Husband: Tell her I'm upset.

Belson: Yeah, but I want you to be convincing.

Husband: Well. [*Pause.*] I'm really disgusted with my choice of a secretary because for the money that I decided to pay—and I payed her on the basis that she was intelligent and could learn—I think I could have gotten somebody who already had experience and I didn't have to train. I'm rather angry at myself for doing that, for wanting to train somebody. She's completely inexperienced with legal and financial matters . . .

Belson: No, no. It has to be something that might be true

	but it might not be true, but you have to come across as though it's true. She knows already that what you're saying about the secretary is true and you know it's true. Do you see what I'm saying?
Husband:	Well, I've got so many things that are true that I've many things to complain about.
Belson:	Let's talk about something that may be true or may not be true, so she won't know.
Wife:	Well, I'm not going to believe it anyway because of the instructions. I do know that he's fabricating.
Husband:	What do you know that I'm fabricating?
Wife:	You're fabricating your upset.
Husband:	That's right. 'Cause I'm not that upset; I'm really not that upset.

The statement "I'm really not that upset" from the husband is the kind of statement that the directive to pretend to have the symptom is aimed to elicit.

Wife:	This is supposed to be—he *doesn't* feel that way, but he's fabricating it to make it *look* like he does feel it.
Belson:	Yes, that's right. Yes. So that when he talks about it during the week, you're never quite sure does he really mean it that much or not.
Husband:	I find that impossible. I . . . I . . . I just find it impossible.
Belson:	Now you see, you just smiled, which means to me that you can do it.
Husband:	Yeah, but I don't know what the hell to do.
Belson:	Let's try it on for size, and we'll see.
Husband:	Try what on for size? Try what? I don't even know how to get started.
Belson:	That's because I want you to start and see. I want you to talk about how disgusted you are with yourself for not doing this and that. You know.
Husband:	Well, I . . . but the point is that you know I . . . I . . .

Belson: Remember that you might be disgusted, but I want
             you to just to pretend.
Husband: OK.
Belson: Because in your heart you're not. That's what I
             mean.
Husband: In my head I may be, but in my heart I'm not.
Belson: Right.
Husband: That's what you're talking about.
Belson: That's right.

The plan was to have the husband try at least four times
to appear inadequate and irresponsible while the wife and the
therapist criticized his performance. Only then would the therapist stop insisting that he continue to pretend.

Husband: Sunday we went to that brunch and I got back feel-
             ing, legitimately feeling, very heavy and a little
             tipsy because of the champagne that we had; I was
             scheduled to go to the office and work, and it was
             very lovely outside and there was a lot of work to
             be done in the garden and I thought, "Well, I'll do
             it for an hour, then I—then I will get dressed and go
             to the office." After an hour's work I made very
             little progress; things were in a shambles . . .
Belson: Use the words *inadequate* and *irresponsible.*
Husband: I was . . . that that pyorrhea bush or whatever you
             call it . . .
Wife: My [*laughs*] pyorrhea [*points to her mouth*].
Husband: That berry bush, I've forgotten the name.
Wife: Pyracantha.
Husband: Pyracantha . . . was tremendous and I cut it down;
             it was overloading the air conditioner. I thought,
             "Oh shit, I've got to get rid of this because if we
             have to use the air conditioning, we're not going to
             be able to use it, I'm afraid." And it was a tremen-
             dous task. So I'm looking at my watch and almost
             an hour has gone by and I'm feeling: "Goddamn,
             I'm irresponsible. I'm worrying about the pyra-

cantha when I could just rip it aside, leave it there, and go to the office like I promised and get it done. But it's so nice out, and I deserve to work in the garden, because it's beautiful and I enjoy doing it and I need my exercise. Oh, the hell with the office."

Belson: You're not coming across as irresponsible enough. It wouldn't be convincing.

Husband: Well, I'm never completely irresponsible because when I don't do something I'm supposed to do, I'm doing something else. I always . . .

Again, this is the kind of statement that the therapist is after.

Belson: But you're not convincing her how irresponsible you were.

Husband: She knows because she came home at five o'clock.

Belson: She's going to read you again next week like . . .

Husband: She came home at five o'clock and she was very angry that I was home, I wasn't at the office.

Belson: Go back and tell her the story, and you have to be more irresponsible. Otherwise, she won't believe you. I'm sounding like I'm critical; I just want you to do a good job, that's all.

Husband: I don't know what else to do. I . . . this is . . . I'm telling . . . I'm not fabricating. I'm telling with my head what was going on. The way I was feeling. And it's not a fabrication. And I don't know how to fabricate these things. I am incapable of fabricating.

Belson: You're as capable of acting a few times in your life as anybody else. [*To wife*] I don't care if he never acts again in his life. I just want him just to be able to do this properly, so that it will be effective in the coming week. Is there anything that you could suggest so that he could be more effective?

Wife: Just keep on thinking about how inadequate you've felt. And tell me about how inadequate you've felt.

This is the kind of statement from the wife that the therapist is after. She is asking her husband to think and to talk about feeling inadequate instead of reassuring him that he is not inadequate.

Belson: Could you give him an example of that? Because he seems to be puzzled.

Wife: I don't know. Thinking about all the piles in the office.

Husband: That's the whole story.

Wife: Well, while you were doing the pyracantha, were you thinking about all those horrible piles in the office?

Husband: Well, sure I was. But I was also thinking of the pyracantha, and I was thinking who the hell will I get to do this. No wonder this guy wanted a hundred and fifty bucks to clean up the yard. You know, it's a lot of work. One lousy bush and a few other trees, it was a four-hour job.

Wife: So concentrate on the part of you that was feeling . . .

Husband: Yeah, but that's not a fabrication; that's my point.

Wife: Well, then I don't know what he wants you to do.

Husband: He wants me to make believe that I'm disgusted and feeling inadequate, when I'm not, when I'm feeling on top of the world. It's very difficult for me to do that. That's my point.

Wife: So you're actually feeling that way?

At this point, the wife seemed to realize what the point of this exercise might be. She was surprised that her husband, instead of feeling "disgusted and inadequate," was feeling "on top of the world." Implicit in the criticism by the therapist and the wife was the fact that the husband was not very believable as an irresponsible and inadequate person. The wife was now behaving in unusual ways. Instead of supporting and reassuring her husband, she was criticizing him for not pretending realistically to be irresponsible and inadequate. The husband then made a third attempt.

Husband: Sunday night, we were in that sexuality course. And after, I looked around, after we left or—afterward, we went to the wine and cheese thing. I was really interested in meeting some of these women. I couldn't seem to latch on to some pretty women and I was feeling kind of dumpy and old. I had a very lovely-looking blond . . .

Belson: No, no. You're smiling. It's not a good job.

[*Husband laughs.*]

Belson: No, no. We have found a good example. In your heart you know that it's not true, but I want you to put on the long face and convince her how women are not interested in you; you must be getting old. We've found a beautiful example.

Husband: Now, I talked with some relatively young women. There was a blonde particularly, I engaged in conversation, and I thought how interesting it would be to go to bed with her, but she didn't have any eyes for me. She just kept looking around for somebody else . . .

Belson: Did you find this convincing?

Wife: [*Laughing*] The edges of his mouth are curved up. They're not down, they're up.

The wife was now even more critical of the husband instead of supporting him. Pretending to be inadequate around work and sex was relevant to the issues that had been discussed previously in the therapy. The more the husband attempted unsuccessfully to pretend to be inadequate around these areas, the more adequate he would be.

Belson: You're not doing a good job.

Husband: Well, I'm laughing, not because of a sense of humor, I'm laughing at myself. I mean, it's the situation that I'm laughing at. The situation right here. But as a practical matter . . .

Belson: What do you mean the situation right here? This is serious business.

Husband: I know it's serious, but it just seems peculiar to me in the sense that I don't understand it, and I'm playing along with sort of a lead to say that it means something but I don't know what.

Belson: [*To wife*] Could you now get him started again with this thing about the women?

Wife: [*Laughing*] Tell me about the woman that was so nice, that blond.

Husband: Well, she wasn't around very often, since that other gal that you saw me with was sticking around and she was seemingly interested in sticking around but I wasn't that interested, but I didn't know how to get out of it. When you came around, I introduced you, so she realized that I wasn't single. So she, the first opportunity she got, she moved away.

Belson: [*To wife*] You do not believe him.

Wife: It's not . . .

Belson: [*To husband*] You're not believable in terms of how inadequate you are with women. It's not believable.

Wife: It says you didn't like her, you didn't think she was that good, and you wanted to get rid of her.

The wife continued her criticism of the husband, who tried once again.

Husband: You were out of the room . . . I was talking to a young lady who's a client. She introduced me to a very lovely young thing who was a teacher of sexuality. And while she was nice and everything, I could see that she looked upon me as an older man. And with no interest beyond a civility there. I was feeling like I lost it, like I don't have any attractiveness to younger women any more.

Belson: Did you find this convincing?

Wife: Well, not really.

Belson: It was better, but not good enough.

Wife: It was better, though, it wasn't as . . .

Belson:	It was definitely better. I must tell you, you're working hard at this, but this was better.
Husband:	It really is? This part?
Belson:	This was almost convincing, almost. But he can't seem quite to do it.
Wife:	Your voice wasn't flat enough, and your mouth was all curved up.

The goal has been achieved. The wife criticized the husband for not appearing properly depressed instead of supporting him in his depression. The husband failed repeatedly at appearing depressed and inadequate. Next the therapist inquired about other directives and found that the wife had pursued the husband sexually.

Belson:	Have you spent a half hour the way you were supposed to do?
Wife:	Yeah, we've done it, most of the time we've done it.
Belson:	And what about the sex? Did she take care of her aggressive sex?
Husband:	Very well.
Belson:	How many times a week?
Husband:	Well, this week it's only been once.
Wife:	What? [*Laughs.*] Twice.
Husband:	Twice? Oh, yeah.
Wife:	He forgets once, he just . . .
Husband:	Yeah, yeah.
[*Wife laughs.*]	
Belson:	You know, there is something that—in the course of all our heavy discussion—you know, you people are very fond of each other. Were you aware of that?
Husband:	In the course of what?
Belson:	I am sometimes so much into all the heavy discussion that I forget that you people are very obviously fond of each other.
Husband:	Yes. I don't know very well what "fond" means, but . . .

Belson: You seem to have an ability to enjoy each other in a very profound kind of a way.

Husband: Yes, I'm, I'm . . .

Belson: I was just—I usually don't remark on what people do, but I decided to do that.

Husband: Once this week I said . . .

Belson: What did you say?

Husband: I even said to Rachel once this week—I don't remember what the occasion was—how much I enjoyed her company as a friend, not only as a wife and a lover but as a friend. It felt good to have her around to share things with her, you know.

Wife: Which I appreciate very much.

Belson: I suspected all along that she fulfilled a great need for you. That's why when I said at the beginning that you [*to wife*] were negligent, that wasn't really criticism as much as how much he needed you to be there. Let me ask you this again; I just want to make sure. My impression was, I might be wrong, is that he's becoming more responsible and finally realizing that he can do it without the therapy. That was my impression. That he's taking care of it. Is this correct?

Wife: It seems to be. He seems to be doing what he's supposed to do.

Belson: That he realizes that therapy is just a waste of his time, and he could probably take care of it himself. Did I hear him correctly?

Wife: That's what I heard him say. Yes.

Husband: As a matter of fact, I was seriously thinking, and more than once it came up in my mind that what the hell am I wasting time here for.

Belson: M-hmm.

Husband: It doesn't help get the work done.

Belson: Well, I think that he finally has spoken a true word, and I think that we should hold him to that, and I suggest that we not have a session next week and that we meet in two weeks.

Husband and wife have expressed clearly that they are happier together and the husband is doing his work. The therapist began to disengage the couple from therapy. If the husband is to sustain a more egalitarian position in relation to his wife, he cannot be defined as a patient who needs therapy.

Belson: I think that you should have the sex three times a week instead of twice a week.

Husband: Oh, come on now, will you; I don't have the strength.

Belson: It's not up to you; it's up to her.

Husband: Oh.

Wife: I don't know if I have the strength.

Belson: Well . . .

Wife: We'll try. We'll see what we can do.

Belson: On the sex, I can be very, very clear. The more you have sex, the more you want it. Three times a week is very important for your physical health. [*Husband and wife laugh.*] And also [*to wife*] I'd like you to take the aggressive stance again.

Husband: I want you to . . .

Belson: I don't want to hear complaints about not enough sex.

Husband: I'm not complaining about not enough sex.

Belson: I'd like it to be three times a minimum. And I'd like you again to take the aggressive stance because that apparently is a turn-on for both. Number three, the half-an-hour conversation about sharing, that's very important. Now the fourth thing, everything is crucial, crucial, I mean there should be a double asterisk around everything. But because you didn't do it last time and because I'm not going to see you for two weeks, it's like super important, ultimately important, crucially important, whatever words you like. It has to be three times each week, and this is what's important: that you complain about your inadequacy and your irresponsibility. But she will not . . .

Husband: This is the point when I'm reaching a point where I'm not feeling inadequate and irresponsible, you want me to complain about it; I don't understand.

Belson: But there will be three times that you'll do it; but she will not know if you are or you are not. Now there could be other times that you really are; but in that nest of time, there have to be three birds that she will not know. But you have to do it the way that you were doing it here when we finally finished. Do a terrific job that she won't know; but you'll know, but she won't know. There is one more thing, unfortunately, that I was so business-like that I forgot. I mean, I was brought up to have a legal mind, as it happens, so sometimes . . .

Husband: Were you trained as a lawyer?

Belson: I was trained as something similar that had a lot of law in connection with it. So I tend to be a little more reasonable. But he . . . But I have found out something. Sometimes I'm so antipsychological that I overlook obvious things. [*To wife*] He happens to be somewhat poetic, and I picked that up in connection with his description about the gardening. What I'd like you to do is, I'd like you on the time next week that you would be here, that you would pick out a place that he would find romantic and have lunch instead of coming here. OK?

Wife: Neat. Fantastic.

Belson: Right, but it should be something that he won't have his instincts disappointed, in regard to the mood.

Wife: That's very nice.

Belson: I owe you a small apology in terms of underestimating you in this regard.

Husband: [*Laughing*] What's so poetic about the garden?

Belson: Well, there are a few other things. You also have a lot of sensitivity towards other things. And it's not just a put on, just to give you an idle compliment because it's not important because I won't be seeing

you very much more. But I think what I had under-
estimated is—because when people come in, sometimes, and they talk a lot about, you know, their
problems and such, sometimes you overlook certain
parts of their personality that tend to get . . .

Wife: Right.

Belson: So, you know what I mean.

Husband: I don't know what you mean.

Belson: Oh, I think you do.

Husband: I don't.

Belson: I don't want to end on such a serious note, but I
think, I guess I feel that—I guess it was a lack in me.
And I really do feel bad about it.

Wife: [*Laughing*] You look it.

Belson: No, I really do.

[*Wife laughs.*]

Husband: I don't know what the hell you're talking about.

Belson: Well, some of the women that are in the group here,
they pointed out what a nice couple you were. And
I was just thinking that you were just a bunch of
complainers.

Husband: Oh, really.

Belson: That's right.

Husband: I just wanted to, since we're throwing bouquets, I
wanted to say—last night I said to Rachel, "If nothing comes out of it, at least a nice improvement in our
sex lives is coming out of this." Rachel was extremely aggressive last night. I was ready to go to
bed; it was one o'clock in the morning, and she was
nudging me at one o'clock in the morning. It was
great. [*Laughs.*]

Belson: You just have to be careful not to discourage her.
That's important.

Husband: No, I don't think she'll be discouraged. I think she
herself finds out how good it is, to be aggressive.

Wife: Yeah, it's fun.

The suggestion that the couple should have lunch together instead of coming to the next session was a further step toward disengagement before termination. The couple came to the final session and reported improvement. They brought their white poodle.

Seventh Interview

Belson: How did you do on the things that we asked you to do, I believe it was a half a month ago.

Husband: Last night for the first time I really sat down and got the stuff together, analyzed it, and then developed at least a year's work, and the rest will come relatively easy.

Belson: I think that you should be congratulated.

Husband: Yes.

Belson: [*To husband*] I mean you should be congratulated.

Husband: She should be congratulated.

Belson: [*To husband*] You should be congratulated.

Husband: Both of us should be congratulated.

Belson: No, no. I don't know, I don't know if the dog is some omen of some sort, that you brought the dog in today.

Wife: [*Laughing*] We didn't bring her; she came herself.

Belson: The dog wanted to join the session to congratulate you also, but I think that that's really terrific.

Husband: Well, I feel it was a breakthrough last night. There's no question. If she hadn't said, "Don't come home until you finish at least a year and even if it's till one o'clock." I think I would have quit at ten thirty because I would have said I was too tired, I deserve to go home, but I stayed till twelve and I got it done.

Belson: M-hmm.

Husband: At least to the point where I knew where I could finish it up.

Belson: Well, that's really terrific.

Husband: Yeah, I think I'm progressed to the point that I'll get it done.

Belson: You seem more serious, and you sound different also, as you talk about it, like you're more serious.

Husband: Well, I'm more confident in the fact that I can get it done.

Belson: [*To wife*] It sounds like he's taking care of his business.

Wife: Yeah.

Belson: That's my impression, that he finally got on his horse.

Wife: Sounds like it.

Husband: And if I get through x and at the same time . . .

Belson: You don't have to apologize for taking care of your work. Did you feel that I was attacking you for taking care of this?

Husband: No, no. Why, did I sound like it?

Belson: It sounded like you were being defensive for doing so well. You don't have to be.

Husband: Well, I have a—I have a . . .

Belson: I think it's terrific.

Husband: I have a penchant for—not a penchant, I have a reluctance to accept credit for doing something I should have done a long time ago.

Belson: M-hmm, well, you could try and get used to that.

Husband: Pardon?

Belson: You could try to get used to it.

Husband: Yeah. But I don't quite feel like patting myself on the back.

Belson: Well, you don't have to . . .

Husband: I'm grateful that I'm getting over it.

Belson: You don't have to pat yourself on the back.

Husband: The feeling of the sickness that I realize I had.

Belson: But you have a right to let other people do that.

Husband: Right, to let other people . . . do what? Oh, to compliment me.

Belson: Yeah. I mean, maybe you don't like to do it yourself, but you have a right to let other people do it. I mean . . .

Husband: It makes me feel like a little boy.

Belson: Oh, in that case I won't do it.

[*Husband laughs.*]

Belson: But I think you should let people do it.

Husband: OK.

Belson: You know, I feel just the opposite. I feel that your . . . I feel that hard work deserves honest praise.

Husband: OK, I agree.

Belson: Are you pleased with what he's done? I mean, am I making too much of it or . . .

Wife: No, I don't think so at all. I think that he's moving along.

Belson: OK.

Wife: And that he's getting . . .

Belson: He's becoming, you know, the way he should.

Wife: He's making inroads into this morass of . . .

Husband: There are six years of irresponsibility here.

Belson: What about you? Have you been taking care of what you are supposed to in terms of his life?

Wife: Certainly.

Belson: How have you lapsed?

Wife: How have I lapsed? I'm going to take credit for what I did.

Belson: OK.

Wife: Not for what I didn't do.

Belson: All right.

Wife: I've been calling him every day, twice a day, and you know yesterday I really put the heat on.

Belson: You did?

Wife: M-hmm.

Belson: That was good.

Wife: Yeah.

Belson: All right, since he's agreed to get through by June the 30th, I think that you have to continue the heat and not to neglect him in that way because you understand that it's just the symbolic thing about the calls, even though it's necessary, but you know he needs to know that you're on his side, I think that's important.

Husband: You know, strangely, I'm not reacting that way.
               I'm reacting in other ways. Last night I was abso-
               lutely afraid to come home without finishing a cer-
               tain part of it.
Belson: Well, that means that you are on the right track.
Husband: By meaning afraid, I didn't want to incur her dis-
               pleasure. I don't like it when she's displeased. I like
               things nice and easy.
Belson: That's terrific. That means that we've chartered a
               successful course.
Husband: [*Sighing*] Yeah, but I resent it; I keep resenting it; I
               don't like it; I feel like a little boy.
Belson: All those things are unimportant.
Wife: Well, I felt like a shrew. [*Laughs.*]
Belson: No, no, you're not a shrew; you're just the oppo-
               site; no, no, just the opposite; you're a concerned
               wife.

[*Later in the interview.*]

Wife: [*To husband*] I thought you should be doing your
               own thing, so I never thought I should be pressur-
               ing.
Belson: It's not pressuring; it's taking a serious interest.
Wife: Well, certainly something had to happen because
               it's just going down hill when you get into that kind
               of difficulty.
Belson: You know, it's a lonely life when people are too
               autonomous. Sometimes there has to be a little
               more togetherness in terms of people's business.
               And even though you and he are in a separate work
               world, it's important to take some interest in each
               other's world in some way. And I think that he
               needed you to do that, and I thought that you were
               being somewhat, somewhat neglectful for not tak-
               ing an interest.
Wife: Well, I certainly hadn't done that.
Belson: Right.
Wife: There's no question about it, so as long as it works,
               I'm going to keep on doing it.

Belson: I don't think that you need me any more; I mean, I have to be frank with you.

Husband: How do you feel about that?

Wife: Well, we had a discussion about it this morning . . .

Belson: And I think that's why you brought in the dog. No, no, you think that you left the door open. No, I think in some way the fact that the dog came out of the car and came in here, in some way you're like saying goodbye. What were you about to say, though?

Wife: I was going to say that David said this morning that he felt that it was a waste of time to continue coming.

Belson: Yeah, I agree.

Wife: And I felt that we should keep coming occasionally just to keep on track.

Belson: Let me tell you what I suggest. I think that, if you don't mind, that I agree with him. I think that he's right. I think that what we should do is we should meet maybe for the last time. I think maybe we should meet for just one more week to make sure everything is still on track, and then if you want to maybe we can meet in the fall or whatever, you know, just to make sure that everything is still OK, and you know, that's about it. 'Cause I really think that you people have worked out things so well. And that you really know what has to be done and you're already doing it. And you don't need me to tell you this any more. So I think that we should follow his suggestions . . .

Husband: [*To wife*] He's full of shocks, you know. You're full of surprises all the time.

Belson: But you know this yourself, that's why I'm surprised myself. I'm surprised that you even said that, because you yourself are coming to the same place I was. You prefer that I say it rather than you say it because, if you said it, you'd probably figure that I might compliment you on it and you didn't want to

	have that. [*Wife laughs.*] It's better that I said it so you can compliment me. But you came to the same conclusion that I did this morning.
Husband:	Yes, I did. I took special pains to talk to her this morning about it.
Belson:	Right. Maybe you don't want to take credit, but meanwhile that was the conclusion.
Husband:	Yeah, I thought there's nothing more that you can do. All I have to do is to get ahead on doing the work. There's nobody who can do it except me and whomever I hired to help me do it.
Belson:	That's right.
Husband:	And it's about time I have to spend some money and hire somebody to get . . .
Belson:	Take the money that you . . .
Wife:	Right, a professional.
Belson:	That's right. It isn't that much of a shift, but the shift that you did make seems to mean that you work together as a team rather than each one going their own separate ways.
Wife:	I feel a lot more . . .
Belson:	I think that you've been more involved in a very nice kind of way.
Wife:	Yes, you know, we had that luncheon last time; it was great.
Belson:	You know, I don't want to tell your wife what to do, but I think that maybe you might want to, you know, on a regular pattern spontaneously do it. I would suggest that you do that.
Wife:	Sure.

The therapy lasted for seven interviews. In follow-ups at four and eight months later, husband and wife were cheerful, and the husband had caught up with the work that he had neglected. The couple had supported each other through the sadness of the death of the husband's mother and the joy of the birth of their first grandchild. The husband said that he now realized he had to face his responsibilities and do his work, and he agreed with the therapist that he should not waste any more of his time in therapy.

The key elements of this therapy were the following:

1. Understanding the Problem

   The man presented as a problem that he was depressed. He said he had felt this way for five years, during which he had completely neglected his work. During those five years, his wife had gone back to school and become a successful therapist. In the past, she had been a housewife and mother, providing her husband with emotional support and a sense of security. The hypothesis was that before the wife went back to school and the daughters left home, the relationship between husband and wife had been centered on the husband's career and the children's growth. As the wife developed outside interests and the daughters left home, the couple were left without common goals, without a theme to hold them together. The husband's depression provided just that. It was a subject that concerned them both, particularly since it affected their financial situation. The depression was within the wife's area of expertise as a therapist and interested her more than the husband's work as an accountant. However, although supportive and kind, the wife failed to help her husband. Her position as a helper made her powerful, but her failure to help put her in an inferior position to her husband, whose power was derived from his helplessness. The husband's symptom elicited a benevolent but unfortunate interaction between husband and wife and stabilized the marriage around unhappiness. It was necessary to arrange that the wife help the husband recover his competence, so that the couple could reorganize in a more egalitarian relationship.

2. The Interventions

   a. *Defining the Problem.* The man was told that he had been misdiagnosed. His problem was not depression; it was irresponsibility, and the goal of the therapy was for him to become responsible once more. It was necessary to redefine the problem for various reasons:

(1) Depression is an internal feeling and less amenable to change than irresponsibility, which can be measured by concrete acts. With a focus on depression, the man was oriented toward internal states. With a focus on responsibility, he became oriented toward action.

(2) The wife and the previous therapist would interfere less with the success of the therapy if this success was on a different problem from the one they had failed to solve.

(3) When a professional man neglects his work, it is reasonable that he would become depressed. To solve the depression, it is necessary first to resolve the neglect.

b. *Putting the Wife in Charge.* Directing the wife to monitor the husband's work served two purposes:

(1) It provided a way in which the wife could succeed in helping her husband actually do something, as compared to her previous unsuccessful attempts to cheer him up.

(2) It exaggerated the wife's superior position to the point where the husband would rebel and take charge of his own affairs.

c. *Requesting That the Husband Pretend.* The therapist requested that the husband pretend to be irresponsible and inadequate and that the wife criticize his performance. The functions of this directive were:

(1) If the husband appeared irresponsible and inadequate, it was because the therapist had requested it; therefore, the wife could not respond in her usual ways when the husband had spontaneously been irresponsible and inadequate.

(2) If the wife had to criticize the husband's performance, she could not be supporting and reassuring him as she had done in the past.

(3) Implicit in the interaction would be the fact that the husband was not believable as an irresponsible and inadequate person because he was *not* irresponsible and inadequate.

(4) When the husband was symptomatic, he was overtly in an inferior position to the wife, but covertly he was in a superior position because she failed to help him. Two incongruous hierarchies were simultaneously defined. With the pretend directive, one aspect of the incongruous hierarchy, the one in which the husband was inferior to the wife, was in play. It was make-believe, and the incongruity was resolved.

3. *The Reorganization*

The relationship between husband and wife was reorganized in a congruous hierarchy. To establish a better balance, the couple were instructed to spend time together talking about each one's work. The wife was defined as neglectful and the husband as responsible and protective with regard to sex. She was required to take the initiative and pursue the husband. Being pursued put the husband in a superior position and made him feel wanted and important. The husband was encouraged to be more overtly demanding of his wife. The husband's success in doing his work was defined as a joint success of husband and wife helping each other. The positive, romantic aspects of the relationship between husband and wife were emphasized throughout the therapy and particularly around the directive to have lunch together instead of coming to therapy.

CHAPTER NINE

※ ※ ※ ※ ※

Summary:
Metaphor and Power

This concluding chapter will review the key elements of this strategic family therapy approach and offer a simplified summary with some additional comments.

The Unit

The approach is part of a family orientation to therapy. The family view has only recently gained a respectable place in the professional world, and the reluctance to accept a unit larger than the individual is puzzling. Somehow it seems to demean the individual to discover that he is only a part of a larger organization. Perhaps this is comparable to the embarrassment of realizing that we are similar to creatures such as ants, bees, and termites, which are component parts in collective societies that behave like organisms. Only with reluctance can a human being look at his own kind and think that, in spite of the

216

uniqueness of each individual, he is only a part, a component of an organization that has an intelligence of its own (Thomas, 1979).

Freud remarked that during the history of science there have been three great blows to man's concept of himself: the first was the discovery that the earth is not the center of the universe; the second was the theory that man descends from animals; and the third was the argument that man is driven by unconscious forces within himself which he is helpless to control. Haley (1967b) has suggested that the fourth blow is the argument that the "cause" of man's behavior is no longer even located within him but in the outer context; that is, the view in which the unit is no longer the individual but a larger unit.

Even more distasteful than the idea that man is no longer the focal point is the idea that the family should be the unit— the collective society with an independent intelligence. Why should not the social unit be the peer group, the friends? What about the work group, the school, or the community? To many of us, these organizations appear to be as important as the family, or even more so. Yet when symptomatic behavior develops, just as when tragedy is to be expressed in the Greek drama, the family is the organism that is usually most relevant. If interventions are necessary into other organizations, it is through the family that they are most effectively carried out.

Power

Once the family began to be accepted as the unit, issues of power also began to be recognized. However, the idea that the behavior of one person is determined by the influence of another has repelled many intelligent thinkers. It has even been said that power may be a myth, a dangerous metaphor to be mistrusted (Bateson, 1980). Yet the influence of one nation over another or the power of the rich over the poor cannot be ignored.

Many people are antagonized by any discussion of power, and they object even more to the idea of the manipulation of power in a field as benevolent as therapy. However, power is an important factor in human relations; therefore, if one is reorganizing families, the issue of power is a main concern. It is difficult to imagine how the relevance of power to human relations can be denied when people lock each other up, murder each other, or devote their lives to helping one another. The objections to power usually derive from thinking about it in terms of people harming one another or influencing one another for selfish reasons. This view, however, has to do with a theory of motivation and not a theory of power. Power can be benign or malignant, depending on how it is used. If one assumes that people are hostile, aggressive, and exploitative, power is a negative concept. If one thinks of people as motivated to be benevolent, helpful, and kind, then power is a means to achieve benevolent ends.

Interpersonal Influence

The issue of power is related to the issue of interpersonal influence, which takes place at levels that are sometimes difficult to comprehend. Take the example of warts as described by Thomas (1980). A wart is the "elaborate reproductive apparatus of a virus." It is a tough overgrowth in which viruses flourish. Yet warts can be ordered off the skin by hypnotic suggestion, even though currently it is thought that there are complex immunological mechanisms implicated in the rejection of warts. Thomas marvels at the ability of the unconscious, which can "manipulate the mechanisms needed for getting around that virus and for deploying all the various cells in the correct order for tissue rejection." He points out that, even if immunology is not involved and all that is involved is shutting off the blood supply locally, this is a tremendous task. If we had a clear understanding of what goes on when a wart is hypnotized away, "we would be finding out about a kind of superintelligence that exists in each of us, infinitely smarter and possessed of technical know-how far beyond our present understanding" (1980, p. 63). Thomas seems to assume that the owner of the wart makes it go away; that the hypnotist tells the "unconscious" of the subject to make the wart disappear, and the unconscious does it. Yet it is the hypnotist who makes the wart go away, after establishing a contract with the subject who permits the hypnotist to influence his autonomous body functions. If we could understand how the contract is made between hypnotist and subject, we would be finding out about a kind of interpersonal influence that is extraordinarily precise and powerful. If we could understand the interaction between the hypnotist and the virus lodged in another person's skin, and the relationship between hypnotist, subject, and virus, we would know infinitely more about the influence that people have over one another. If it is possible that one person can influence another so that the subtle and complex mechanisms necessary to eliminate warts will take place, what other kinds of influence are possible?

Helpfulness

The protective and helpful aspects of power and of interpersonal influence have been emphasized in this book. It has been proposed that family members influence each other in helpful ways that are often unfortunate: instead of resolving a problem, they only distract from it, preventing a resolution and creating a new problem.

A child's disturbed behavior helps the parents by focusing their concern on him, providing a respite from the parents' own troubles and a reason to overcome their own difficulties. For example, a mother may become involved with her problem child instead of being concerned about improving her husband's shortcomings or instead of being involved in her career in a way that the husband might find upsetting. A child's difficulties can make a father feel needed at those times when he feels rejected by his wife. These ways in which the child protects the parents make the child appear to be helpless because of his disturbed behavior, yet he is powerful as a helper to the family.

Symptomatic behavior in a spouse can be protective of the other spouse by making the other the helper and defining him as the competent person in the marriage. The disturbed behavior can also be helpful by eliciting benevolent interaction and preventing a separation.

There are many ways in which people can protect and

help one another. For example, when someone is attacked, one can step in and attack the attacker, or one can draw the attack on oneself, or one can collapse and draw attention away from the victim and on to oneself. Or one can even attack the victim oneself in a less harmful way, and so replace the attacker. Protection has many forms and does not appear to be always kindly and benevolent. Some ways of protecting are quite indirect, and some actually involve hurting others. It is possible, for example, to help someone overcome one kind of pain by inflicting another kind of pain. Helpfulness can be unfortunate to the object of the help and quite different from the kind of help preferred. Certain forms of protectiveness do not solve a problem but create a new, and often worse, difficulty.

The question arises: Is not symptomatic behavior often so excessive and exaggerated that it is almost impossible to imagine that a child would go to such extremes in an attempt to solve a parental problem that often appears mild in comparison? Again, an example from biology is appropriate. Bateson (1980) and others have remarked that nature is always excessive. Man produces millions of sperms in order to have one survive. Fish lay millions of eggs so that only a few may hatch, and millions of seeds are scattered so that one tree may grow. Nature produces too much in order to ensure its objectives. Symptomatic behavior could have the same characteristics and be exaggerated to ensure a relatively minor objective.

Thomas (1980) has proposed that the things that go wrong with a complex social system may be the result of someone's efforts to be helpful. He suggests that the best intervention, instead of trying to move in and change things around, could be "to reach in gingerly and simply extract the intervener" (1980, p. 90). The intervener, whom Thomas refers to as the "meddler," acts from outside the system and intervenes into it. One of his examples is syphilis, a disease in which all that has to be done for a cure is to reach in quickly and eliminate the intervener—the microorganism that causes the illness. Before it was known that the spirochete causes syphilis, medicine was the meddler, adding insult to injury in its ineffectual attempts to cure the patient. Another example in Thomas (1980) is Professor Calhoun, who demonstrated that malignant social pathology occurs when rats live in crowded conditions. Thomas points out that the trouble was not the tendency of crowded rats to go wrong, but "the scientist who took them out of the world at large and put them into too small a box" (1980, p. 92). These considerations have two implications for the work of the therapist. One is that, even though the therapist must meddle, he should at least meddle with caution. Second, to remove the meddler can be to intervene and meddle in a way that is most unfortunate (as in hospitalization). The solution is not as simple as with the case of syphilis or the case of Professor Calhoun.

An alternative that has been proposed in this book is to identify the meddler, the helpful one in the family, and to intervene so that the nature of this helpfulness can change and become more benign for all concerned. The task of identifying helpfulness is, however, a complex one. Helpfulness occurs in sequences that involve several family members. A child, for example, behaves in symptomatic ways which are helpful to his parents. The parents focus on the child to help him to overcome his problems. This helpfulness by the parents perpetuates the function of the child's symptomatic behavior, and he becomes more helpless in a way that is helpful to the parents. Helpfulness is a joint endeavor; there is never only one meddler in the family.

Planning Ahead

It may be difficult to accept the idea that a child can be so intelligent that he can plan a symptom as a way of helping his parents. It is difficult to conceive that a child who develops a symptom is planning the reaction of others to his behavior. Does the child know that the father will recover from his own problems to help him? Is it an occurrence based on trial and error? Is it the father who elicits the symptomatic behavior in the child, so that he can then be helpful to the child and, while becoming a competent parent, recover from his own difficulties?

Although it may appear improbable that such planning ahead can occur in human interaction, children clearly do have that intelligence. In fact, so do the birds of the air and the beasts of the field. Take for example Thomas's (Ferris, 1980) description of a beetle, the "mimosa Girdler." Thomas says:

> The reason I like her so much is she's a good example of planning ahead, of real forethought in a creature that obviously can't have much of a central nervous system. She is attracted, first off, to mimosa trees. Doesn't live on any other tree. She climbs up the mimosa trunk, goes out on a limb, and cuts a longitudinal slit with her mandible, then lays eggs in the slit, which almost immediately heals over so that it can't be seen. She then goes back onto the limb and spends a couple of hours digging a girdle around the limb. It's a job of cabinetwork, like a beaver's. Having done that, she's finished. The girdle is just deep enough to kill the limb. It cuts the circulation off. She departs. The limb dies. The next wind could break it off. And after it falls, the larvae now can hatch, because they're in deadwood. And the cycle begins again. Now, how did evolution achieve these two separate and—when you think about it, or when she thinks about it—quite unrelated acts of behavior? It looks as though it's really been thought out. She wants to lay her eggs in the mimosa because it is somehow attractive. They can't live in live wood, and the nicest way to kill the wood is to girdle it [1980, p. 128].

What could be the complexities and mysteries of the ways humans plan ahead if the little beetle does it with such sophistication!

The beetle has a plan, but she cannot help having a plan; she cannot stop following the plan. It may well be that the child helps the parents but cannot stop helping the parents; he cannot not help. The child might have the illusion that he can stop, that he is acting deliberately, but in fact he may be part of a system with a purpose of its own.

Hierarchy

Another aspect of power that has been emphasized in this book is in relation to hierarchy and organization. Just as power can be malign or benign depending on the theory of motivation, the existence of a hierarchy in which some people are superior to others can also be seen as undesirable or benevolent. One's view can depend on the function and the purpose attributed to those in higher positions. Once, in a group of student therapists, a Baptist minister commented on the advantages of his religion, saying, "No one is above me to tell me what to do." Later, in private, one of the teachers, a Catholic, reflected, "These Baptist ministers are so alone; no one is above them to help them." The Baptist and the Catholic had different views of the function of a superior.

In any organization, there is hierarchy in the sense that one person has more power and responsibility than another person in determining what happens. Parents have legal responsibility for providing for and taking care of their children. As the children grow into adolescence, parents are expected to relinquish some of this power, so that the children gradually take increasing responsibility for their own lives. When adolescents become young adults, their parents no longer have legal responsibility for them, and the relationship shifts to one of increasing equality between parents and children.

In a marriage, the spouses usually deal with the hierarchical issue by dividing areas of power and responsibility. This division can be done in different ways. For example, one spouse might make all the decisions having to do with money, while the other spouse makes all the decisions involving relatives. In another couple, one spouse might have power over the decisions involving children, while the other spouse makes the decisions involving friends. In these ways, several hierarchies are defined in a couple; one of the spouses is superior to the other in certain areas but inferior to the other spouse in other areas.

The hierarchical organization of a family includes the members dominating, taking responsibility, and making decisions for others. It also includes helping, protecting, comforting, reforming, and taking care of others. By the nature of their position in the hierarchy, parents help and protect their children more frequently than the children help and protect their parents. In this sense, parents have more power than their children. In a marriage, spouses help and protect each other at different times in different situations.

When a child presents symptomatic or problem behavior, the parents express their concern in helpful, protective, or punitive ways. The disturbed behavior of the child gives him power over the parents, who focus their concern on him and yet fail to help and to change him. In this sense, the child has power over the parents, often determining what the family can do, what they will talk about, how time will be spent, and so forth. Yet, because the child is disturbed or symptomatic, the parents have to take care of him even more. In this sense, there are two conflicting hierarchical arrangements in the family. Both parents and child are *simultaneously* in a superior and an inferior position in relation to each other. The hierarchical incongruity may become a hierarchical reversal if the parents lose all power over an adolescent or young adult who dominates them by terrorizing them through violent, delinquent, or bizarre behavior.

When it is a spouse who develops symptomatic or problem behavior, two incongruous hierarchies are simultaneously defined in the marriage. In one, the symptomatic person is in an inferior position because of helpless and disturbed behavior, and the other spouse is in the superior position of helper. Yet at the same time, the symptomatic spouse is in a superior position by not being influenced and helped, while the nonsymptomatic spouse is in the inferior position of being an unsuccessful helper whose efforts fail and whose life can be organized around the symptomatic spouse's needs and problems.

A symptom is an incongruent message in the sense that the symptomatic person behaves in an unfortunate or inappropriate way and denies that he has control over this behavior because it is involuntary. To quote Haley (1963, p. 5): "From the communication point of view, symptomatic behavior represents an incongruence between one level of message and a metacommunicative level. The patient does something extreme, or avoids doing something, and indicates that *he* is not doing it because he cannot help himself." A symptom is an incongruous message, but in the wider context it can be seen as appropriate to an incongruous position in a hierarchy. If a person is simultaneously defined as powerful and helpless, he will behave in symptomatic ways that will reflect that incongruous hierarchical position. When one person is powerful and yet helpless in relation to others, those others must be correspondingly powerful yet helpless; power and helplessness can be defined only in relation to others. An incongruous hierarchy is the organizational structure in which symptomatic behavior takes place.

Metaphor

People communicate in analogical ways; their messages can be assigned meaning only in a context of other messages. An analogical message usually has a second referent different from the one explicitly expressed, and it also carries an implicit request or command. For example, when a wife says to her husband, "I have a headache," she is explicitly making a statement about an internal state, but she may be analogically expressing her dissatisfaction with her situation. She can also be requesting that the husband help her with the children.

All human behavior can be thought of as analogical and metaphorical in different ways and at various levels of abstraction. A behavior is analogical to another behavior when there is a resemblance between them in some particular, even though they may be otherwise unlike. A behavior is metaphorical for another behavior when it symbolizes or is used in place of another behavior. Symptomatic behavior can be considered analogical and metaphorical in certain specific ways:

1. A symptom may be a report on an internal state and also a metaphor for another internal state. For example, a child's headache may be expressing more than one kind of pain.
2. A symptom may be a report on an internal state and also an analogy and a metaphor for *another person's* symptoms or internal states. For example, a child who refuses to go to school may be expressing his own fears and also his mother's fears. The child's fear is analogical to the mother's fear (in that the fears are similar) and also metaphorical (in that the child's fear symbolizes or represents the mother's fear).
3. The interaction between two people in a family can be an analogy and a metaphor, replacing the interaction of another

dyad in the family. For example, a husband may come home upset and worried, and his wife may try to reassure and comfort him. If a child develops a recurrent pain, the father may come home and try to reassure and comfort the child in the same way that the wife was previously reassuring and comforting him. The father's involvement with the son in a helpful way will preclude his involvement with the wife in a helpless way, at least during the time in which the father is involved with the son. The interaction between father and son will have replaced the interaction between husband and wife.

4. The system of interaction around a symptom in one family member can be a metaphor for and replace another system of interaction around another issue in the family. Mother, father, and siblings may helpfully focus on a child's problem in a way that is analogical to the way they focused on the father's problem before the child's problem developed. The focus on the child's problem precludes the interaction centered around the father's problem.

5. There may be a cyclical variation in the focus of interaction in families—sometimes centered on a symptomatic child, sometimes on the problem of a parent or on a marital difficulty; but the interaction remains the same in that there is helplessness and incongruity.

The distinction between the literal and the metaphorical levels of messages is an issue of contemporary psychopathology. A concern with metaphor has characterized the development of psychoanalysis, the theories of schizophrenia, and Gestalt psychology. These theories have been plagued by confusions between what is communication and what is thinking about communication. Korzybski (1941) and the movement of general semantics offered some clarification when emphasizing that the map is not the territory. The whole of psychoanalysis is a theory of metaphor that confuses map and territory, where the oedipal drama, for example, is not thought of as a metaphor or a map but is taken as a literal event. Schizophrenia has been described as a difficulty in discriminating between the literal and the metaphorical level of messages, and generations of therapists have struggled to understand the metaphors of the schizophrenic in the belief that that understanding would lead to a solution to the mystery of psychosis. All the psychodynamic and experiential therapies are based on understanding the metaphor of adult language and of children's play.

The contribution of this book is within this tradition of interest in metaphors, but it introduces new complexities by describing metaphorical sequences of interaction. A system's metaphor and a metaphor in a dream are not of the same order. To focus on the metaphor expressed by a sequence of interaction is of a different order from focusing on the metaphor expressed in a message or an act. There is a shift to a different level of analysis when metaphorical communication is thought of as expressed not only by individual messages but also by relationships and by systems of interaction.

Strategic family therapy shares with the individual psychodynamic and experiential therapies the focus on understanding the metaphor. With the family therapies it shares a concern with the organization of the family. The two concerns come together in a strategic therapy based on changing interactional metaphors and manipulating power in families.

References

Ackerman, N. *Treating the Troubled Family.* New York: Basic Books, 1966.

Ascher, L. M. "Paradoxical Intervention in the Treatment of Urinary Retention." *Behavior Research and Therapy,* 1979, *17,* 267-270.

Ascher, L. M., and Efran, J. S. "Use of Paradoxical Intervention in a Behavioral Program for Sleep Onset Insomnia." *Journal of Consulting and Clinical Psychology,* 1978, *46* (3), 547-550.

Attneave, C. L. "Therapy in Tribal Settings and Urban Network Intervention." *Family Process,* 1969, *8,* 192-210.

Bateson, G. *Steps to an Ecology of Mind.* New York: Ballantine Books, 1972.

Bateson, G. *Mind and Nature.* New York: Bantam Books, 1980.

Bateson, G., and Jackson, D. D. "Some Varieties of Pathogenic Organization." In D. D. Jackson (Ed.), *Communication, Family and Marriage.* Vol. 1. Palo Alto, Calif.: Science and Behavior Books, 1968.

Bateson, G., and others. "Toward a Theory of Schizophrenia." *Behavioral Science,* 1956, *1* (4), 251-264.

Bell, N. W. "Extended Family Relations of Disturbed and Well Families." *Family Process,* 1962, *1,* 175-193.

Berger, H. G. "Somatic Pain and School Avoidance." *Clinical Pediatrics,* 1974, *13,* 819-826.

Boszormenyi-Nagy, I., and Spark, G. *Invisible Loyalties.* New York: Harper & Row, 1973.

Bowen, M. "The Use of Family Therapy in Clinical Practice." In J. Haley (Ed.), *Changing Families.* New York: Grune & Stratton, 1971.

Bowen, M. "Family Therapy After Twenty Years." In S. Arieti (Ed.), *American Handbook of Psychiatry.* Vol. 4. New York: Basic Books, 1975.

Bowen, M. *Family Therapy in Clinical Practice.* New York: Aronson, 1978.

Dicks, H. *Marital Tensions.* New York: Basic Books, 1967.

Duhl, F., Kantor, D., and Duhl, B. "Learning, Space and Action in Family Therapy: A Primer of Sculpture." In D. Block (Ed.), *Techniques of Family Therapy: A Primer.* New York: Grune & Stratton, 1973.

Ferris, T. "Hopeful Prophet Who Speaks for Human Aspiration." (An interview with Lewis Thomas.) *Smithsonian,* 1980, *11* (1), pp. 127-142.

Framo, J. "Symptoms from a Family Transaction Viewpoint." In N. Ackerman, J. Lieb, and J. Pearce (Eds.), *Family Therapy in Transition.* Boston: Little, Brown, 1970.

Gehrke, S., and Kirschenbaum, M. "Survival Patterns in Family Conjoint Therapy." *Family Process,* 1967, *6,* 67-80.

Haley, J. *Strategies of Psychotherapy.* New York: Grune & Stratton, 1963.

Haley, J. (Ed.). *Advanced Techniques of Hypnosis and Therapy: The Selected Papers of Milton H. Erickson.* New York:

Grune & Stratton, 1967a.

Haley, J. "Toward a Theory of Pathological Systems." In G. Zuk and I. Boszormenyi-Nagy (Eds.), *Family Therapy and Disturbed Families*. Palo Alto, Calif.: Science and Behavior Books, 1967b.

Haley, J. *Uncommon Therapy: The Psychiatric Techniques of Milton H. Erickson*. New York: Norton, 1973.

Haley, J. "The Development of a Theory: A History of a Research Project." In C. Sluzki and D. C. Ranson (Eds.), *Double Bind*. New York: Grune & Stratton, 1976a.

Haley, J. *Problem-Solving Therapy: New Strategies for Effective Family Therapy*. San Francisco: Jossey-Bass, 1976b.

Haley, J. *Leaving Home*. New York: McGraw-Hill, 1980.

Hawkins, R. P., and others. "Behavior Therapy in the Home: Amelioration of Problem Parent-Child Relations with the Parent in a Therapeutic Role." In J. Haley (Ed.), *Changing Families*. New York: Grune & Stratton, 1971.

Herr, J., and Weakland, J. *Counseling Elders and Their Families*. New York: Springer, 1979.

Jackson, D. D. (Ed.). *Therapy, Communication and Change*. Palo Alto, Calif.: Science and Behavior Books, 1968a.

Jackson, D. D. (Ed.). *Communication, Family and Marriage*. Palo Alto, Calif.: Science and Behavior Books, 1968b.

Jackson, D. D., and Weakland, J. "Conjoint Family Therapy: Some Considerations on Theory, Technique and Results." *Psychiatry*, 1961, *24*, 30-45.

Kempler, W. *Principles of Gestalt Family Therapy*. Oslo: A. S. J. Nordahls Trykkeri, 1973.

Korzybski, A. *Science and Sanity*. New York: Science Press, 1941.

Lacqueur, H. P., Laburt, H. A., and Morong, E. "Multiple Family Therapy: Further Developments." In J. H. Masserman (Ed.), *Current Psychiatric Therapies*. Vol. 4. New York: Grune & Stratton, 1964.

Laing, R. *The Politics of Experience*. New York: Pantheon Books, 1967.

Laing, R. *The Politics of the Family*. New York: Random House, 1969.

Liebman, R., Minuchin, S., and Baker, L. "An Integrated Treatment Program for Anorexia Nervosa." *American Journal of Psychiatry*, 1974a, *131*, 432-436.

Liebman, R., Minuchin, S., and Baker, L. "The Use of Structural Family Therapy in the Treatment of Intractable Asthma." *American Journal of Psychiatry*, 1974b, *131*, 535-540.

MacGregor, R., and others. *Multiple Impact Therapy with Families*. New York: McGraw-Hill, 1964.

Madanes, C., Dukes, J., and Harbin, H. "Family Ties of Heroin Addicts." *Archives of General Psychiatry*, 1980, *37*, 889-894.

Minuchin, S. *Families and Family Therapy*. Cambridge, Mass.: Harvard University Press, 1974.

Minuchin, S., and Montalvo, B. "Techniques for Working with Disorganized Low Socioeconomic Families." *American Journal of Orthopsychiatry*, 1967, *37*, 880-887.

Minuchin, S., and others. *Families of the Slums*. New York: Basic Books, 1967.

Minuchin, S., and others. "A Conceptual Model of Psychosomatic Illness in Children." *Archives of General Psychiatry*, 1975, *32*, 1031-1038.

Minuchin, S., Rosman, B. L., and Baker, L. *Psychosomatic Families*. Cambridge, Mass.: Harvard University Press, 1978.

Montalvo, B. "Aspects of Live Supervision." *Family Process*, 1973, *12*, 343-359.

Montalvo, B. "Observations on Two Natural Amnesias." *Family Process*, 1976, *15*, 333-342.

Montalvo, B., and Haley, J. "In Defense of Child Therapy." *Family Process*, 1973, *12*, 227-244.

Palazzoli, M. S., and others. *Paradox and Counterparadox*. New York: Aronson, 1978.

Papp, P. "The Greek Chorus and Other Techniques of Family Therapy." *Family Process*, 1980, *19*, 45-57.

Patterson, G. R. *Families: Applications of Social Learning to Family Life*. Champaign, Ill.: Research Press, 1971.

Patterson, G. R., Ray, R., and Shaw, D. *Direct Intervention in Families of Deviant Children*. Eugene: Oregon Research Institute, 1969.

Rabkin, R. *Strategic Psychotherapy*. New York: Basic Books, 1977.

Rubinstein, D. "Family Therapy." *International Psychiatry Clinics*, 1964, *1*, 431-442.

Satir, V. *Conjoint Family Therapy*. Palo Alto, Calif.: Science and Behavior Books, 1964.

Satir, V. *Peoplemaking*. Palo Alto, Calif.: Science and Behavior Books, 1972.

Sigal, J. J., Barrs, C. B., and Doubilet, A. L. "Problems in Measuring the Success of Family Therapy in a Common Clinical Setting: Impasse and Solutions." *Family Process*, 1976, *15*, 225-233.

Singer, M. "The Origins of Schizophrenia." *Excerpta Medica International*, 1967, Congress Series No. 151.

Sojit Madanes, C. "Dyadic Interaction in a Double Bind Situation." *Family Process*, 1969, *8*, 235-259.

Sojit Madanes, C. "The Double Bind Hypothesis and the Parents of Schizophrenics." *Family Process*, 1971, *10*, 53-74.

Speck, R., and Attneave, C. *Family Networks*. New York: Pantheon Books, 1973.

Stuart, R. B. "Operant Interpersonal Treatment for Marital Discord." *Journal of Consulting and Clinical Psychology*, 1969, *33*, 675-682.

Thomas, L. *The Lives of a Cell*. New York: Bantam Books, 1979.

Thomas, L. *The Medusa and the Snail*. New York: Bantam Books, 1980.

"Towards the Differentiation of a Self in One's Own Family." In J. Framo (Ed.), *Family Interaction: A Dialogue Between Family Researchers and Family Therapists*. New York: Springer, 1972.

Watzlawick, P., Weakland, J., and Fisch, R. *Change*. New York: Norton, 1974.

Weakland, J. "Family Therapy as a Research Arena." *Family Process*, 1962, *1*, 63-68.

Zuk, G. *Family Therapy: A Triadic Based Approach*. New York: Behavioral Publications, 1971.

Index

■ ■ ■ ■ ■

A

Ackerman, N., 10

Adolescent: authority given to, by parents, 133-137; behavior of, metaphorical, 125; disruption by, 128, 133-134; drug use by, 139-140; and expulsion from home, 134-135; and hospitalization, 143-144; and organicity, 145; parents put in charge of, 122-146; power of, 124-125; redefinition of problem of, 130-131; self-destructive, 136-137; straightforward approach to, 125-126; and suicide, 135-137; summary of therapy for, 145-146

Analogical-digital communication, dimension of, 6-7, 9, 10, 11, 12, 13, 15, 17, 21

Ascher, L. M., 12

Attneave, C. L., 13

B

Baker, L., xxiv, 18

Bankhead, J., xxiv, 70n

Barragan, M., 78n

Barrs, C. B., 10

Bateson, G., xii, xiii, xxiii, 6, 15, 73, 126, 217, 220

Bed wetting, case example of, 70-72

Bell, N. W., 13

Belson, R., xxiv, xxv, 33n, 178-215

Berger, H. G., 18

Binge eating and vomiting: case example of, 39-48; interventions in, 47-48

Boszormenyi-Nagy, I., 10

Bowen, M., 14, 66